The illustrated history of
AIR TRAVEL

Brian Walters

Crescent Books
New York

First British edition published by
Marshall Cavendish Limited 1979

© Marshall Cavendish Limited

Library of Congress Cataloging in Publication Data
Walters, Brian.
   The illustrated history of air travel.
   1. Air-travel--History. I. Title.
TL720.W34   387.7'09   78-27892
ISBN 0-517-27626-7

This edition is published by
Crescent Books, a division of Crown Publishers, Inc.

Printed in Singapore

Front endpapers: *The Dornier
Do X flying over the Rhine en
route for Amsterdam on the first
stage of her Atlantic flight in 1930.*

Back endpapers: *African chiefs at
Croydon airport inspecting Imperial
Airways Short L.17 'Syrinx'.*

Title page: *Imperial Airways
Handley Page HP42 'Hannibal'
over Croydon airport in 1931.*

This page: *Pan Am's Boeing 314
'Yankee Clipper' on arrival at
Southampton after her transatlantic
survey flight in 1939.*

Overleaf: *British Airways
Concorde which entered service in
1976 after 20 years research.*

Introduction

IN THESE DAYS of mass air travel, when it is possible to breakfast and dine the same day 50,000 feet above opposite ends of the earth, it is difficult to image the sense of adventure, or at least occasion, that even a short air journey evoked only a generation ago. It is even harder to believe that air travel in any real sense did not exist a generation before that.

The astonishing pace of development of the machines that conquered the air is the main story of this book. From a struggling 100 mph or so with a mere score of passengers over stage lengths of a few hundred miles in the 1920s – to 600 mph with 500 passengers over 5000 miles or more today is progress indeed. And, short of some unforeseen catastrophe, is there really any doubt that the splendid Concorde is trail-blazing a supersonic aerial network that will serve the coming generations?

The future is unlikely ever to produce as varied and continuously colourful a saga as the period covered by this book. Its pages take the reader from the first tentative ventures off the ground by intrepid inventors and experimenters, through the eras of the converted bomber, the stately airship and flying-boat. Stage by stage it follows the story into the present age of the 'liner' of the skies, with scheduled services at supersonic speeds a matter of routine for at least two of the world's leading airlines.

The air travel business will no doubt continue to improve in efficiency and perhaps also profitability but, is it becoming less interesting as economics are reducing the aeroplane to a handful of international designs and airports to a uniform cosmopolitan standard? One must hope that for the future these economic pressures do not rob the aircraft enthusiast of the variety and changes in aircraft and air travel that have made its history so fascinating.

Contents

1. Steps to Success

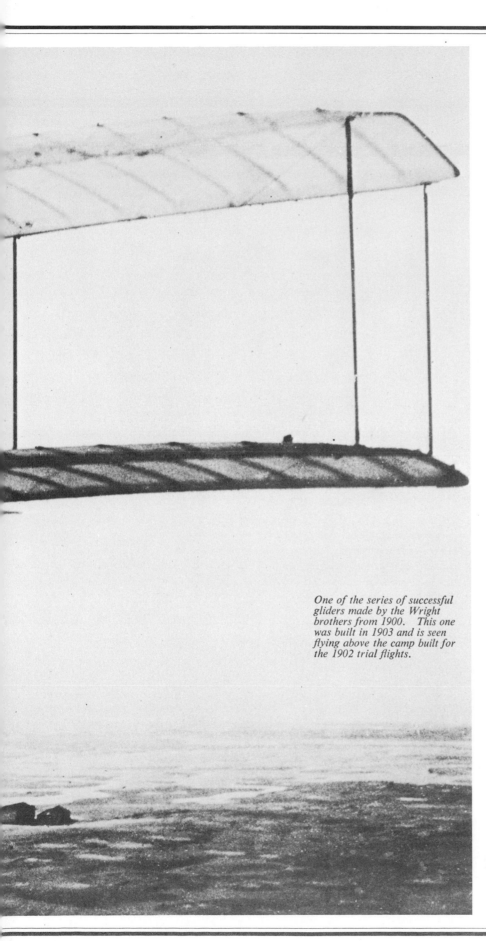

One of the series of successful gliders made by the Wright brothers from 1900. This one was built in 1903 and is seen flying above the camp built for the 1902 trial flights.

FOR THOUSANDS OF years, Man's imagination has been fired by the idea of travel. The earliest tribes migrated to new lands to establish independent territories and some performed the most amazing voyages across oceans in the flimsiest of craft. New generations evolved new methods of travel but it has taken thousands of years for air travel to become perhaps the ultimate in Man's ingenuity. In the gigantic span of our history aviation has developed at an incredible pace in barely seven decades.

The frail Wright brothers' craft which took to the air in 1903 is rightly credited as being the world's first successful powered aeroplane but it was by no means the first attempt to conquer the air. Always adventurous and ever anxious to master the environment, the air had long presented men with a challenge. For example, it is said that thousands of years ago the Chinese were the first to build a device capable of lifting a man into the sky——a kite. Others claim that the mysterious gigantic figures carved on a plain in Peru by a lost civilisation could only have been planned from the air, and recently a crude hot-air balloon built of local materials was flown to prove the possibility of the theory.

A wooden model of a bird discovered in Saqqara, Egypt, has led to the suggestion that some sort of glider might have existed as long ago as 400 BC. For the model is of no ordinary bird, its body having a shape more like that of a modern light aircraft. Aviation can be said to have had as wide an appeal as maritime travel in Asia, Africa and South America hundreds of years before the recognised pioneers in the United States and Europe.

The drawings of 'aircraft' by Leonardo da Vinci are well known and later aviators have admired the sketches which reveal some of the brilliance of the great 15th-century Italian inventor. From Leonardo's pen came signs pointing the way for later designers; devices with flapping wings, helicopters and gliders.

Of course, some trusting souls thought that it would be sufficient to stick some feathers onto their arms and, launching themselves from a high point, flap their 'wings' to success. Alas, many a broken head showed the futility of this approach although recent attempts at man-powered flight have proved to be more successful and the £50,000 Kremer prize offered for flying a mile over a figure-eight course on muscle power alone has at last been won. The legend of Icarus has underlined Man's longing to emulate the

birds but wax and feathers have long been discarded as a practicable means of air travel.

In 1709 a Jesuit priest demonstrated a hot-air balloon to the King of Portugal. Laurenco de Gusmao planned to build a man-carrying hot-air balloon but there is no record of his having done so. Indeed, his model is reputed to have caught fire and damaged some of the furnishings in the royal palace. The later efforts by the Montgolfier brothers in France were more successful and their name will be forever linked with this means of air travel just as the Wrights' name is now associated with successful heavier-than-air flight.

Beginning with tethered flights the Montgolfier brothers and others built improved designs until free flights became possible. Later, hydrogen was substituted for hot air and proved to be a more reliable means of remaining aloft. Whatever the method of gaining lift, however, a balloon has distinct disadvantages, the greatest of which is uncertainty about where it will go. The vagaries of the wind mean that the balloon is largely a means of travelling on a mystery tour, and it is as a sport that ballooning thrives today in craft which are very similar to those produced nearly 200 years ago. During the great siege of Paris in 1870 ballooning provided a means of flying out mail over the surrounding Prussian forces.

Once self-contained engines small and light enough became available, a logical development of lighter-than-air travel was the airship; indeed the powered balloon was to provide the first means of regular air passenger services. Abandoning the spherical shape of the balloon, designers built elongated airships under which passengers and engines were suspended in ' gondolas '. Once again it was French inventiveness which turned theories into practical 'aircraft'. In 1852 Henri Giffard produced a craft powered by a 3hp steam engine and his success led others to produce more-powerful airships. However, this method of air travel, like others, was awaiting the advent of a really compact lightweight power source and the internal-combustion engine ultimately provided the answer.

Experimenting with new devices is usually expensive; in early aircraft development many hours of laborious work were often dashed to pieces within minutes of the first flight, but that was the way lessons were learned. Fortunately the imagination of wealthy patrons has often been fired by farsighted scientists and it was a rich young Brazilian who furthered the development of the airship. Initially a keen balloonist, Alberto Santos-Dumont set about building an airship fitted with a motor-cycle engine and, undeterred by a series of crashes, produced several 'dirigibles'—cigar-shaped craft in which the fabric was supported by a rigid frame. His persistence finally brought its reward when he won a 100,000-franc prize by piloting the Santos-Dumont No 6 around the Eiffel Tower in Paris.

It is the name of Count Ferdinand von Zeppelin, however, which is most closely associated with the airship. In a large floating hangar on Lake Constance, Zeppelin devoted his energies to the design and construction of an airship nearly 400ft in length. Misfortune befell several of Zeppelin's early designs but his tenacity eventually bore fruit when in 1910 his company began regular air services from Hamburg to several other German cities. In just over a year between 1912 and 1913 about 19,000 passengers were carried without a single accident. Dirigibles went on to play an important role in the development of international air services but the R101 and *Hindenberg* disasters (of which more later) sounded the death-knell for this type of air transport.

As lighter-than-air craft developed, proponents of the heavier-than-air machines were by no means idle. As early as 1799 Sir George Cayley had applied his fertile mind to the task of designing an aircraft. Much of his work and theories have earned him the respect of later aviators and one of his designs is credited with carrying a man safely across a valley in 1853. The 'pilot' of the craft was one of Sir George's coachmen and by all accounts he was by no means enthusiastic about his historic role. The glider was fitted with a wheeled gondola in which the unwilling coachman sat working two flapping wings. Pushed down a hillside, the craft carried the terrified elderly coachman to the other side of the valley, thus making him probably the first man to fly in a heavier-than-air craft.

Inventors in several countries produced designs for powered aircraft but, as with the dirigibles, a suitable power plant simply was not available. Steam-powered craft no more than hopped into the air, and it was not until Wilbur and Orville Wright fitted a petrol engine to their *Flyer* that a practical aeroplane at last opened up possibilities for travel by air and fired other experimenters in many parts of the world to fresh endeavours.

As scientists awaited the advent of the internal-combustion engine, work continued on the refinement of aerodynamics. Gliders of increasing efficiency were produced and the name of Otto Lilienthal is closely associated with monoplane and biplane gliders of the late 1890s which have inspired designers to this day. Like ballooning, hang-gliding—as it is called today—is a sport which enjoys great popularity. Many of today's designs are refinements of Lilienthal's gliders which advanced the art of flying 80 years ago.

With the benefit of hindsight we might be surprised at the lack of domestic interest in the Wright brothers' achievements, for although they were soon making flights of up to 24 miles few seemed to share their enthusiasm for powered flight and the Wrights went back to making bicycles. Santos-Dumont, however, was a man of drive and energy and the enthusiasm which he had applied to dirigibles he turned to heavier-than-air craft. His first machine, the 14 bis, was built in 1906; it was of canard form and incredibly ugly even for those days, driven by an engine at the rear with elevators and rudders forward of the wing, giving it the appearance of flying backwards. His later design, the *Demoiselle,* is considered to be the first aircraft to enter series production, the enterprising Brazilian considering the design to be suitable for others to buy and fly. Encouraged by the success of Santos-Dumont several manufacturers entered the aircraft business and the impetus for the development of aviation crossed the Atlantic from the United States to France.

Various French pioneers advanced the science of aeronautics but the next pinnacle of achievement was attained by Louis Blériot. He had built—and crashed—many aircraft but was determined to win the Daily Mail prize of £1000 offered to the first pilot to fly the English Channel. In 1900 he sprang to fame by flying his frail Blériot XI across the 22 miles of water which separate Calais from Dover. Without compass, and uncertain that he was on the right course, Blériot was relieved to sight the cliffs of Dover about 20 minutes after leaving the coast of France. Alarmed by the stronger winds near the British coast he flew through a gap between high cliffs and planted his machine on English soil—a pioneering flight which was to inspire budding aviators all over the world.

Zeppelin LZII 'Viktoria Luise' pictured at Friedrichshafen just before she joined LZ10 'Schwaben' in service with Delag in April 1912. The two airships cruised together from Mannheim to Heidelberg, but 'Schwaben' was destroyed by fire in June 1912.

9

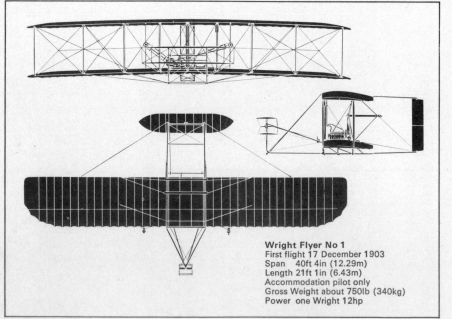

Fired by the success of the French, new companies sprang up in several countries and names which became firmly established in aviation history offered their first designs: A. V. Roe, de Havilland; Handley Page, Sikorsky, Junkers and others gave a much-needed impetus to the development of the aeroplane.

Although many aviation characters, like 'Colonel' S. F. Cody brought the new science to the public's attention it was still widely regarded as a pastime for daredevils and sportsmen. Certainly there was little serious thought given to the potential of air travel, although it was a time when many young enthusiasts embarked upon careers which would bring fame to some, fortune to a very few and excitement and satisfaction to all.

It took some time for the enthusiasm generated by the French to cross the Channel, and it was Cody—an American— who

Wright Flyer No 1
First flight 17 December 1903
Span   40ft 4in (12.29m)
Length 21ft 1in (6.43m)
Accommodation pilot only
Gross Weight about 750lb (340kg)
Power one Wright 12hp

claimed the credit for the first flight in England. Cody could neither read nor write but he was an aviation enthusiast par excellence; he demonstrated a man-lifting kite to the Royal Navy, worked on an airship for the British Army and in 1908 made the maiden flight of British Army Aeroplane Number One at Farnborough. The tree to which his machine was tethered to measure the horsepower stands to this day at the airfield which has been the centre of British aviation research ever since.

Some could see the potential benefits of aviation however, and speeding the mails was to be the method by which many routes were pioneered in the United States, Britain, Italy and even as far afield as India. Most of these early ventures were short-lived. The aircraft were frail and unreliable, few pilots had the skill to cope with bad weather and, last but not least, the services failed to make money. Between 1911 and 1914 some

passenger aircraft emerged from the drawing boards of designers in various parts of the world. In Russia a young engineer named Igor Sikorsky built several large airliners including the *Grand* and *Ilya Mourometz*. The latter was unique in having an open balcony upon which the passengers could walk!

Back in the New World, an attempt to start a regular passenger service was made in Florida. Using a Benoist flying-boat carrying one passenger at a time, an airline operated a service across Tampa Bay for a fare of $5, and attracted 1200 customers before fading into oblivion.

The days of wood and string aeroplanes were numbered however, for the 1914-18 war was about to accelerate the development of aviation. It is a fact of life that the greatest advances in aviation, as in much else, have been brought about by the demands of war. Conversely it might be said that civil

A successful early French design was the series of monoplanes built by the Deperdussin company, whose 1913 racing machine broke the 200 km/hr 'barrier' and set a dozen world speed records. This picture shows a 1910 Deperdussin replica maintained in flying condition by the Shuttleworth Collection in Bedfordshire in the air over Shuttleworth's Old Warden aerodrome in October 1976.

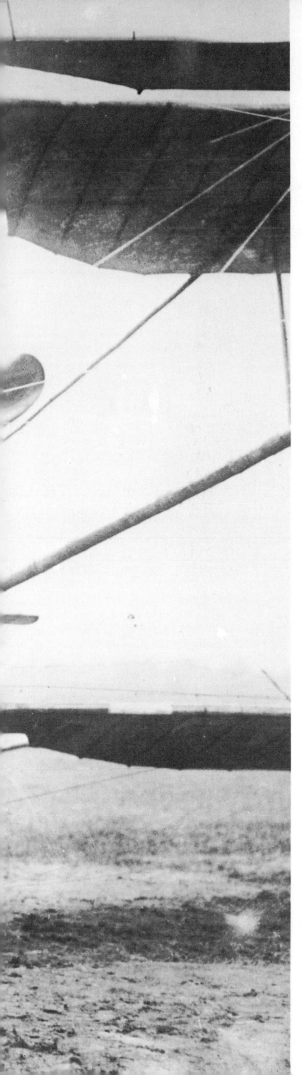

aviation has benefited from the research and development made necessary by military needs. Whichever explanation is accepted, it is a fact that the first serious use of aircraft as a means of transport came about as a result of the First World War.

The use of aircraft in warfare was initially spurned by generals, who considered that the battlefront was no place for daredevils and sportsmen with their unreliable craft which were as fragile as Meissen porcelain. The need fathered the deed, however, and scout and fighter aircraft were soon developed in Britain, France and Germany. Pilots demanded— and got—aircraft which were stronger, more reliable, and faster than anything seen before. Furniture factories all over Europe turned their skills to the construction of aircraft and literally thousands were delivered to the air forces of France, Germany and Britain, and later the United States. Large aircraft, too, were developed as bombers. Sikorsky's great airliners donned military uniform and in Britain Handley Page produced the 0/400 long-range bomber. Capable of carrying out raids on Germany, the 0/400 later proved to be suitable for use as an airliner. Indeed, the type carried 1800 passengers during the war, flying between Lympne and Marquise, near Calais. The Germans used the Zeppelin to carry their bombs to England and later the Gotha aircraft carried on this task.

The war ended eventually but it took some time for the authorities to realise that aviation had an important part to play in peacetime. One of the first post-war 'airlines' was in fact run by the Royal Air Force. During the Paris Peace Conference which culminated in the Treaty of Versailles, the RAF Communications wing flew about 1000 passengers and many bags of mail between England and France. Using converted DH4 and DH9

Historic flight by S. F. Cody in England in January 1912, when he flew his biplane for seven miles at a height of 70 to 80 feet carrying four passengers at a total pilot-and-passenger load of 738 lb; this picture shows the start of the flight at Aldershot.

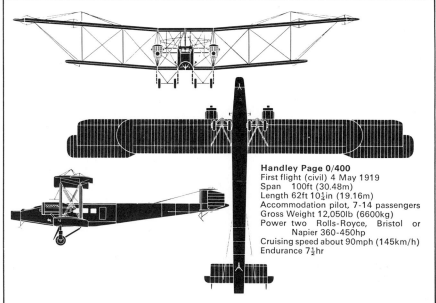

Handley Page 0/400
First flight (civil) 4 May 1919
Span   100ft (30.48m)
Length 62ft 10¼in (19.16m)
Accommodation pilot, 7-14 passengers
Gross Weight 12,050lb (6600kg)
Power two Rolls-Royce, Bristol or
            Napier 360-450hp
Cruising speed about 90mph (145km/h)
Endurance 7½hr

aircraft the service proved that reliable communications were possible using 'airliners' currently available.

There was an abundance of surplus aircraft at the end of the war and there were many skilled pilots anxious to find employment in the element which they had grown to love. Some enlightened governments could foresee the benefits which airlines could bring and gave financial support to budding operators. In France the terrible destruction of the war had ravaged surface communication and air services were quickly established to fill the need: by August 1919 six airlines had become established in France. In common with other European countries, France pressed converted bombers into service, the Breguet 14 and Farman Goliath bearing much of the early post-war service demands.

In Germany, too, the need for air communications was recognised. Backed by state subsidies, city authorities and chambers of commerce encouraged the foundation of airlines, which soon resulted in a large network throughout Germany. At one time there were as many as 30 airlines, almost all very small and inefficient, which one by one

ceased operation. Europe's leading airlines which survived this testing period soon realised that some order was called for and they formed the International Air Traffic Association, which has evolved into the present-day IATA.

Many of the ex-military aircraft were totally unsuited to carrying passengers. An AEG aircraft was used to open a service between Berlin and Weimar in February 1919. Wrapped in a leather coat and a thick woollen blanket and wearing a helmet, fur gloves and goggles, the passenger sat astride a wooden plank which served as a seat. Small wonder that a tot of brandy was proffered to passengers about to embark on a journey. Clearly such standards would not be tolerated for long and the airlines called for more up-to-date aircraft.

In Great Britain a similar pattern emerged and several airlines were formed using demobilised bombers. One such company was Handley Page Air Transport which naturally used its own 0/400 to establish routes to the Continent. First off the mark, however, was Aircraft Transport and Travel (AT and T). Using DH4 and DH9 machines the company opened a service between

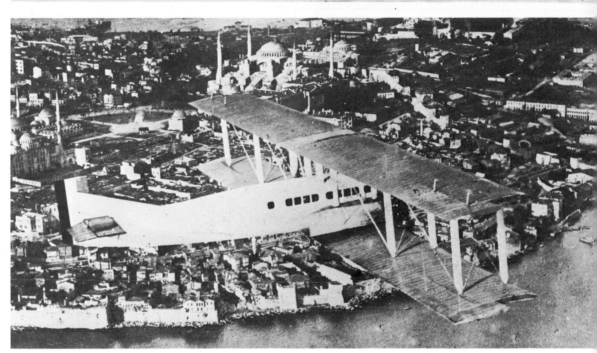

Hounslow and Le Bourget, a journey which could take $2\frac{3}{4}$ hours, flying as low as 200 feet to avoid clouds. The navigational aids of today were quite unknown in the early 1920s and it was common for pilots to ' navigate ' to their destinations by flying above railway lines; as a further aid to pilots many stations had their names painted on their roofs.

A collision between two airliners flying in opposite directions along a road led to the realisation that rules of the air would be necessary. Although railway lines have long since been abandoned as a means of navigation, a rule established in those pioneering days is still observed by pilots of light aircraft; as the captain of an aircraft sits in the left-hand seat in the cockpit it is customary to fly keeping the guiding feature to the left. This ensures that the railway line, or whatever, is kept in sight and a pilot coming in the opposite direction will have the same feature on his left leaving ample clearance between them.

In the early days of flying in the US pilots sat at the right of the cockpit, so the rule would have been reversed, but eventually the left-hand rule became universal. Handbooks were provided for passengers to enable them to pick out such features as gasworks, rivers and so on which were generally visible from the low heights at which airliners flew in those days.

Although passenger air travel at that time was mainly for the rich and adventurous, airlines soon learned that higher standards of comfort and reliability would be necessary if air travel was to be taken seriously and compete successfully with surface transport. Not having suffered destruction on the scale of much of Continental Europe, Britain ended the war with its network of roads and railways reasonably intact. Also, as distances between cities were not so great as on the Continent, internal air routes stood less chance of success. It was only on the Channel crossing that British airlines could offer very serious competition to traditional forms of transport.

Aircraft development and production suffered some lean years at the end of the war with the sudden cessation of military production, but aircraft manufacturers entered the 1920s with a great challenge to produce comfortable, fast and, above all, reliable airliners.

2. The Seeds are Sown

THE YEARS FOLLOWING the First World War are arguably the most exciting in the history of air transport. It was a time of innovation and experiment without the benefit of experience. The pioneering spirit filtered down to the most lowly workers in the infant airlines, for all could sense that they were building the foundations of a great industry.

Aircraft design was still something of a hit-or-miss affair but pioneers of outstanding skill began to produce aircraft which became classics in their own time. The country which gave birth to the aeroplane however momentarily lost the leadership in airliner design. Ironically, defeated Germany established a position of some dominance in the supply of airliners and, in fact, became a pacesetter in design improvement.

Some order had become necessary in Germany where already the huge number of airlines had been whittled down to two—Deutsche Aero Lloyd and Junkers Luft-

verkehr. But the government grew tired of paying subsidies to keep them in business and obliged the two airlines to merge, and in 1926 to form Deutsche Luft Hansa (forerunner of the present Lufthansa). The new company carried on a policy which Professor Hugo Junkers had long practised—a close involvement in foreign investment.

Junkers was a professor of heat engineering at Aachen Technical University until 1912; he was attracted to the new science of aeronautics and evolved several theories which were to revolutionise aircraft design. Junkers's chief engineer, Otto Reuter, applied the professor's theories in the design of the little F13 airliner, which was developed from a wartime ground-attack aircraft. The F13 monoplane was ahead of its time both structurally and aerodynamically, with wings of cantilever construction that eliminated the wires and struts previously necessary to keep wings and fuselage together. It could carry four passengers in a comfortable cabin

Above: De Havilland DH66 Hercules built to the order of Imperial Airways from 1926 to take over from the RAF the scheduled Cairo-Karachi airmail service. Hercules aircraft were also used to found Australian and South African routes.

Right: A Philips Telecommunications promotional picture showing a 1920s installation of its AD6 radio equipment, with access through a removable panel on the fuselage of Fokker FVIII.

which was both heated and ventilated; the seats were fitted with safety belts, another innovation.

The F13 was first flown in 1919 and over 300 were eventually built although the type was nearly killed at birth by the Inter-Allied Aeronautical Commission of Control. The commission was set up to ensure that Germany did not build warplanes and it was understandably suspicious of an aeroplane which was clearly fathered by a military machine. To avoid being forced to stop production, Junkers shifted the production line from Dessau to Danzig, and even to Moscow where a young engineer named Tupolev helped to build the F13.

Eventually the Allies relented and the little F13 poured forth from the Junkers factories to be operated by carriers as far afield as New Guinea and Bolivia. As well as being used to pioneer passenger routes in many parts of the world, it was also adopted for some mail services in the United States during the 1920s. At a time when wood and fabric were common construction materials the F13 was a pioneer of the use of a sheet-metal skin, the corrugated aluminium used becoming a characteristic of Junkers aircraft. Indeed, the F13 generally is considered to have been the world's first all-metal airliner.

Far from putting the Germans at a disadvantage, the restrictions imposed by the Treaty of Versailles seem to have stimulated the country's designers to produce non-military aircraft which found widespread acceptance.

The French and British it seems expended too much energy in the development of wartime designs; long after metal had been adopted by the Germans and Americans as the definitive material for aircraft construction, wood and fabric continued to be used in France and Britain.

Until the formation of Imperial Airways, airlines in Britain received little official encouragement. As Secretary of State for Air, Winston Churchill decided that airlines could not expect state subsidies, so the many small carriers that came into being after the war struggled to make ends meet. Aircraft Transport & Travel (AT&T) ceased operation in December 1920 and in February 1921, in an endeavour to force a change in government policy, Handley Page Transport and the Instone Air Line suspended their services on the London-Paris route. This drastic measure was successful and, with the promise that state support would be forthcoming, services were resumed within a month. Nevertheless they realised that their

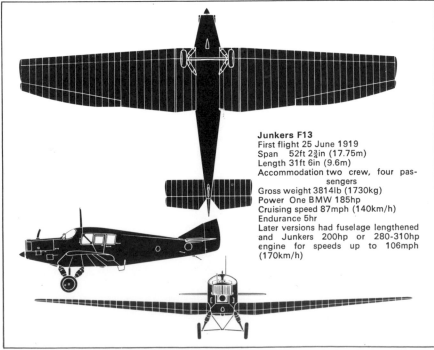

Junkers F13
First flight 25 June 1919
Span 52ft 2¾in (17.75m)
Length 31ft 6in (9.6m)
Accommodation two crew, four passengers
Gross weight 3814lb (1730kg)
Power One BMW 185hp
Cruising speed 87mph (140km/h)
Endurance 5hr
Later versions had fuselage lengthened and Junkers 200hp or 280-310hp engine for speeds up to 106mph (170km/h)

interests would be best served by co-operation instead of competition and the two airlines agreed to operate the Paris service on alternate days.

This did not entirely solve the problem; at one time five airlines including the French were operating on the London–Paris route and order was clearly necessary if competition was not to keep all in a weak state. A revised subsidy scheme from 1 October 1922 allocated definite routes; Instone transferred its operations to the London-Brussels-Cologne service, the newly formed Daimler Airways took the Manchester-London-Amsterdam route and Handley Page was allocated that to Paris.

As in Germany, some British aircraft manufacturers found that one way of ensuring a use for their aeroplanes was to form their own airline. AT&T was a subsidiary of the Aircraft Manufacturing Company and Handley Page was also an early exponent of this policy, while in April 1919 Blackburn Aircraft formed the North Sea

Upper: *A poster promoting the early French airline Lignes Farman in the early 1930s, depicting its then new three-engined Farman F300-series Silver Star Class airliners. The four big cabin windows each side could be opened and a notice on the wall 'absolutely' forbade passengers to throw anything therefrom.*

Above: *The little Boeing 1919 B-1 seaplane was used for the first US private airmail contract between Victoria BC and Seattle. It covered 350,000 miles of flying and wore out six engines in 10 years of service.*

Aerial Navigation Company. Like many other airlines, this one, which was renamed North Sea Aerial & General Transport six months later, was short-lived as a regular operator and it turned to other activities. One serious stumbling-block to the successful operation of airlines in the pioneering days was the difficulty of maintaining regular schedules in the winter months. Bad weather played havoc with planned operating times and business dropped, many passengers returning to the comfort and reliability of the railways.

In 1922 it was recognised that something drastic would have to be done if the airlines were to survive at all and the Civil Air Transport Subsidies Committee was appointed in January 1923. Its report led at last to the formation in 1924 of Imperial Airways—a national airline which incorporated all the principal carriers and earned a government subsidy of £1 million to be used over a period of 10 years. Its very name indicated the ambition of the new airline—to forge links with the many nations which comprised the British Empire at that time. Indeed, Britain's pre-occupation with improving communications with its far-flung territories was to be at the expense of developing the European network of Imperial Airways. German domination of some Continental air routes did not seem to concern the British. Aircraft for Imperial Airways, for the most part, had to have the range to link the United Kingdom with the chain of airfields extending east to India and

beyond and south to Egypt and South Africa.

In 1921 the Royal Air Force Desert Air Mail service linked Cairo with Baghdad. Flying over the largely featureless desert called for navigational skills which were lacking at that time and a simple solution was found. Taking a cue from the 'railway navigation' which was common in Europe at that time, the RAF ploughed furrows across the desert. When Imperial Airways took over responsibility for mail services in January 1927 the furrows continued to be a valuable navigational aid.

De Havilland DH66 airliners were put into service on the route to Baghdad and Basra, calling at Gaza, Station H3 on the oil pipeline, Rutbah Wells (for an overnight stop) and finally Baghdad. For the passengers and crews alike the journey was something of an adventure, for they flew over tribes which were hostile to aircraft—not just British aircraft but *any* aircraft. Taking pot-shots at passing airliners was the custom for rifle-toting tribesmen who had no desire to enjoy the 'benefits' of an alien civilisation.

Diplomatic wrangles have long been a feature of the world of air transport and many persist still. Probably the first of any significance was a difference of opinion with Italy which obliged Imperial Airways to fly its eastbound passengers first to Marseilles where they picked up a P&O ship for Port Said; Mussolini, the Italian dictator, would not allow British airliners to enter his country from France and their performance did not permit them to cross the Alps. In Egypt another aircraft waited to take the passengers to the Gulf and beyond. In 1929 the Short Calcutta flying-boat helped to reduce the journey time by flying from Genoa to Alexandria. The route remained somewhat tortuous, however, for the passengers began by flying from London to Basle, where they took a train to Genoa. In November 1929 Armstrong-Whitworth Argosy aircraft were used to establish a link to Salonika where a flying-boat waited to take passengers on to Egypt.

The experiment was short-lived, however, as bad weather forced the adoption of a Cologne-Athens rail link after only two flights. The big gawky Argosy had been used in October 1927 to inaugurate the Silver Arrow service between London and Paris. It introduced new standards of comfort and gourmet meals were served by a steward—a novel feature in those days.

Elsewhere in Europe other nations were building airlines, some of which have lasted to this day while others did not survive for long. Always a nation of individuals, the French created a multitude of airlines operating in North Europe and to the French territories in North Africa. It was not until the next decade that complete order was brought to the airline industry by the creation

19

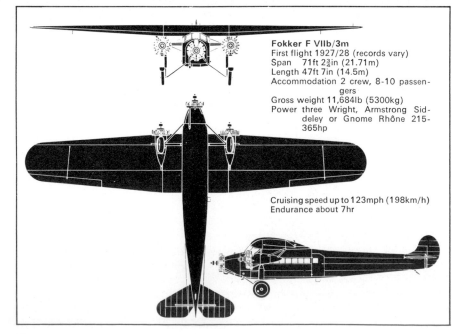

Fokker F VIIb/3m
First flight 1927/28 (records vary)
Span 71ft 2¾in (21.71m)
Length 47ft 7in (14.5m)
Accommodation 2 crew, 8-10 passengers
Gross weight 11,684lb (5300kg)
Power three Wright, Armstrong Siddeley or Gnome Rhône 215-365hp

Cruising speed up to 123mph (198km/h)
Endurance about 7hr

of Air France in 1933. Air Union had been founded 10 years earlier to merge Cie des Messageries Aériennes and Cie des Grands Express Aériens.

Anthony Fokker sprang to fame with his First World War fighters which were flown with devastating effect by such famous aces as the ' Red Baron ' von Richthofen. Fokker had established a factory and flying school in Berlin before the war and, although his native Holland was neutral during the conflict, he remained in Germany to design and produce several types of warplanes. With the hostilities over, Fokker returned to Holland and set up a company which has made a mark for itself as a producer of transport aircraft. KLM had been established as the Dutch national airline as early as 1919 and was a regular customer of Fokker from the early years.

The Fokker FII was, like the Junkers F13, a four-seat single-engined airliner, and was soon followed by the larger and faster FIII which carried five passengers. These aircraft were the forerunners of a series of high-wing airliners which sold in many countries including the United States. The FVII tri-motor airliner was particularly successful and used on many pioneering flights, including the first flight over the North Pole by Byrd. Used by many United States airlines, the wooden-winged Fokker FVII suffered a disastrous accident in 1931 when a TWA machine disintegrated. In-flight failures were by no means unknown in the early years, even the highly successful Junkers F13 won a dubious claim to fame when a British-registered aircraft broke up in flight. The entire structure of the crashed machine was pieced together at the Royal Aeronautical Establishment, Farnborough, the first time that this method of accident investigation was used.

The investigation was successful and established that failure of the tailplane was the cause of the crash.

Early Belgian attempts to found an airline were not successful but in 1923 Sabena was formed to take over SNETA and operate services to Amsterdam and Basle using Farman Goliaths, de Havillands and Breguet 14s. The Belgians quickly recognised the potential of aircraft to improve communications in the Congo—an area with a poor railway network and a river steamer system which guaranteed that long journeys were tedious in the extreme. In 1920 LARA (Ligne Aerienne du Roi Albert) was formed and provided a welcome improvement in communications within the Congo using flying-boats. Sabena later took over the task and opened landplane services in 1926 and 1927.

Italy established several airlines in the late 1920s. Domestic and international routes grew apace until by the end of the decade Italy was third in terms of the number of passengers carried, after Germany and France (Britain, more concerned with developing intercontinental routes, was fourth.)

Having set up his own airline in 1921 using 60 F13s, Junkers used the same type to help launch airlines in Austria, Danzig, Denmark, Estonia, Finland, Latvia and Sweden. Known as the Transeuropa Union the 'Junkers' airlines spanned Europe from north to south. Fitted with wheels, skis or floats, the tough ubiquitous little F13 helped to launch many airlines in Europe and elsewhere.

Russia was an ideal country for the formation of airlines, for surface transport between cities was for the most part poor. Using a motley collection of British and German aircraft, a Russian Volunteer Air Fleet was formed in 1924. About two years earlier, however, a Russo-German airline—Deruluft—began operations with Fokker F13s from Berlin into Moscow. The Germans were keen to aid the new airline, seeing it as a step towards a possible link with Shanghai via Siberia. In the Central Asian states of the Soviet Union, camels were a common form of transport and once again it was an F13 operated by Junkers and Luftverkehr which was used to open a route from Moscow to Tiflis. A year later Dornier Komet aircraft opened a route from Kharkov to Kiev, reflecting the growing influence of Germany in the development of Soviet air services.

Through its national airline Lufthansa Germany aided the Danish airline DDL, the Austrian OLAG and CLS in Czechoslovakia. The German airline also helped the formation of the Spanish airline Iberia and Balair in Switzerland. What became known as the German Continental System involved airlines from Finland and the north to the Balkan countries. Poland, however, broke free of this system to form LOT in 1929. In the late 1920s airlines were established in Yugoslavia, Hungary, Romania and Bulgaria. Thus this new form of transport was well and truly established in Europe by the end of the decade.

The development of the airline industry was by no means limited to Europe. Far away in Australia, air transport offered a welcome improvement to the communications between cities separated by hundreds of miles of empty country. The varying gauges of the railways in the different states made surface transport tedious and the long distances between urban centres encouraged the formation of airlines. Most did not last long but Queensland and Northern Territory Air Services prospered and became the efficient and respected overseas airline of Australia—QANTAS.

In nearby New Guinea the densely forested and mountainous terrain made travel difficult or even dangerous, for some of the natives acquired a taste for unwary travellers. A journey from Edie Creek to the coastal settlement of Salamanta could take 10 days on foot along rough paths over the 4000ft mountain ridge and understandably there were plenty of customers when an air service over the 35-mile route was begun. A fare of £25 was considered infinitely preferable to the risk of disease, fever or even the cooking pot.

That vast distances could be flown by aircraft had been convincingly demonstrated as early as 1919 when a Vickers Vimy was flown by two brothers from Hounslow Heath to Darwin—a distance of over 11,000 miles—to win a £10,000 prize for the first Australians to fly from the United Kingdom to Australia. Captain Ross Smith and Lieutenant Keith Smith completed their journey in 28 days—a journey which can be flown in almost as many hours today.

Although it might be thought that the Canadian vastness would lend itself to the development of air services, in fact most of the population lived within 100 miles of the border with the United States and were served by the excellent Canadian National and Canadian Pacific railway network. Communications in the far north relied on dog-sleighs and canoes as their principal means of transport and many years were to elapse before the aeroplane made a significant contribution to communications in the area. As on the other side of the border, it was as a means of carrying mail that aircraft first began to develop routes in Canada.

In Japan, a country long cut off from the rest of the world, several airlines sprang into existence in the early 1920s. The pattern of development which evolved in many countries proved to be the case in Japan too. Most of the country's small airlines were absorbed in 1928 into the new national airline Japan Air Transport Company, the forerunner of today's Japan Air Lines.

Latin America is a continent where air transport has long played a vital role. Distances between cities are large. Most of the early settlements were on the coast and those that ventured inland lived an isolated existence. In Colombia, for example, a tortuous rail and river journey from the port of Barranquila to the capital Bogota, 8500ft high in the mountains, could take up to 14 days. In 1919 German settlers decided to acquire some aircraft and nine months later two Junkers F13s fitted with floats were used in an attempt to establish a service. However, even with only two passengers aboard, the little aircraft refused to rise from the waters of the Rio Magdalena. After several runs at full throttle the F13 taxied back to the landing stage and all the baggage was off-loaded. Thus lightened, the floatplane finally lifted into the air only to land an hour later with steam gushing from the radiator.

It was the high temperature in Colombia sapping the engine power that defeated the F13, but two years later a successful scheduled service was established using the bigger more powerful Junkers W34. With this machine the tedious journey overland could be avoided by making the air journey of only eight hours.

In 1924, encouraged by its success in Colombia, the Sociedad Colombo Alemana de Transportes Aereos (SCADTA) joined with Deutsche Aero Lloyd in forming the Condor Syndikat Berlin. This organisation studied conditions in South America with a view to opening an 'interamericana' network from Colombia to the United States via Central America to be operated by SCADTA. Deutsche Aero Lloyd's interests lay in the establishment of a gateway for a proposed transatlantic service to South America. To further this aim the Condor Syndikat bought two Dornier Wal flying-boats. The role of the flying-boat will be more fully dealt with in the next chapter but it must be noted that this type of aeroplane was used extensively during formative years of airline services.

A year later, in 1925 Junkers aided the establishment of Lloyd Aero Boliviano and once more it was the F13 which was used to pioneer routes in Bolivia. Successful German enterprise in Colombia and Bolivia was repeated in Brazil where in 1927, the Sindicato Condor formed by Lufthansa became the first airline to be established in the country, flying Dornier Wal flying-boats. In the same year Varig was founded, initially using one of the Condor Syndicate's flying-boats. Later Varig put Dornier Merkur floatplanes into service flying on coastal routes from Rio de Janeiro.

German and British attempts to open routes in the Argentine were less successful but the French, having mounted proving flights from Rio to Buenos Aires, established a network of services from the Argentinian capital. Latignes Latecoere founded a sub-

sidiary in the Argentine and by the late
1920s Aeropostale had established routes
to Paraguay and Chile. Encouraged by
this success, Aeropostale began services in
Venezuela.

Meanwhile, from its base in the United
States, Pan American Airways was adding
more and more to the number of cities
served by its airliners. After several attempts
at establishing links with Mexico Pan American bought CMA, a Mexican airline, which
enabled it to fill a vital gap in its network.

The wild terrain in South America encouraged the growth of airlines and aviation
has been an important element in the development of the continent from the earliest
days. What might be called economic
imperialism played a part too, for Germany
was anxious to achieve a dominant position
in Latin America. The United States was
equally anxious to protect its interests and
viewed the new air mail routes to Europe
with some alarm, for until Pan American
Airways began services in 1927 the Europeans
made all the running in the development of
air transport in Latin America.

It is little short of astonishing that the
country which gave birth to the aeroplane
should have delayed so long in its development of air transport. As symbols of
national prestige, instruments for imperial
communication or advantages over land or
sea transport, airlines were being established
all over the world, yet the United States
seemed like a sleeping giant, a leading
industrial nation which had nevertheless lost
its lead in aviation. A major factor in this
was that, spared the ravages of the 1914-18
war, the United States railway system offered
formidable competition to fledgeling airlines.
In the early 1920s airliners were little more
than converted bombers capable of only
about 80mph and the United States main-
line railways were fast, comfortable and
reliable, and linked all the major cities.

Hence, as a means of passenger transport
the aeroplane had little appeal. With few
exceptions, therefore, the earliest efforts in
the United States were directed to the
establishment of mail services. Initially the
US Army undertook the task but costs
proved to be high and reliability low. The
Post Office Department acquired a hundred
war-surplus US-built DH4M aircraft as well
as some Glenn Martin machines and
Liberty-engined Handley Page bombers. At
first the mail was carried only by day, the
bags being put on to trains to continue the
journey by night.

Although the long distances between such
cities as New York, Chicago and San
Francisco encouraged the growth of air mail
services, night flying would be necessary if
the maximum advantage was to be taken of
aircraft. To that end airfield lighting was
provided at the many stops along the way,

revolving beacons aided night-time navigation, and aircraft were fitted with landing
lights. In 1923 the first night mail services
between New York and Chicago were begun.

In 1925 Congress passed the Kelly Air
Mail Act, which opened up the opportunity
for private operators to take over air mail
routes. By the following year lighting had
been extended over the entire coast-to-coast
route and gradually private companies took
over routes formerly operated by the US Air
Mail. One company which succeeded in
gaining a contract was the Robertson Aircraft Company, an operator which employed
a young pilot named Charles Lindberg.
Already an experienced pilot despite his few
years, Lindberg survived a number of serious
incidents. One day he set off in a de Havilland biplane carrying a cargo of mail. To
keep beneath the clouds, he had to fly at
500ft and gradually as darkness fell the
weather forced him to fly lower and lower.
In total darkness, Lindberg was unable to
see even the beacons which lit the transcontinental route. He only occasionally
glimpsed the ground as he flew on through
falling snow, and he decided to make an
unscheduled landing. Dropping a parachute
flare he hoped to be able to pick out a suitable
landing space. Unfortunately the flare dropped like a brick and the momentary blinding
glare only served to make matters worse, so
Lindberg decided to climb and abandon the
aeroplane. Leaping from his machine, he
landed safely on a barbed wire fence which
cushioned his fall and, after a night's stay at
a nearby farm, he recovered his three sacks
of mail and flew them on to his destination
in a spare aircraft.

On the US West Coast, Standard Airlines
managed to make a living flying passenger
services. Using a single-engined Fokker
machine, the airline prospered by flying film
stars from Hollywood to their weekend
homes in Phoenix, Arizona.

It was not Clyde Kelly's intention with the
1925 Act to assist the growth of the airlines.
He sponsored the Contract Mail Act because
the railways were his backers and wanted
the mail business to be taken away from the
government. It was believed that the small
private airlines would not be able to succeed
in operating efficient mail services and that
the business would revert to the railways.

Later in the same year the Department of
Commerce encouraged the formation of the
Joint Committee of Civil Aviation and it
later recommended the development of a
national aviation policy. The Morrow Board
set up at the behest of President Coolidge
came to the same conclusion as the Joint
Committee and this led to the separation
of civil from military aviation. Herbert
Hoover, then Secretary of Commerce, was
delighted with the new policy decision which
resulted in the Air Commerce Act of 1926.

Effectively this enabled the government to regulate the airlines which had mushroomed as a result of the Kelly Act. In a year the number of operators had grown from 290 to 420 and about 300 aircraft went into service.

One company which successfully tendered for a Post Office contract was the Boeing Airplane Company. Dissatisfied with the performance of the Liberty engine, Boeing selected the Pratt & Whitney Wasp radial engine to power its Model 40 mail carrier. To meet its contract date, Boeing needed to produce 25 of the new aircraft in about six months. Services were scheduled to begin on 1 July and although by the beginning of June only one aircraft had been delivered all were ready by the end of the month.

Initially the Model 40 carried only two passengers but a 'stretched' B version introduced later could carry a total of four. To everyone's astonishment, the Boeing machines were very efficient and in their first two years of operation they carried 1300 tons of mail and about 6000 passengers.

As the decade progressed America began to catch up with the Europeans, for the mail subsidies encouraged the development of more efficient aircraft. In the late 1920s the Ford Trimotor became a widely used passenger-carrying aircraft. Based on the Fokker design, the Ford differed in being built entirely of metal. The wooden Fokker quickly lost favour after a disastrous crash and, although noisy and uncomfortable, the Ford was very strong and reliable. Today few of the famous 'Tin Goose' airliners survive, but one has found a place of rest in the Smithsonian Aviation and Space Museum in Washington. Rescued from a field in Mexico, the Ford Trimotor had been used as a home—complete with a chimney poking through the roof!

The mail subsidies encouraged the formation of an international airline as well as domestic carriers. Backed by an impressive list of industrialists, Pan American Airways was founded in 1927 and, using a borrowed Fairchild floatplane, began a scheduled service from Key West in Florida to Havana in Cuba. Juan Trippe, Pan American's president, was one of America's most important airline personalities. A man of great energy and vision, Trippe was to remain at the head of the airline until the late 1960s.

The Postmaster-General, Walter Brown, firmly believed that strong airlines were necessary for the development of the industry and his methods of support were to be the subject of severe criticism. Be that as it may, Brown chose Pan American Airways as the monopoly airline for international routes and backed it as an instrument of economic force. With Lindberg as a technical adviser Pan American set about the development of routes to the Caribbean and Latin America and the company's Miami flying-boat base

became a major gateway to central and south America.

Lindberg may be regarded as the catalyst which unleashed a worldwide enthusiasm for air travel. In May 1927 he flew alone across the Atlantic, linking New York with Paris and in the process caught the imagination of millions throughout the world. Here at last was a demonstration that aircraft were not hazardous machines but capable of flying very long distances. The Atlantic had indeed been flown non-stop once before—in 1919 when Alcock and Brown piloted a Vickers Vimy bomber from Newfoundland to Ireland. Lindberg's passage was 1600 miles longer and his $33\frac{1}{2}$-hour flight was made at a time when aviation was seen to have grown up.

Certainly in the late 1920s the New York Stock Market began to witness wild investment in the airline business. Large conglomerates came into existence. The Boeing Aircraft and Transport Company, for example, was combined with several other aircraft firms to form the United Aircraft and Transport Company, forerunner of today's United Airlines. Alas, many investors lost heavily, some buying shares at $97 saw them double in value in five months but three years later their holdings were only worth $6 a share. The Wall Street crash burnt the fingers of many who regarded the airline business as a way to make a fortune; it never has and probably never will.

In 1929 the Fairchild Aircraft Company, anxious to protect its relations with a struggling airline, sought the help of Wall Street experts and within a short time the Aviation Corporation was formed and attracted $35 million from investors. The new corporation bought everything in sight starting with its parent. All manner of small airlines, flying schools, airport construction companies, even radio stations, were snapped up by the company, which is known today as the AVCO Corporation. In an endeavour to bring some order to this motley collection of airlines, all were gathered into one new carrier—American Airways.

Further major upheavals were to take place within a few years, but already the sleeping giant was on the move. In 1928 Germany still had the largest airline in the world and all its airliners together carried 100,000 passengers in that year. In the, same year United States airlines flew 60,000 passengers, Britain 27,000 and France 22,000. A year later Germany carried 120,000 but the United States had shot up to 160,000. The figures for Britain and France remained low down in the scale. This rapid growth of the American airline industry was a portent of things to come; the leadership of the air transport world had moved back across the Atlantic to the birthplace of the aeroplane.

Above: *The Handley Page W8, 9 and 10 series of three-engined airliners for up to 15 passengers provided a wide variety of services from the early 1920s. The first of the W8f (Hamilton) development, using a Rolls-Royce 360 hp engine in the nose and two Siddeley 240 hp engines on the wings, was bought by the Belgian airline Sabena, who had more of the same type built under licence in Belgium. Here one of the Sabena Hamiltons, ' Princesse Marie Rosé,' is shown.*

Left: *In 1933 the French Dewoitine D332 Emeraude all-metal eight-passenger monoplane set up several fast intercity timings in Air France service, including Paris-Algiers in six hours, Paris-Dakar in 25 hours, and Paris-Saigon in a flying time of 48 hours, before crashing on the return flight from Saigon in December 1933.*

3. Ships of the Air

As aircraft gradually developed into practical airliners, the airship continued to enjoy some enthusiastic support. Although the first airship to be built and flown was in fact, French, Count Ferdinand von Zeppelin's name will always be associated with this type of air transport. His airships were the first to carry passengers on a regular scheduled basis. Between 1910 and the outbreak of the 1914-18 war the airships of Deutsche Luftschiffahrts AG (Delag) carried no fewer than 35,000 passengers. The 25-seat airships were based at Friedrichshafen on Lake Constance and flew a circular route via Baden-Baden, Frankfurt, Dusseldorf, Hamburg, Potsdam, Gotha and back to Friedrichshafen.

Zeppelin's first airship, the LZ1, flew in 1900 powered by two 16hp Daimler engines. It was 390 feet long and had a rubberised-silk envelope covering an aluminium framework about 30 feet in diameter. There were 16 hydrogen gas balloons installed in the airship to provide an important safety feature; in the event of the failure of one of the gas bags it was intended that stability would be maintained by those remaining. The LZ1 was not without its problems but Zeppelin persevered and after some years Delag ordered a series of passenger-carrying airships, the LZ7 being typical of the craft used. The LZ7 was capable of cruising at 36mph and remaining airborne for 40 hours, giving a maximum range in still air of about 1400 miles. The plywood-lined and carpeted cabin was an integral part of the airship's frame and included facilities such as a toilet and washroom; it was to be a long time before conventional airliners were to offer such comforts. Passengers sat in wicker chairs by large windows which were slightly angled to permit good downward vision. The windows could be opened during flight.

During the 1914-18 war, Zeppelins were used for several military roles, including bombing. Although not noticeably successful in causing damage, they did cause some alarm and despondency, introducing aerial bombardment of civilian populations for the first time in warfare. During the war, several Zeppelins fell into the hands of the British and French, giving them the opportunity of studying the German designs.

In July 1919 the British R34, then the largest airship in the world, flew from Edinburgh to New York; it covered the 6300 miles in 183 hours in the hands of a crew of 30. Two years later, the R34 broke up and was destroyed, and of the 49 people on board only five survived.

Considerable rivalry existed between the French and Germans to establish a fast mail run to South America. However, at that time aircraft simply did not have the range to fly nonstop across the Atlantic and therefore a relay system involving ships was devised. From Toulouse in France, mail was flown to Dakar in Senegal, where a fast ship sailed to Natal in Brazil and on to Rio de Janeiro. The Germans used a similar combination, carrying mail in Dornier Wal flying-boats to Las Palmas whence a ship continued to a position off the coast of Brazil to meet another Dornier.

Despite this 'hare-and-tortoise' system, the journey from Berlin to Rio still took eight or nine days, so the *Graf Zeppelin* was introduced into the chain. Mailbags were flown by Lufthansa aircraft to Friedrichshafen whence the Zeppelin took them on to Recife. Syndicato Condor assumed responsibility in Brazil and flew the mail on the final leg to Rio. This combination reduced the journey time to a total of five days and had the added advantage that the airship could carry passengers. Between 1930 and 1937 the mighty airship crossed the South Atlantic 144 times and carried about 1000 passengers.

During day flights the *Graf Zeppelin* could carry 150 passengers. For longer journeys involving night flying passengers enjoyed a standard of luxury equal to that of an ocean liner. Twenty-five twin-berth cabins were located on the upper deck along with a restaurant on the port side and a lounge to starboard. Large angled windows ran the full length of the promenade and despite speeds of up to 90mph the windows could be opened without causing a draught. The airflow over the vast hull ensured that the passengers could enjoy a splendid view in comfort. A smoke-room, bar, toilets and shower baths were located on the lower deck, where the kitchen and messes for the officers and crew were also situated.

In 1923 the Vickers Company proposed to the British government a building programme involving six airships. It was intended that they should be used to provide a link with the countries forming the British Empire but although the project was accepted, a change of government brought about a change in policy. The new government was not convinced that airships could best be built by private industry and proposed a competitive programme whereby one airship would be built by the Air Ministry factory at Cardington and another by Vickers.

The privately built R100 was the first to be completed and it flew to Canada in 1930

Above: *Airship LZ127 'Graf Zeppelin' pictured in May 1930, the month in which it made a nonstop South Atlantic crossing from Seville in Spain to Recife in Brazil. The airship started scheduled service between Friedrichshafen and Recife in March 1932.*

Left: *A corner of the spacious dining room of 'Graf Zeppelin' with views of the ground through large angled windows.*

The Germans had more success. Hugo Eckener enthusiastically promoted the virtues of the Zeppelin and undertook some remarkable journeys to demonstrate his faith in this type of transport. A new company, the Luftschiffbau Zeppelin, was formed and in 1928 built the LZ127 *Graf Zeppelin*. A year later Eckener made a nonstop flight in the new airship from Germany to Palestine. During the journey, Eckener took the craft down to 1000 feet below sea level, over the Dead Sea. On the run home via North Africa the *Graf Zeppelin* completed the journey in three nights and two days without refuelling. Further to demonstrate the superiority of the airship over aircraft, in 1929 Eckener flew the *Graf Zeppelin* around the world in 21 days, carrying 20 passengers and a crew of 41.

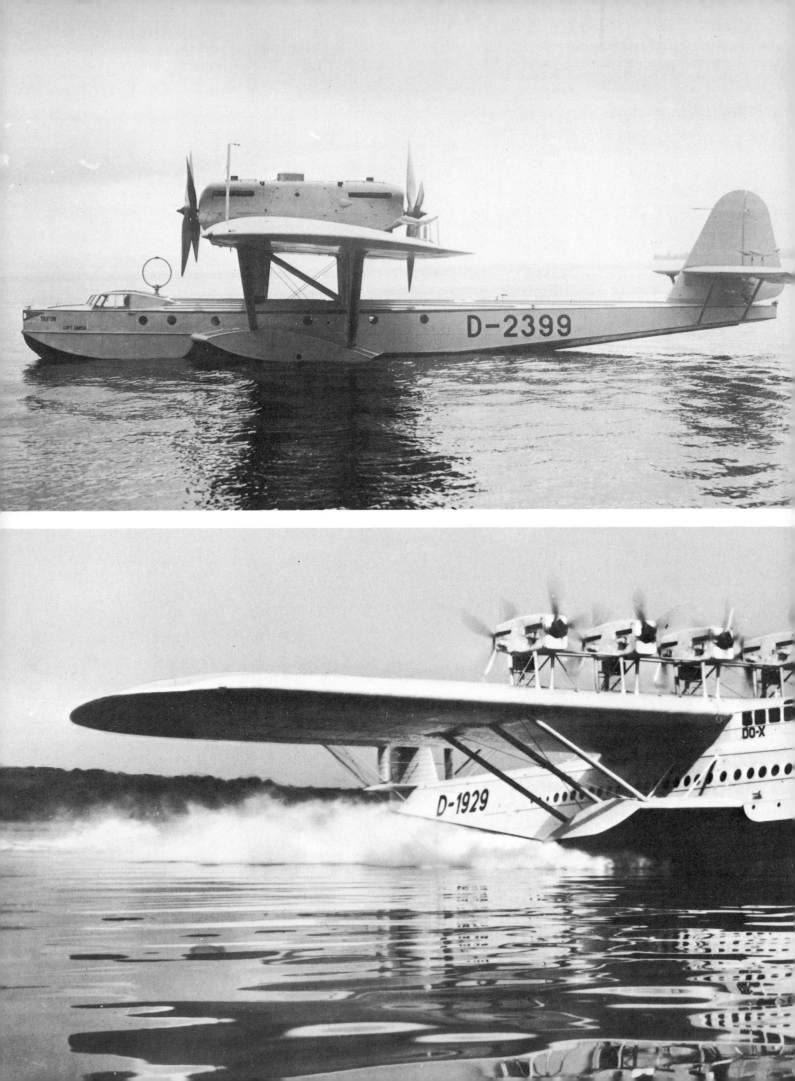

to demonstrate the viability of the project. The R100 had three decks and was equipped with enough cabins to carry 100 passengers; there was a 56-seat dining-room. Spurred on by the success of the R100 the Cardington team hastened to complete the R101 and it was quickly given its first trial. Immediately it was clear that there was a design weakness, for there was insufficient lift and it was decided to insert an extra section.

Impatient to prove the ability of the Air Ministry designers, the Secretary of State for Air decided to head an official delegation to India on the inaugural flight of the R101. Despite the misgivings of the Cardington builders, it was decided to go ahead with the visit and, with the Airworthiness Certificate handed to the captain only at the start of the flight, the great airship began its journey. As the R101 approached France it encountered strong headwinds and made only slow progress. As darkness fell observers expressed surprise at how low the R101 appeared to be. Nearing Beauvais the captain realised that the airship was in a dive and anxiously called for the nose to be raised. Despite efforts, however, the mighty ship ploughed into a forest and burst into flames; only six of the 54 on board survived the holocaust.

Next day only the smoking skeleton of the R101 remained and Britain's interest in the airship as a means of maintaining links with the Empire evaporated. It seems likely that in the heavy winds and buffeting encountered over France, a large section of the fabric of the R101 was torn. The exposed gas bags sprang leaks and with buoyancy lost, the fate of the airship was sealed. It is fair to conclude that the rivalry between the two teams contributed to the over-hasty preparation for the ill-fated flight of the R101. Certainly the disaster effectively ended any further British interest in airships as a means of transport and the R100 was withdrawn from service and dismantled.

The United States, too, had some unhappy experiences with large airships. As war reparations, Germany supplied the country with three Zeppelins which used helium instead of hydrogen to provide buoyancy. It was hoped that by switching to helium the danger of fire would be eliminated but accidents and losses still occurred. The US Navy's *Shenandoah* first flew from Lakehurst, New Jersey, in 1923 and although helium-filled it, too, was to suffer a disastrous crash. In 1925 while flying to take part in an air show, the *Shenandoah* was caught in a storm and the great ship was tossed about like a feather. The stresses proved too much for the airship which was broken and fell to the ground with much loss of life. Not surprisingly, enthusiasm for this form of transport rapidly declined in the United States thereafter. However, 'blimps'——non-rigid airships——gave good service in the US Navy during the 1939-45 war, serving in some numbers as convoy escorts.

Although airship accidents were not unknown in Germany, there remained a considerable enthusiasm for this type of transport. Indeed, the success of the Zeppelin was regarded with pride by the Germans who had established a clear lead in airship design. The *Graf Zeppelin*, like the USS *Shenandoah*, had, in the course of its operational life, inadvertently blundered into a storm and although the huge airship rose and fell uncontrollably, it did not suffer any major structural damage. Encouraged by the record of the *Graf Zeppelin*, the Germans decided to build another giant airship, the *Hindenberg*, which first flew in 1936 and marked a milestone in the history of air transport. It had an air of opulence which has never since been equalled, even in the Jumbos of today.

Although much of the furniture was of tubular aluminium to save weight, great comfort was provided and many of the luxurious details found in the best hotels were provided on the *Hindenberg*. The carpeted public rooms were equipped with comfortable couches and the windows were fitted with curtains. The dining-room was 50 feet square and seated 34. Lace cloths covered the tables, which carried silver

cutlery and fine china especially made for the *Hindenberg*. Each table was decorated with flowers and passengers were offered the finest wines and cuisine. A mural depicting the adventurous flights of the *Graf Zeppelin* decorated the walls of the dining-room. Passengers were expected to conform to German discipline and keep to the appointed hours for breakfast, lunch, afternoon tea and dinner.

Entertainment from a baby grand piano (made of aluminium) added a final touch of elegance more expected of an ocean liner than an airship. For those used to taking a morning 'constitutional' around the deck of a ship, 200 feet of promenade was provided on the *Hindenberg* and passengers were able to enjoy a panoramic view of the passing scene as the great airship made its way majestically only a few hundred feet above ground. Notices exhorted passengers not to throw objects out of the windows!

To enable passengers to enjoy the starlit scene at night, the curtains of the public rooms were drawn to shut out the glare of artificial light. Because some countries objected to unauthorised aerial photography, passengers were obliged to hand in their cameras on boarding the airship but on leaving the three-mile limit of territorial waters the cameras were handed back. In common with ships' passengers, those on board the *Hindenberg* could send telegrams by radio during the journey and a system of pneumatic pipes hastened letters to the mail room.

The airship's main public rooms closed at 11 pm, but energetic night owls could make merry until three o'clock in the morning in one bar and smoking-room. Sore heads and other ills could receive attention in the free sick bay. The smoking-room was pressurised against the possible entrance of hydrogen and matches were not permitted. An electric

lighter was provided and if pipe smokers required a flame they had to seek a light from the steward. An air-lock door sealed off the smoking-room from the rest of the ship and the stringent safety measures were considered sufficient to prevent an accident.

The *Hindenberg* could carry up to 150 passengers and 45 crew but was arranged for only 50 passengers on transocean flights. It could also carry over 55,000lb of mail or cargo. Initially it was fitted with 25 cabins in the centre of the airship. Although comfortable they did not have windows (unlike those on the *Graf Zeppelin*) and this design feature was not very popular with the passengers. Later a further nine cabins were added, each fitted with a window. Although much was done to provide comfort for the passengers, some found the three-day journey somewhat tedious. To provide some relief, it was one of the tasks of the chief steward to conduct passengers on a tour of the airship. Small parties were shown the stores—gas cells, fuel and water—and the spare engine and propellers.

The largest airship to be built, the 800ft-long *Hindenberg* was also to be the last to carry passengers, for after making 10 transatlantic crossings, disaster struck in 1937. Its journey almost over, the airship approached the mooring mast at Lakehurst; customs and immigration officers were strolling across the field when a sudden sheet of flame shot into the sky. Within minutes the mighty *Hindenberg* had crashed to the ground a flaming mass of twisted metal and exploding gas. Over seven million cubic feet of hydrogen fed the holocaust from which, incredibly, 61 of the 97 people on board survived.

Thus, in one spectacular disaster the impeccable safety record of the Zeppelin line came to an end, and with it the airship too. To this day the airship has its enthusiastic protagonists who consider it could be an efficient means of transport. It is argued that helium is much safer than hydrogen and that if the *Hindenberg* had been so equipped the airship might still be a familiar sight today. Fate decreed otherwise and a brief passage of aviation history was over.

The early years of aviation saw the rise and fall of another method of air transport— the flying-boat. Many airlines pioneered services using floatplanes or flying-boats, for the simple reason that airfields were few and far between. In the United States some of the earliest air transport services utilised water-based aircraft; the Aeromarine Model 75, for example, was used to open services from Florida to Havana as long ago as 1919, carrying passengers, mail and freight. As America concentrated its efforts on establishing internal mail services, elsewhere flying-boats were playing an important role in opening routes between major cities, for in

the late 1920s the flying-boat was considered to be the best type of airliner to develop as a long-distance transport; it did not need a runway and in an emergency it might safely put down on the sea. In practice it was not quite like that but for a brief period in air transport history the flying-boat was to enjoy both the support and affection of its passengers.

In their endeavours to forge links with South America, the French and Germans employed flying-boats with some success. Jean Mermoz and Antoine de Saint-Exupery achieved fame as a result of their courageous pioneering flights over the Atlantic, while the Germans devised ingenious ways of using floatplanes and flying-boats. Still with speeding the mails in mind, they catapulted aircraft from special ships used as ocean airbases. The ships were used to refuel the mail planes and send them on their way to Natal on the Brazilian coast.

It was the British and Americans who took the development of the flying-boat to the ultimate. Already employed to provide links in the chain of services operated by Imperial Airways, flying-boats assumed an even greater importance in the late 1930s. Ordered principally to operate the Empire Air Mail scheme, the Short C-class flying-boats brought a splendid standard of luxury for passengers. Initially 28 of the all-metal flying-boats were ordered but they were so successful that Imperial Airways placed a contract for a further 11. Australia's Qantas and Tasman Empire Airways of New Zealand also ordered C-class flying-boats.

The flying-boat station at Hythe, near Southampton, became the base for the Imperial Airways long-distance network. Services to India and Australia, to Egypt, East and South Africa began at Hythe and it was no longer necessary for passengers to take a relay of different airliners across Europe and the Middle East.

The atmosphere on board the big flying-boats was not unlike that of a friendly club, and such was the leisurely pace of the flights that passengers got to know one another well. As the lumbering machines made their way along the routes, passengers could admire the view from a promenade cabin and the relatively short range of the aircraft obliged many stops on a long journey. Overnight stops were taken in first-class hotels, giving further opportunity for passengers to become acquainted with each other. The bonds established during these leisurely journeys led to reunions being held from time to time. The aircraft were spacious, the deep hull permitting two decks to be accommodated within the fuselage. The pilots, radio operator and flight clerk were located on the upper deck, while smoking, midship, promenade and aft cabins were on the lower deck, as were the kitchen and toilets. The

Right: *One flying-boat that did not make it was the Saro Princess, here seen in flight in 1952. The Princess was designed to carry 100 or more passengers on transatlantic and similar long routes using 10 Bristol Proteus turboprop engines, but delays in engine development and, more particularly, misjudgment of the speed with which big landplanes and suitable airports would be developed ensured its obsolescence before production orders were placed.*

Above: *The Short C-Class Empire flying-boat represented a big advance in commercial aircraft development, and possibly the only means at the time by which the British Government's decision of 1935 to carry all mail within the Empire without surcharge could be implemented. Imperial Airways took the unprecedented step for such an advanced concept of ordering 28 straight off the drawing board, but optimism was rewarded by a troublefree development and long successful life. The picture shows the second C-class machine built, a long-range version named 'Caledonia', over Rochester where it was built.*

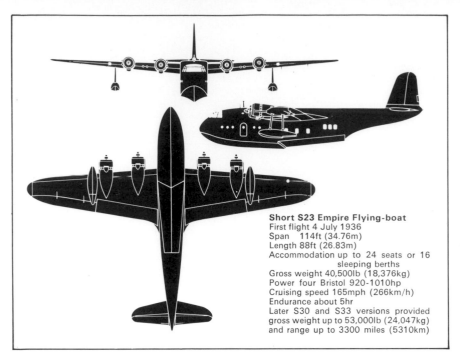

Short S23 Empire Flying-boat
First flight 4 July 1936
Span   114ft (34.76m)
Length 88ft (26.83m)
Accommodation up to 24 seats or 16
sleeping berths
Gross weight 40,500lb (18,376kg)
Power four Bristol 920-1010hp
Cruising speed 165mph (266km/h)
Endurance about 5hr
Later S30 and S33 versions provided
gross weight up to 53,000lb (24,047kg)
and range up to 3300 miles (5310km)

The big flying-boat era in the US started in the mid-1930s and through the war years PanAm founded many of its early services with flying-boats, using Martin, Sikorsky and Boeing aircraft. Sikorsky's first successful boat was the amphibious VS-38 of 1928, of which 114 were built. One of the last of the series was the VS-44 illustrated.

steward (no stewardesses were employed at that time) provided refreshments and other attention during the flight. Cocoa, sandwiches, Bovril and coffee were available free of charge but cigarettes and alcoholic beverages had to be paid for. For the duration of the journey, sunglasses, playing cards, books, children's games and so on could be borrowed.

On routes where night flying was scheduled bunks could be erected, providing opportunity for passengers to sleep in comfort. But Imperial Airways also paid great attention to improving cabin seating. Its engineers devised adjustable seats to enable passengers to adopt a posture most suitable for their particular needs. What is taken for granted today was considered a great advance in the 1930s. Patented by Imperial Airways, the seats were also manufactured under licence by Junkers in Germany.

Pan American Airways relied heavily upon flying-boats in the early days, its Clippers becoming a familiar sight over the Caribbean and Pacific. Beginning with Sikorsky aircraft, the airline went on to use the Martin 130 and finally the Boeing 314. Serving Honolulu and Hong Kong, the majestic boats featured seats which could be folded down to become beds. During long journeys passengers could help themselves to iced water in the pantry. Just before the outbreak of the 1939-45 war attempts were made to open flying-boat services between the United States and England. The range of the C-class flying-boats was not adequate, however, and Imperial Airways experimented in the use of in-flight refuelling, using the hose system developed by Sir Alan Cobham. Pan American Airways grew impatient of operating a joint transatlantic service with Imperial Airways, although the two airlines

did co-operate in the establishment of flying-boat services between Bermuda and New York.

So, the American airline began a service to the British Isles in May 1939, using a Boeing 314 capable of carrying 74 passengers and a crew of 10. The war ended development of the giant Boeing but three were operated by British Overseas Airways Corporation (BOAC)——the successor to Imperial Airways.

The apparent absence of limitation on take-off and landing runs of flying-boats had inspired several designers to produce large and magnificent aircraft. but by the end of the middle 1940s, influenced by wartime long-range bomber developments, it was becoming clear that landplanes would supplant them. There is a lot of unavoidable drag in any flying-boat. To provide the fuselage with a boat-shaped hull results in a large comfortable airliner but it cannot be so streamlined——and therefore so fast and

economical—as a landplane, which can tuck its drag-inducing wheels away into the wing.

In 1929 Dornier flew its 12-engined DoX flying-boat designed to carry 170 passengers. Although it was a splendid sight, the DoX was not a success and it ended its days in a museum. Claude Dornier had built many successful flying-boats, including the Wal used to open up routes in South America, but the much bigger DoX never saw regular passenger service. It could almost be called a flying ship, for it had a 'bridge' rather than a cockpit and separate cabins for the navigators, engineers and the captain.

Nearly 20 years later, in 1947, the American eccentric Howard Hughes personally piloted the first—and only—flight of the flying-boat *Hercules*, powered by eight 3000hp Pratt & Whitney Wasp Major engines; the great aeroplane has remained locked in a hangar ever since its maiden flight. The wooden-hulled *Hercules* was intended to provide capacity for 700 passengers, although the first and only machine was equipped as a cargo plane.

The ultimate giant flying-boat—alas, no less a failure than the DoX and the *Hercules*—was the Saunders-Roe Princess intended to carry more than 100 passengers between Southampton and New York. It was designed to have 10 Bristol Proteus gas-turbine engines driving four pairs of contra-rotating propellers and two simple propellers. It flew in 1952 but developments in landplane and airport runway design rendered the Princess obsolete before it could carry a single passenger.

A few flying-boats are still to be found in service in some parts of the world—serving remote communities on the River Amazon, for example. Essentially the days of the graceful flying-boats have ended but their place in history is assured and they are remembered with nostalgia by those who were fortunate enough to experience the elegance and excitement of those great ships of the air.

4. The Giant Awakes

MOMENTOUS DECISIONS WERE taken in the 1930s, decisions which have had a major influence on air transport to this day. For the unchallenged dominance of the United States aircraft manufacturing industry and the giant size of the country's airlines are due entirely to policies adopted by American politicians during the 1930s.

Encouraged by the mail subsidies provided by the Kelly Act of 1925, many airlines sprang into existence; within a year of the Act becoming law the number of operators had increased to over 400. Most came into being because their owners were aviation enthusiasts but this has rarely been sufficient to guarantee the survival of an airline and by the end of the decade most had fallen by the wayside.

The appointment of Walter Brown as Postmaster General brought order to the prevailing chaos. A controversial figure, Brown had a clear notion of the way the airlines should develop and he ruthlessly set

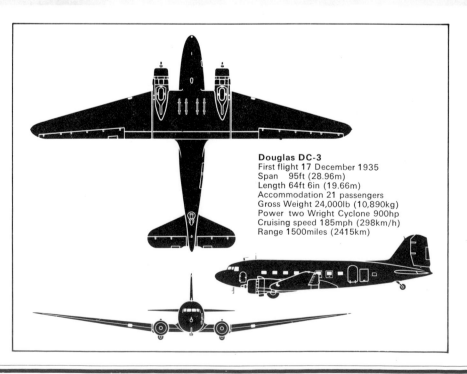

Douglas DC-3
First flight 17 December 1935
Span 95ft (28.96m)
Length 64ft 6in (19.66m)
Accommodation 21 passengers
Gross Weight 24,000lb (10,890kg)
Power two Wright Cyclone 900hp
Cruising speed 185mph (298km/h)
Range 1500miles (2415km)

First of the production all-metal twin-engined low-wing transport aircraft was the Boeing 247, introduced in 1933 for United Airlines. The Boeing fell short of its original design concept however, carrying only 10 passengers instead of the 14 planned, and because production capacity was unable to cope with the demand, the Boeing lost its lead to the similar Douglas design.

about eliminating weak operators. Only the big business conglomerates were invited to tender for coast-to-coast routes, for Brown was convinced that the future lay with large financially strong airlines and there would be no place for small local operators on trunk routes, however efficient they appeared to be.

The Post Office was paying increasingly high mail subsidies and some carriers were suspected of posting bricks and directories in order to boost their air mail revenue. The passing, in 1930, of the Watres Act changed the basis of mail payments to that of available space rather than the weight carried. This had the effect of encouraging the use of larger aircraft which were capable of carrying passengers. In this way it was predicted, correctly as it turned out, that airlines would be encouraged to buy larger more-economical airliners. It was reasoned that an airline so equipped would provide an improved passenger service and ultimately would require a smaller subsidy, or none at all.

The Watres Act gave the Postmaster General dictatorial rights and Brown had every intention of using them to the full. In particular, he exploited one provision of the Act which permitted him to extend or consolidate routes 'when, in his judgment, the public interest will be promoted thereby'. Such a provision gave Brown virtually carte blanche for the execution of his plan to redraw the airline map of the United States. Nearly every small operator was excluded by the manipulation of such rules as that which called for the award of mail contracts to the lowest responsible bidder who had flown a daily schedule over a 250-mile route for a six-months' period. It was for Brown to judge who was a 'responsible' bidder and in May 1930 he arranged a series of meetings which have become known as the 'Spoils Conference'. Only favoured airlines were invited; indeed, representatives of small airlines who attempted to enter the conference room were politely but firmly told that there was no place for them.

Brown was determined to establish three main transcontinental routes: Northern, Central and Southern. The selected major carriers were given the opportunity of sharing the principal mail contracts among themselves—although Brown insisted that the Central route would be awarded only to a combination of Western Air Express and Transcontinental Air Transport. Brown was not the only stubborn personality in the world of aviation, however, and Harris Hanshue, Western's president, was unwilling to be forced into a merger. 'Pop' Hanshue

was a man of unbounded energy and his airline was one of only a few to survive from the swashbuckling days of expansion in the 1920s. Transcontinental Air Transport, too, was an enterprising airline and employed the services of Charles Lindberg to survey passenger routes from coast to coast, using a combination of rail services and TAT Ford Trimotor flights.

By withholding a mail contract between Kansas City and Los Angeles Brown eventually forced a merger between the two airlines and when Transcontinental & Western Air was formed in July 1930 he duly awarded the contract which formed the final link in the transcontinental route. The Northern route went to United Airlines and the Aviation Corporation (today's AVCO) was granted the Southern route.

When the alert Controller-General of the United States suggested that the Post Office Department had illegally awarded some of the routes because no-one was invited to compete for the bids, Brown simply devised new specifications which were so stringent that no other companies could begin to compete and the original contract winners were once again successful.

Brown was single-minded in his determination to engineer the formation of strong airlines. He saw nothing wrong in manipulating the rules so that large carriers were promoted at the expense of small ones and indeed it must be said that history has proved him right. For the airlines have outpaced every other type of transport in the United States and the rest of the world looks to America for innovation in most branches of the airline business.

President Herbert Hoover's administration came to an end in 1932 with the election of Franklyn D. Roosevelt to the presidency. Brown's policies were continued, however, until 1934 when some of his blatant acts of support for big business were revealed in a sensational Senate Committee of Enquiry chaired by Senator H. L. Black.

A young reporter had earlier begun to dig into what appeared to be the seamier side of the Spoils Committee's activities. In a casual conversation with a friend Fulton Lewis learned that although Ludington Air Lines had put in a bid for a route at 25 cents a mile, the contract was awarded instead to Eastern Air Transport which had bid 89 cents a mile.

Ludington Air Lines was established in 1930 and quickly became an efficient operator, managing to become profitable in carrying passengers even without a mail subsidy. Far from being impressed by the lower bid, however, Brown was convinced that the airline could not have expanded satisfactorily on the income provided by such a low figure and he chose Eastern as the carrier most likely to grow and develop the network. Although encouraged by his editor to delve into the story, Lewis's reports never made the headlines. His file was sent to the head office of the publishing chain where William Randolph Hearst decided to put the matter 'on ice'.

When Senator Hugo Black began his hearings into the Brown administration of the mail contracts, the detective work carried out by the young journalist came to light and Hearst was persuaded to part with the file. Charges of malpractice by Brown were made by the Black Committee but although favouritism in the award of contracts was clearly revealed, the former Postmaster General was cleared of fraud. The public scandal brought disgrace upon Brown and for a time it seemed that his draconian measures to create strong airlines would be reversed. Not all those concerned with the Spoils Conference went uncensured, for William MacCracken of Western Air Express who chaired one of the meetings refused to let the Black Committee see his records. Indeed, for having destroyed some of the documents pertaining to the conference he was jailed for 10 days.

President Roosevelt took precipitate action as a result of the Black Committee's findings and instructed his Postmaster General, James Farley, to cancel all the current contracts. The President ordered the Army to carry out the task of flying the mails but the inexperienced pilots and inadequate aircraft were unequal to the task and there were many accidents in which several men were killed. Clearly the military solution to the problem was not the answer and within a month the Army mail flights were cancelled.

It was decided to begin again and award fresh mail contracts. Farley called a meeting to which 45 operators were invited. The large 'conglomerate' airlines which took part in the Spoils Conference were specifically debarred from taking part but by severing their connection with the aircraft manufacturers, · American, Eastern, TWA and United were able to participate in the meeting. Huge losses had been suffered by the airlines after the loss of the mail contracts and their very survival depended upon their separation from the giant business corporations. For the most part, the new airlines had new presidents to run them, too. Boeing cut its link with United, North American sold its shares in TWA, AVCO withdrew from American Airlines and General Motors abandoned its holdings in Eastern and Western. In this way the Big Four airlines were able to retain their transcontinental routes, and the work begun by Brown was in fact carried on by Farley.

Other airlines brought into being by the 1934 conference have survived to this day, retaining most of the routes allocated at that time; they include Braniff, Delta and Northwest. Henceforth the airlines were to be responsible for their own destiny and they no longer had an obligation to support the 'corporate aircraft manufacturer'. With hindsight, this was one of Brown's less successful policies, for although his administration had built 34 mail routes and a network of 27,000 miles operated by airlines strong enough to sponsor new aircraft, the competitive element in aircraft design was largely swept aside.

By the vertical integration of aircraft manufacturing and operation (a pattern exemplified in some parts of Europe, after all), the airline was inevitably directed to buy the product of the aircraft division. Even if the high cost of the airliner resulted in losses for the airline, the holding corporation did not mind for it simply applied for a higher government mail subsidy. The airlines' losses cancelled out the manufacturer's profit so that

Competition for the Boeing 247 came from the Douglas company, whose DC-1 was also introduced in 1933 and could carry four more passengers for the same operating costs. The DC-1 became the prototype of the DC-2, 20 of which were ordered by TWA and of which over 200 were built as a prelude to the epoch-making DC-3.

the holding company was able to avoid paying federal taxes—a complex but effective method of tax evasion. Farley's new ruling ended this connection between airline and manufacturer so that both had to stand on their own feet. It is a curious quirk of history which led to the design of the most significant airliner ever built——the Douglas DC-3.

Needing an airliner capable of flying passengers from coast to coast, United Airlines turned, of course, to Boeing, which designed the Model 247. Regarded as the first modern American airliner, the 247 was of all-metal construction and could carry 10 passengers in a degree of comfort unknown hitherto in the US. The Boeing 247 could cruise at 160mph and carry a full load of passengers from coast to coast in $19\frac{3}{4}$ hours; it was not, however, a particular success. Originally intended to be powered by the new Pratt & Whitney Hornet engines, United Airlines instead preferred the trusted but lower-powered Wasp motor. As a consequence the 247 could only carry 10 passengers instead of the 14 originally intended.

United's president, William Patterson, signed a contract for 30 aircraft, ultimately increasing the order to 70. This effectively prevented competing airlines from ordering the same type because Boeing was fully committed to the production of the Model 247 for United. Thus when TWA and American came to consider the purchase of a transcontinental airliner, Boeing could clearly not supply their needs and so they turned to Douglas.

Jack Frye, president of TWA, proposed that a three-engined airliner should be built. The airline had been well served by the Ford Trimotor but a modern machine was necessary if the company was to remain competitive. The young Donald Douglas had other ideas. He was confident that his twin-engine design would give a good performance using the Wright Cyclone engine. In his early aviation career Douglas had shown considerable design ability and in the mid-1920s he was able to attract the financial backing to form his own company. It was his good luck that Boeing could not build enough 247s to satisfy the needs of TWA, for the DC-1 could carry four more passengers at the same operating costs. Like the 247, the DC-1 flew for the first time in 1933 and it served as the prototype for the DC-2 which appeared a year later. The venture was an enormous gamble for Douglas; the debt he incurred in the development of the airliner was not covered even by the initial TWA order for 20 aircraft. Nevertheless he went on to build 220 DC-2s before the famous DC-3 was evolved.

Although earlier in the field, only 75 Boeing 247s were built. Even so, the 247 incorporated technical advances first seen in the Boeing Monomail and B-9 bomber. Its ability to climb with a full load on one engine was a welcome safety feature and the use of variable-pitch propellers was another notable advance which singled the 247 out as

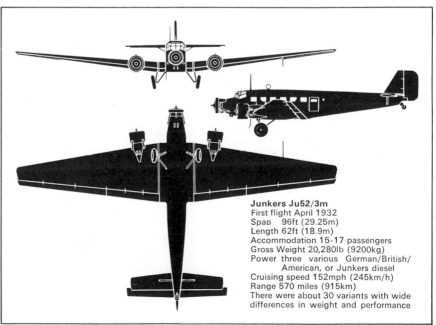

Junkers Ju52/3m
First flight April 1932
Span 96ft (29.25m)
Length 62ft (18.9m)
Accommodation 15-17 passengers
Gross Weight 20,280lb (9200kg)
Power three various German/British/
American, or Junkers diesel
Cruising speed 152mph (245km/h)
Range 570 miles (915km)
There were about 30 variants with wide
differences in weight and performance

Above: *European designers also took to the low-wing monoplane concept but were not yet committed to all-metal construction. In 1934 Savoia Marchetti introduced the SM73 three-engined 14-passenger transport which was bought by several foreign as well as Italian airlines. Belgian Sabena bought an early production batch, as illustrated, and others were built under licence in Belgium.*

Left: *A major French design of the mid-1930s, the Bloch 220, was a clean all-metal monoplane for 16 passengers developed for Air France's main European routes, Air France was the only purchaser and ordered 16, but some were taken over by the Germans during the war and some of the survivors of the war were converted to 221s by replacing the original Gnome Rhône engines with Wright Cyclones.*

a pioneer. As the precursor of the modern airliner it has a place of honour in Washington's Aviation and Space Museum.

The Douglas commercial airliners, however, were to prove to be the springboard from which many airlines were at last to become modern efficient carriers. Impressed by the DC-2, American Airlines asked Douglas to produce a version capable of accommodating sleeping berths. Called the Douglas Sleeper Transport, the aircraft was basically a DC-2 with a widened fuselage. As a day version of the DST, the DC-3 became a 21-passenger airliner—a machine which has become an all-time 'great'. Adopted by most leading airlines of the day (including United, which no longer had to remain loyal to Boeing), the DC-3 was built in greater numbers than any other transport aeroplane. It was used extensively during and after the 1939-45 war; 11,000 were built in the United States and a further 2000 were manufactured under licence in Russia and Japan.

The DC-3 is an aircraft which has earned the affection of successive generations so that, over 40 years after it first appeared, the DC-3 is still in service in considerable numbers. Budding airlines still use the ubiquitous machine to get established before moving on to something more modern and complex. The DC-3 has seen service in all parts of the world, in all climates and terrain.

Indeed, it could be called the Volkswagen of the air—except that it is infinitely prettier and might well survive longer. With the DC-3, Douglas became a major supplier to the world's airlines, a position it occupies to this day.

The foundations upon which American dominance in the air was built were laid in the 1930s by Brown and Farley, who devised policies which ensured that the United States would become the acknowledged leader in aviation. Aided by mail subsidies, the United States caught up with and passed Europe in airliner design and operation. The policy of ploughing back revenue earned from mail subsidies into the development of new designs paid dividends. With Europe preparing once more to go to war, the resurgence of American activity in airliner design was to have far-reaching effects.

President Roosevelt took advantage of the new broom which swept the airline industry by setting up regulation agencies to control the business. The Federal Aviation Administration was concerned with the safety aspects of aviation while the Civil Aeronautics Authority handled route applications. After further deliberations the CAA evolved in 1940 into the Civil Aeronautics Board and from that time any airline with or without a mail contract had to obtain route certification from the CAB.

In the same epoch-making decade America made another contribution to aviation; in 1930 United Airlines became the first airline to employ air hostesses. Initially all were registered nurses and wore the appropriate uniform. Miss Ellen Church is acknowledged as being the first of many thousands of young women who attend to the needs of airline passengers. The first hostesses had other duties, too—they carried bags, cleaned the cabins and even helped to push the aircraft into the hangar at the end of the day.

As America built larger and more efficient airlines so the process of rationalisation in Europe gathered pace in an endeavour to reduce the losses which most airlines were suffering.

In France four major airlines, with government backing, combined to form Air France. The constituent companies—Air Orient, Air Union, Farman and CIDNA—between them owned about 260 airliners of 35 different types; quite obviously fleet standardisation was to be an urgent task of the new airline. Old slow aircraft started to be replaced by new machines such as the 150mph Wibault Penhoët 282 and later the Bloch 220.

The Bloch 220 was capable of carrying 16 passengers at 212mph—proof that innovation was taking place in the Old World as Air France, which was formed on 30 August 1933, set about extending its network to include all the major capitals in Europe. It was soon providing stiff competition for other airlines

The Junkers G38 introduced into regular Lufthansa service in 1931 was the biggest landplane of its time. With a wingspan of over 144ft and a length of 76ft, it is justly dubbed jumbo of the 1930s and both the passenger load of 34 and the range of over 2000 miles were impressive for the early 1930s. So was the arrangement of seats in the thick wing roots and extreme nose from which up to eight passengers had excellent forward views. Only two were built but they were used on various Lufthansa European routes up to and into the war years.

which were generally operating slower aircraft. One type which helped Air France to become a leading European airline was the series of Dewoitine tri-motor machines. The first flown in 1933, was the Dewoitine D332, which was followed by the D333 and later the D338. All were sleek airliners which gave good service, as indeed did Wibault and Breguet machines, and some remained in operation until after the war.

Italy soon followed the example of France by forming a nationalised airline. Ala Littoria was established in 1934 by combining a number of smaller airlines. Societa Aerea Mediterranea was one carrier which was absorbed in the new airline, contributing Caproni and Savoia Marchetti flying-boats. Another flying-boat operator, SANA, had an established network of services to Africa using Dornier Wal and Super-Wal aircraft. A route from Genoa to Alexandria was flown parallel to the Imperial Airways Empire route,

and Italy's colony in North Africa, Libya, was also linked to the mother-country by SANA's flying-boats.

Although these airlines were absorbed into the new government-backed carrier, a monopoly was not established. The Fiat-owned Avio-Linee Italiane maintained its independence operating Savoia Marchetti SM73s, Fiat G18s and a single DC-2, leaving the new national airline the task of modernising its fleet. Italian, German and Dutch airliners made up the Ala Littoria fleet but the airline was encouraged to sponsor the development of new Italian aircraft. Some of the three-engined Savoia Marchetti airliners produced in the late 1930s were designed to meet the needs of Italy's national airline.

Holland's KLM continued to grow during the 1930s, led by Dr Albert Plesman, a man of considerable vigour and vision. The company established fast links to the Dutch colonies in the east for, unlike Imperial Air-

Top left: *Most numerous of the European transport aircraft of the 1930s was the Junkers Ju52, which started life in October 1930 as a single-engined cargo aircraft able to take a variety of German or British engines but was quickly developed into the famous Ju52/3m three-engined 15/17-passenger airliner. Total production of the type has been calculated as approaching 5000, though most were purely military transports, but they figured prominently in many airline fleets until well into the 1950s.*

Above left: *The long-lived Fokker family of high-wing monoplanes was also built in large numbers from the early 1920s onward, but in great variety compared with other makes. Probably most widely used was the FVIIb/3m, one of which is shown making the first Belgium-Zaire scheduled service in 1935.*

ways which operated a series of hops from one British area of interest to another, KLM was concerned mainly with providing a reliable service with Batavia. Having faithfully supported Fokker for many years, in 1934 KLM concluded that the reliable but outdated tri-motors had to be replaced. The company turned to Douglas and selected the new DC-2, an aircraft which quickly won fame for both the manufacturer and the airline.

To commemorate the centenary of the foundation of the Australian State of Victoria, Sir MacPherson Robertson offered £15,000 in prize-money for an air-race from England to Australia. The race was won by a de Havilland Comet racer which took nearly 71 hours for the journey of over 11,000 miles. To everyone's surprise the Dutch DC-2 came second in the race, dramatically showing the world just what a modern airliner could do. Small wonder that Plesman decided to build

up a fleet of 14 DC-2s, beginning a close relationship with Douglas which has lasted to this day.

The qualities of the DC-2 enabled KLM to expand its network to include Prague, Vienna, Budapest and Oslo; at the same time the company stepped up the frequency on its existing routes, serving London, for example, eight times a day. Spurred on by the success of the DC-2, KLM ordered 11 DC-3s from Douglas. Although Amsterdam was not a major European capital in comparison with London, Paris or Berlin, KLM nevertheless led Europe in the introduction of the latest and best of American airliners.

Over the border in Belgium, Sabena did not follow the Dutch example; it turned instead to Italy for a fleet of Savoia Marchetti SM73 three-engined 18-passenger airliners, with which it linked Brussels with Leopoldville in the Belgian Congo. Later the popular Junkers Ju 52/3m was added along with

Above: *As late as the middle 1930s British designers were still producing big biplanes for Imperial Airways, like the Short L17 Scylla shown. It had seats for 39 passengers and was built for London-Paris/Brussels services but only two were built in 1933-34.*

45

Savoia Marchetti SM83s capable of cruising at 250mph.

In Switzerland, too, the 1930s were the years of consolidation and modernisation. In 1931 Balair and AdAstra combined to form Swissair, a company which looked to the New World for modern equipment. In 1932 Swissair ordered the Lockheed Orion, a single-engined aircraft which was faster than the competition although it could only carry six passengers. Impressed by the record of KLM's DC-2, the Swissair carrier selected the same type and later ordered the DC-3 too.

In Scandinavia, Denmark was perhaps the most enterprising in terms of civil air transport. Using Fokker FVIIs in the early 1930s, DDL later bought German Focke-Wulf FW Condors and built up a network that included London, Amsterdam, Hamburg, Hanover, Berlin, Vienna and, of course, her Scandinavian neighbours. In Norway, DNL operated a domestic network, beginning a service which has since become a vital link for the country's scattered communities. DNL was set up by Fred Olsen and other shipping companies which could foresee an important future for air transport. Sweden's airline, ABA, followed the example of several other European carriers in selecting American equipment. Once more it was the DC-3 which was chosen and this type was operated by ABA for several years.

Some East European and Baltic airlines made progress during the 1930s. The Polish airline LOT bought DC-3s and some Lockheed 14 airliners and expanded its network as far as Tel Aviv.

Neighbouring Russia decided to reorganise air transport and in 1932 Dobroflot gave way to Aeroflot which began a rapid programme of expansion. From the beginning Aeroflot was unusual in being made responsible for a number of non-airline tasks. Crop-spraying, aerial survey and patrol work, for example, became a regular feature of the airline's activities. The network of air services in the Soviet Union developed so quickly that by the end of the decade the country had almost caught up with Germany as the leading air transport nation outside the United States. In 1935 Russia imported the DC-3 and was so impressed that a licence agreement for local production was concluded. The Russian-built version was designated Li-2, of which more than 1000 were built.

There were few indigenous aircraft in Russia at that time but a young engineer who was later to produce many airliners designed the massive ANT-20 *Maxim Gorky* in 1934. The prototype of this transport monoplane was powered by no fewer than eight engines, six on the wings and two in tandem mounted above the fuselage. Capable of carrying 60 passengers, the only production version of this massive aircraft remained in service with Aeroflot until 1941. The young man's name was Andrei Tupolev.

One of the Czechoslovakian airlines, CLS, joined the ranks of DC-3 operators, while the other, CSA, preferred the Savoia Marchetti SM73. Italy and Germany emerged as the principal competitors of the United States aircraft industry. By 1939 there were 11 European airlines using American designs and 13 others were committed to the use of German or Italian machines. Britain and France made little impact in markets outside their own countries; indeed, as we shall see later, American airliners were soon to see service with a British airline.

Romania embarked on a major expansion programme in 1934 when the government airline LARES was revitalised, taking over SARTA, an airline founded by the French Potez company. The new airline selected equipment produced by Douglas, Lockheed and Savoia Marchetti and embarked on an expansion programme to include Athens, Milan, Berlin and Warsaw in its network.

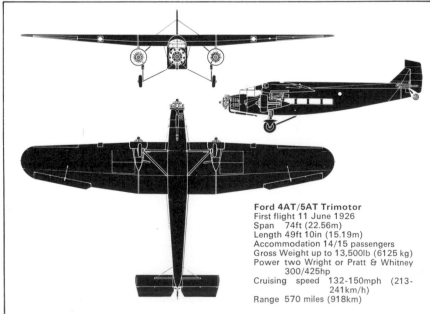

Ford 4AT/5AT Trimotor
First flight 11 June 1926
Span 74ft (22.56m)
Length 49ft 10in (15.19m)
Accommodation 14/15 passengers
Gross Weight up to 13,500lb (6125 kg)
Power two Wright or Pratt & Whitney 300/425hp
Cruising speed 132-150mph (213-241km/h)
Range 570 miles (918km)

In Britain, alas, the government did not include a personality with the drive and vision of America's Walter Brown—Sir Sefton Brancker died in the R101 airship disaster in October 1930—and the development of air transport was influenced largely by the major concern of Imperial Airways in developing the Empire routes with such machines as the Armstrong Whitworth XV (Atalanta) and the Empire version of the big Handley Page biplane—the HP42. Otherwise IA showed interest in only the fashionable European cities, such as Paris, and did little to expand its Continental network.

The insularity of Imperial Airways can be illustrated by its selection in 1931 of the HP45, the European version of the HP42 airliner. Without question a splendid aeroplane, the HP42 was the largest biplane airliner and the 45 carried 40 passengers in new standards of comfort. It was, however, comparatively slow and its four Bristol Jupiter 550hp engines provided a cruising speed of only 100mph. Its ability to land at a slow speed made it a very safe airliner but although it was the last word in airline comfort it failed to provide one of the fundamental requirements of a modern airliner—speed.

The Short Scylla biplane was another airliner which Imperial Airways ordered into service but, like the HP42, it was a lumbering giant which was simply not competetive with its European contemporaries. In the Atalanta, mentioned above, Imperial Airways found a more modern machine. The same company designed the Ensign, another high-wing monoplane, this time aimed also at European operation, but it was not delivered to Imperial Airways in time to make a significant contribution before the outbreak of the 1939-45 war.

Imperial Airways' disinterest in the development of European routes led to attempts by several small airlines to open routes to the Continent. Most were too small and financially weak to sustain their services for more than a short time but some did succeed in making a significant contribution to air

Facing page: Andrei Tupolev's original giant of 1934, the eight-engined ANT-20 'Maxim Gorky', was destroyed in a collision with a small aircraft but a second, and only production, machine of the same name could carry 60 passengers and was in Aeroflot service from 1939 for a few years.

Below: Foreign visitors meet at Paris Le Bourget in May 1939 while warclouds gather and the French build air-raid shelters at the airport. The aircraft are, left to right, Lufthansa Ju52/3m, Imperial Airways DH91 Albatross 'Fortuna' and KLM DC-2.

also had the elegance and excellent performance which typified many of de Havilland's designs and it was used in many countries for several years. Nearly 700 had been built when production ended in 1946. Unfortunately Hillman's enterprise and energy were lost to aviation when he died in 1934. A year later his airline was absorbed into British Airways which was formed from several small airlines.

Encouraged by Hillman's example, a number of other operators, some of them also associated with the coach business, formed airlines to serve popular coast resorts in Britain. Few survived for very long as their services were, by their very nature, seasonal.

The railways, looking towards the time when airliners would provide severe competition, had obtained air powers in 1929 and in 1934 formed Railway Air Services with the collaboration of Imperial Airways and later that of Coast Lines Shipping group. Using the popular and economical DH84, DH86 and DH89 airliners RAS established routes between the major cities in the United Kingdom, and also in conjunction with British Airways and British & Foreign Aviation such regional operations as Scottish Airways and Great Western & Southern Air Lines. Generally this enterprise must be considered a success, for it continued in operation for 14 years until it was finally absorbed into British European Airways in 1947.

Jersey Airways was seemingly a 'holiday' airline which was however a successful all-year-round operation. It was founded in 1933 by W. L. Thurgood, a bus operator and coachbuilder, and could offer a much faster service than the Channel steamers operated by the railways. Within a year of its formation the airline owned a fleet of eight DH Dragons and had carried 25,000 passengers using the beach at St Helier as its Jersey aerodrome. Whitehall Securities obtained an interest in 1934 and early in 1935 the four-engined DH86 Express was put into operation. The railways retained their major activity in Channel Island services by acquiring an interest in Channel Island Airways, the holding company, and complete control of the airline in 1934.

Captain Gordon Olley was instrumental in setting up several small airlines during this period, and they came into the British & Foreign Aviation group in due course. His own Olley Air Service remained in existence for several years until absorbed into the British United Airways group after the 1939-45 war.

British Airways, which was controlled by Whitehall Securities, having reached agreement with the railway companies on setting up Scottish Airways had little interest in developing domestic routes and concentrated its efforts on building up a network of services

transport. Edward Hillman formed Hillman Airways in 1932, bringing a refreshing new approach to airline operation. Hillman was a successful motor-coach operator and he applied a simple 'no frills' principle to running his airline. He regarded his pilots as no more than aeroplane drivers and they were expected to help in the general administration of the airline. Hillman introduced a low-cost service from Romford, near London, to Paris at a return fare of £5.50, compared with the £8.10 Air France fare, and his services attracted many passengers.

Anxious to operate an efficient airliner, Hillman did much to encourage de Havilland to build the DH84 Dragon and was the first to put the type into service. This little twin-engined biplane led to the DH86 four-engined machine and to the DH89 Dragon Rapide, an airliner which was the first of British design to sell in quantity overseas. The DH86 was used by Imperial Airways and Qantas Empire Airways to link Singapore with Australia and also operated other IA light traffic routes. The eight-seat Rapide

Development of a classic: The Douglas DC-2 (facing page upper) was developed from the DC-1 in 1934 to meet a TWA order, but was quickly seized on by other airlines as a big advance in design and efficiency. For American Airlines the DC-2 was developed in 1935 into the DST (Douglas Sleeper Transport) and equipped with 14 berths, to become in essence the first of the immortal DC-3s (lower picture); above, typical of the hundreds of DC-3s still in regular service 30 and even 40 years after its introduction is this one of Fiji Airways pictured at Nadi airport in 1969.

to the Continent. Primarily concerned with providing a competitive service, British Airways did not consider the support of British industry to be one of its obligations. Consequently it selected new and secondhand Dutch, American and German airliners for its fleet. The Fokker FXIIs (four from Crilly Airways and two from KLM) were joined in 1937 and eventually supplanted by the new Lockheed Electra.

The Electra was one of the new breed of American airliners which was to make an important contribution to the development of air transport. It could carry 10 passengers and its two Pratt & Whitney Wasp Junior engines provided a top speed of 203mph. A total of 148 Electras was built and the type led to the development of the Lockheed 12 and 14 airliners.

In 1937 British Airways brought three Junkers Ju52/3Ms (two from Swedish AB Aerotransport) into service to operate mail services to Berlin via Hanover. Gradually the airline penetrated deeper into the Continent, adding new cities to its network and using Lockheed 14s on some of the new services. Not all attempts to open new routes were successful; plans to fly to Lisbon had to be abandoned when Spain maintained the refusal to allow British aircraft to fly over its territory, which had frustrated Crilly's plans early in 1936.

Growing criticism of Imperial Airways in Europe became an embarrassment to the government of the day. Under the chair-

manship of Lord Cadman, a committee was set up to investigate the situation and make recommendations. Reporting in February 1938, Cadman proposed that Imperial Airways should be designated as Britain's long-distance Empire carrier and British Airways should be given European routes. The recommendations were not adopted, although agreement was reached between the government and British Airways for the latter to survey with a view to operating routes to West Africa and South America. For a time some European routes were divided between the two airlines, and some were operated jointly, until yet another merger was brought about when both were nationalised under an Act of 1939 to form British Overseas Airways Corporation. Meanwhile subsidies had been announced for internal services in December 1938 and, most importantly, the Empire Air Mail scheme involving the large fleet of Short C-class flying-boats, which had been announced in 1934 and introduced in 1937, was completed in 1938.

With war clouds gathering over Europe once more, some airliner designs were never given the chance to prove themselves. One such was the four-engined de Havilland DH91 Albatross, an airliner which had a beautiful aerodynamic shape but, surprisingly, was made of wood. American and German designers had long decided that all-metal airliners had many advantages over wood and fabric. The Albatross set up several speed records in Europe but the war prevented its

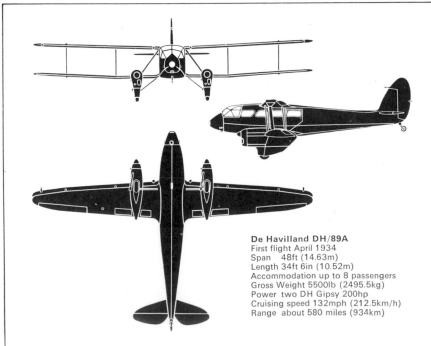

De Havilland DH/89A
First flight April 1934
Span   48ft (14.63m)
Length 34ft 6in (10.52m)
Accommodation up to 8 passengers
Gross Weight 5500lb (2495.5kg)
Power two DH Gipsy 200hp
Cruising speed 132mph (212.5km/h)
Range about 580 miles (934km)

further use as an airliner. In the twin-engine field de Havilland built the DH95 Flamingo.

Germany was the one country outside the United States which had a successful aircraft industry and a thriving national airline. It must be remembered that the Hitler regime in Germany was bent on becoming a world power, if not on achieving world dominance. Consequently the establishment of international air routes had an importance beyond that of mere commerce. Similarly the design of fast airliners was undertaken with the probability that some of the types would be developed for military use. For Germany, no less than the other countries we have surveyed so far, the 1930s were years of impressive expansion and technological advance.

Junkers continued to produce advanced airliners of excellent design. The little F13 had played an important part in the early development of air transport but larger machines were needed. In the late 1920s the

Classic also in its own sphere, and equally a mainstay of the world's commercial aviation for several decades, is the de Havilland DH89A Dragon Rapide. Virtually a scaled-down version of the DH86 Dragon, the Rapide first flew in April 1934. It provided seats for six to eight passengers, depending on fuel load, and was quickly adopted for a wide variety of duties from VIP transport, air ambulance and twin-engined trainer to small-airline flagship fleet. In the 10 years of production nearly 750 Rapides were built.

company produced the three-engined G31 developed from the earlier G24. The G31 was capable of carrying 15 passengers and it had a well-equipped galley; Lufthansa provided a steward for the first time in 1928. Formerly with the Mitropa railway company, Albert Hofe was not the first airborne steward, for the early airships had provided a cabin service, but he might well have been the first to be carried in an airliner.

The G31 was, in turn, to be developed into one of the industry's 'greats', the Ju52/3m. Affectionately referred to as 'Auntie Ju', the Ju52/3m became the principal aircraft of the Lufthansa fleet and was adopted by many other airlines. It was widely used during the 1930s and in the 1939-45 war and over 4000 were built.

Hugo Junkers dreamt of building a giant airliner capable of carrying up to 1000 passengers across the Atlantic. Gradually his ideas were toned down until in 1928 he began work on a large aeroplane that could carry 30 passengers. The result was the G38 which might be called the Jumbo of the 'thirties, for it had a wingspan of over 260 feet. The wing was $7\frac{1}{2}$ feet thick at the root, which allowed some passenger seats to be placed in the wing, with windows in front, and also enabled engineers to have access to the engines during flight. Two of the big G38s were built and they regularly operated such routes as Berlin-London.

It was the Ju52/3m, however, which became the mainstay of the Lufthansa fleet. The three-engined airliner, built with the characteristic corrugated sheeting, could carry 17 passengers and attracted orders from airlines in many parts of the world. It could land on small airfields but its cruising speed of 150mph was rather slow. So the Junkers designers produced a completely new machine the Ju90, the prototype of which first flew in June 1937. Gone were the corrugated sheeting and the ugly three-engine configuration; in their place was a four-engine design employing the smooth stressed-skin construction favoured by American aircraft builders. The Ju90 could carry 40 passengers and was the first Lufthansa airliner to carry air hostesses.

In earlier chapters we have looked at the efforts made by Germany to establish a service to South America. In this, the Zeppelin played an important part but in 1934 experiments began using floating flying-boat bases from which heavily-laden aircraft could be launched by catapult. Initially the mail service took four to five days from Berlin to Buenos Aires; the flying-boat made its way to a ship midway between Bathurst and Natal. Landing on the ocean, the Dornier flying-boats were recovered by the ship and, after refuelling, they were catapulted on their way to South America. This system was employed for some years and experiments also took place in the North Atlantic with a view to establishing a mail service to New York. The ships *Westfalen* and *Schwabenland* were the only vessels to be owned and operated by an airline in this way.

The North Atlantic catapult experiments had first employed the liner *Bremen*. A Heinkel He12 floatplane was launched about 250 miles short of New York and after a $2\frac{1}{2}$-hour flight the aircraft delivered the mail well ahead of the ship's arrival. In 1937 further trials were carried out using four-engined Blohm & Voss Ha139 floatplanes and the floating bases which bore the Lufthansa symbol on their funnels. Although these trials were successful, a further technical advance overtook the floatplane experiment and rendered the idea obsolete; in 1938 a Focke-Wulf FW200 Condor flew non-stop from Berlin to Floyd Bennett Field, New York. The journey took 24 hours, but the success of this landplane sounded the death-knell of flying-boat and floatplane operations. The 1939-45 war, however, put paid to the Condor's pioneer flights and the aircraft found new employment as an ocean patrol machine in the service of the Luftwaffe.

In the Far East, Lufthansa concluded an agreement with the Chinese transport ministry in 1930. The agreement provided for the formation of a joint company to be called Eurasia Aviation Corporation and Lufthansa's contribution was to provide the aircraft. In 1931 Junkers F13s and W33s were sent to China and regular mail services began linking Shanghai and Nanking, Peking and Manchouli. Despite poor facilities and sometimes hostile tribesmen, experimental route-proving flights continued until the Sino-Japanese war effectively brought operations to an end in 1937. Lufthansa continued to fly trial services in the Far East to such cities as Bangkok, Hanoi and Tokyo.

During the early 1930s several faster airliners joined the Lufthansa ranks. The Heinkel He111 achieved speeds of 260mph and could carry 10 passengers. Although designed as an airliner, its shape was to become better known as a bomber with the Luftwaffe. Similarly the Junkers Ju86 twin-engined transport was ultimately to find a military role. Even the little single-engined four-passenger Heinkel 70 was considered to have a potential as a light bomber. It had a retractable undercarriage and was used to carry passengers on special 'lightning' services between Berlin, Hamburg, Cologne and Frankfurt. In 1933 the little Heinkel established eight speed records with a top speed of 240mph.

There is little doubt that Germany's ambitions under Hitler accounted for her success in civil air transport, but success it was and by the end of the 1930s she enjoyed an unchallenged position of dominance in Europe.

5. Air Transport at War

THE OUTBREAK OF war in Europe in September 1939 effectively froze the development of air transport in most parts of the world. Even neutral countries could do little to expand their air services for in most cases there was nowhere safe for them to fly. This was particularly true of Swissair, which ceased operations for the duration of the war, Switzerland being surrounded by warring nations.

So important had air transport become, however, that it had a major part to play in the conduct of the war—in the front line, as well as a supporting role at home. The dynamic impetus which had established a strong domestic airline industry in the United States was allowed to continue, although channelled into the war effort, with the result that by the end of the decade American airlines accounted for 70 per cent of total world air traffic.

It is a commonly held but fallacious view that, as the war progressed, Britain came to an agreement with America whereby the latter would produce transport aircraft leaving British manufacturers with the task of building combat machines. No such agreement was made, but Britain's most immediate needs were for combat aircraft and many fine designs were produced. For the most part America supplied all the necessary transport aircraft, the ubiquitous DC-3 (or C-47 in military guise) bearing the brunt of the needs in all theatres of war.

Development of transport designs was not curtailed only in Europe. Some United States designs which showed great promise in the late 1930s either failed to survive the war as ongoing projects, or had to await the war's end before reaching successful development.

In the Model 307, Boeing once again had a technical success but a commercial failure. Using the wings and tail surfaces of the famous B-17 Flying Fortress, the 307 was the first airliner with a pressurised cabin which enabled it to be operated above most of the rough weather at which other passenger aircraft were obliged to fly. The fuselage of circular section accommodated 33 passengers and the aircraft could cruise at 220mph at over 15,000ft. Named the Stratoliner, to emphasise the fact that passengers were flown at high altitudes, only eight Boeing 307s saw airline service. Pan American Airways and TWA operated them briefly before the aircraft were drafted into military service. It says much for the reliability of the type that several were still flying in airline service in the 1960s.

The Boeing 307 was a victim of the war in that airlines were not in a position to develop

new routes for a long-distance airliner—it had a range of over 2000 miles—and Boeing found itself heavily committed instead to the production of the B-17 bomber.

Lockheed's 049 Constellation first flew during the war but did not enjoy significant success until the late 1940s. The Douglas DC-4 fared better than the Boeing and Lockheed four-engined airliners. The prototype of the Skymaster, as the DC-4 became known, first flew in 1938 and a scaled-down version was later placed in production. The DC-4 was a four-engined development of the DC-3 designed to meet the requirements of major US carriers. When production began, however, military needs had become paramount and the type immediately entered service with the US Army Air Force as the C-54. Production ended in 1947, by which time 1163 machines had been built, and of them 300 Skymasters were made available for airline use after the war.

Another American aircraft which began life as a commercial transport but was quickly adapted for military duties was the Curtiss CW-20. After its first flight in 1940 its potential as a military freighter was recognised and, as the C-46 Commando, it was ordered into quantity production. Powered by two 2000hp Pratt & Whitney engines, the Commando's 'double-bubble' cabin could accommodate bulky military cargo with comparative ease. Over 3000 were built and saw service in many parts of the world, proving particularly useful in the Far East area. Many were 'demobilised' after the war and gave valuable service to airlines, particularly in the United States and Latin America.

As Europe erupted into the Second World War its airlines were affected immediately. The United States did not enter the war until the Japanese raid on Pearl Harbor in 1941. This devastating attack catapulted America out of her isolationist stance and the nation's energies and inventiveness were at last channelled into the task of fighting a global war.

Britain's newly formed British Overseas Airways Corporation (BOAC) put on uniform as it were, and was to play a vital role throughout the war maintaining links with many parts of the world. The experimental North Atlantic services came to an end as did the Empire Air Mail flying-boat services. The Short C-class flying-boats continued in operation, however, linking the United Kingdom with West and East Africa, flying from Foynes in Ireland via Lisbon.

For a brief period the Ensign replaced the slow HP42 on the Paris run but when German forces occupied the French capital of course the service ended. The few Albatross and Ensign airliners were pressed into military service and further development of the types ended. Similarly the Fairey FC-1 four-engined airliner project was abandoned.

Two British transport aircraft did serve with the Royal Air Force in the early war years but they were clearly outclassed by contemporary American designs. The Bristol Bombay was a high-wing transport aeroplane with a fixed undercarriage; 50 were built and saw service in the Middle East. The Handley Page Harrow was of similar configuration and was originally designed as a bomber. In transport service it was operated as a troop carrier and the type was used during the evacuation of wounded paratroops from Arnhem.

BOAC continued to develop a network of services and by 1943 had established a flying-boat base at Poole in Dorset. A year earlier BOAC opened the 'horseshoe' route

Above: The outbreak of WW2 severely curtailed European air services and virtually ended the career of the majestic, if somewhat rococo, Handley Page HP42 Hannibal class of Imperial Airways, the prototype of which is pictured after its first flight in November 1930. Despite its comparatively low speed and outdated biplane design, the European HP42 and Empire-route HP42E, or HP45, versions introduced new high standards of safe, quiet and comfortable travel.

Left: In America, as well as the ubiquitous DC-3, many wartime services were continued with Lockheed Electras and Lodestars, which were produced in fair numbers between 1934 and 1938. Here a KLM Electra is pictured on delivery in 1938, just before its entry into service on the Dutch airline's Far East route to Batavia.

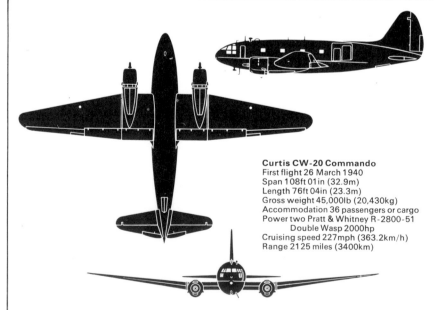

Curtis CW-20 Commando
First flight 26 March 1940
Span 108ft 01in (32.9m)
Length 76ft 04in (23.3m)
Gross weight 45,000lb (20,430kg)
Accommodation 36 passengers or cargo
Power two Pratt & Whitney R-2800-51
Double Wasp 2000hp
Cruising speed 227mph (363.2km/h)
Range 2125 miles (3400km)

from Durban, South Africa to Australia and New Zealand. Using C-class flying-boats the airline flew via Cairo, Basra, Karachi, Rangoon, Bankok and Singapore. The later fall of Singapore to the advancing Japanese broke the flying-boat link—albeit briefly. Some C-class flying-boats were lost to enemy action but others which were stranded in the Far East were taken over by Qantas for services in Australasia.

The acquisition of Catalina flying-boats allowed BOAC to resume services to Australia. Specially converted aircraft were able to fly non-stop from Perth to Colombo, Ceylon (Sri Lanka), and on to Africa. Converted Liberator bombers later supplemented the service operated by the Catalinas.

The C-class flying-boats gave sterling service with BOAC during the war, for as well as linking Britain with West and East Africa, they were used to fly between Lagos and Cairo. In 1943, however, landplanes—in the familiar shape of the DC-3—took over services from the United Kingdom to Lisbon and West Africa.

The countries which went to make up the Empire did not escape the drastic measures taken by the military authorities to obtain transport aircraft. In South Africa, for example, the 28 Lockheed Lodestars and 18 Junkers Ju86s operated by South African Airways were gradually commandeered to carry troops to the battles raging at the other end of the continent.

When Germany occupied Holland the indomitable Dr Plesman took KLM to Britain and continued to fly services for the Allied cause. Based at Bristol, his airline maintained links with Lisbon and Gibraltar and continued to operate until the war ended in 1945. Seven KLM airliners managed to escape from Java before the island was taken by the Japanese. On arrival in Australia they were pooled with the motley transport fleet which was formed in that country. Included among the 'refugee' KLM aircraft was a DC-5, an unusual high-wing Douglas design of which only a few were built.

Neighbouring Sabena also evacuated as many of her fleet to Britain as possible. The types included Savoia Marchetti 83s and DC-3s, some of which were shot down in Britain. Later the fleet was transferred for service in North Africa but fell into German hands. The Congo fleet of Sabena aircraft fared better, however, making an important contribution to the war effort by maintaining links in the area. Its African network extended to around 20,000 miles by the time the war ended.

When Germany took over Vichy France in 1942, Air France ceased to exist, its fleet and personnel being taken over by Lufthansa. The Free French forces, however, supported the establishment of military airlines in Africa and the Near East, operating services

between Damascus and Cairo and between
Algiers and Dakar. Later Khartoum,
Tananarive and Pointe Noire were added to
the network.

Neutral Sweden continued to operate
international services for as long as possible
although ABA lost two DC-3s shot down
during the war. Moscow and Berlin remained on the network radiating from Stockholm until hostilities obliged the abandonment of most international routes, though
London continued to be served throughout
the war. Reciprocal services to Sweden by
BOAC were from 1943 flown by Mosquito
bombers converted to carry passengers.
They were not the last word in passenger
comfort but the 800-mile trip was completed
in about two and a half hours. The speedy
wooden 'airliner' could carry up to half a ton
of mail and freight, showing its heels to any
enemy fighter sent up to intercept it.

Portugal played an important role during
the Second World War, for Lisbon was
served not only by Pan American Airways,
BOAC and KLM but also by Lufthansa.
Thus the city became the point at which the
protagonists met. The country's own airline, Aero Portuguesa, managed to continue
operations although with increasing difficulty as it became impossible to obtain spares
for its French Wibault airliners. The airline
was superseded by TAP in 1944 which began
operations with a service to Casablanca
using Lockheed Lodestars.

In neighbouring Spain, Iberia was established in 1940 with the help of Lufthansa.
German aircraft were operated by the airline
although only domestic services were flown
until the end of the war.

It is ironical that with the outbreak of war
Europe's strongest airline became one of the
smallest, its network truncated by the
fighting which began to tear the Continent
apart. Lufthansa's services were largely
limited to neutral countries such as Sweden,
Switzerland, Spain and Portugal. The
description of a flight from Berlin to Barce-
lona in 1944 is an example of the hazards
which the airlines of both sides had to risk
during the war. A Junkers Ju90 took off
from Templehof bound for Munich but the
darkness on arrival was such that the pilot
was unable to see properly and the aircraft
was damaged in a heavy landing. The next
day, a relief Ju90 continued the journey
flying low over the Gulf of Genoa in an
endeavour to elude patrolling fighters. Flying a few feet above the sea, the pilot hoped
to avoid detection but a Spitfire did pick out
the dark shape of the airliner in the bright
moonlight. For a time the fighter seemed
uncertain of the identity of the low-flying
airliner but satisfied that it belonged to the
enemy, he opened fire. The first burst hit the
starboard outer engine and the propeller
disintegrated. Perhaps the Spitfire was running out of fuel but, in any event, it did not
press home the attack and the Ju90 limped
to its destination on three engines. From
that moment, Lufthansa aircraft were forbidden to fly in bright moonlight.

To the delight of Pan American Airways,
Germany was obliged to relinquish its airline interests in South America. Bolivia,
Peru, Ecuador and Colombia all had airlines
which were linked with Germany but it
became impossible to retain German control
and Pan American was able to swallow them
up into its own expanding organisation.

When Italy joined the Axis powers in 1940,
the aircraft of Ala Littoria were absorbed by
the military forces and the airline effectively
ceased to operate.

As Japanese forces poured into South East
Asia and across the Pacific, Greater Japan
Air Lines was formed to operate services to
the conquered territories. At the end of the
war the airline ceased operations entirely.

The Far East services of Qantas continued throughout the war, its Catalina and Liberator aircraft flying the Eastern leg of the 'horseshoe' route which BOAC operated from Durban.

Within hours of the United States' dramatic entry into the war, the country's domestic airlines were called to the aid of the nation. Contingency plans which had been worked out several years previously were called into action. Airliners in mid-flight were re-routed and their passengers or cargo disembarked. Soldiers or military equipment were taken aboard and flown to war duties. The contingency plans worked smoothly and thousands of troops were flown secretly to areas which were considered vulnerable.

Although many aircraft and crews were drafted into military service, the airlines managed to remain in existence. Indeed,

President Roosevelt signed an executive order which would have nationalised the entire airline industry. However, the president of the Air Transport Association persuaded Roosevelt that the airlines could do an effective job of running wartime transport services without government direction and the order was withdrawn. The energy which had built up the airlines was quickly turned to the nation's war effort and helped to form the United States Military Air Transport Service (MATS). The splendid DC-3 and later the DC-4 became the mainstay of the domestic and international network.

As the C-47, or Dakota as it was called by the RAF, the Douglas transport was called upon to undertake all manner of duties, flying in all parts of the world in all types of climate. The American aircraft industry responded to the call to help the war effort

Probably the only passenger aircraft developed in Britain during the war was the Short Sandringham flying-boat, as a sort of grandchild of the famous C-class boats, many of which themselves continued in wartime service with British or Commonwealth operators. Development of the Sandringham started in 1942-3 when Sunderland 3s were demilitarised and equipped to carry priority passengers and mail on joint BOAC and RAF Transport Command services. Refurbished Sunderlands and new Sandringham's went on to re-establish BOAC's Empire routes and five Sandringhams were built for South American airlines and delivered in 1945-6. The picture shows a Sandringham still in service with Antilles Air Boats in 1977 on a visit to Cowes.

with the same enthusiasm as the airlines. Requested to build transport aircraft in large numbers, production of the DC-3 reached a peak of five aircraft a day. New techniques in design and production were devised which helped the United States to become the unchallenged leader in aircraft production. Safety and economy became accepted features as aircraft became as commonplace as other forms of transport.

Although the United States carriers were obliged to shrink to a shadow of their prewar size, they nevertheless did remain in being ready to resume their services when the opportunity arose. Some routes were established especially for Army contracts and the technical services of the airliners were put at the disposal of the nation. Some military aircraft were serviced by airlines and some modification programmes were undertaken by experienced engineering departments.

MATS personnel were for the most part former airline executives and the airlines helped to establish the organisation until it became self-supporting. The fact that North and South America were far from the battle-front enabled airlines in both continents to remain in existence. Mexico and South America had steadily expanded their airline operations aided by American, German and French airlines (each of which had very definite motives for so doing).

As Postmaster Brown's chosen instrument, Pan American Airways had a free rein to develop a network throughout Latin America. Brown had forced one of his famous shotgun weddings upon the New York, Rio and Buenos Aires Line when, backed by leading industrialists, the airline negotiated mail contracts with the Argentine government. The embryo airline was forced to sell out to Pan American Airways before foreign air mail contracts were granted.

Poor, and lacking technical expertise, the South American countries had encouraged foreign investment but Brazil insisted that airlines formed in its country should be registered, so Pan American formed a subsidiary called Panair do Brasil. One by one, small local carriers were 'picked off' by the American giant. Joining forces with the Grace organisation—a large shipping and banking group—PanAm formed Panagra and by the start of the Second World War the airline and its associates had a network extending around the east and west coasts of South America. The threat posed by the presence of French- and German-founded carriers was eliminated with the outbreak of war. Pan American Airways had achieved a virtual monopoly in the area.

From its earliest days, PanAm relied on flying-boats to establish new routes. Airfields were, for the most part, non-existent and the airline had to be entirely self-reliant in providing facilities for handling the flying-boats. With the acquisition of six Boeing 314s, PanAm pioneered new routes, finally adding New Zealand to its network in 1940.

Having forged links from Los Angeles to Hong Kong and China, PanAm had developed navigational and weather-forecasting techniques which were to be invaluable to the military authorities. When American forces later operated air transport services 'over the hump' between China and Burma, the earlier experience of PanAm's pioneering aircrews was to be extremely useful.

As well as maintaining links with an industry geared to war production, air transport for the first time played a direct role in modern warfare.

It is a sad fact of life that war is often the spur which accelerates the development of new designs and techniques. In the 1939-45 war this was especially true of the aeroplane. As German forces invaded Poland and later Western Europe, air transport was used for the rapid deployment of troops and gliders were used as invasion instruments for the first time. The little DFS230 assault glider carrying about 10 soldiers took part in many daring and successful attacks. Over 1000 DFS230s were built. The bigger Gotha 242 glider was capable of carrying 21 troops and about 1500 were built. A powered development of the twin-boom Gotha 242 was produced but was not a success.

The Messerschmitt Me321 was an ungainly machine with a wing span of 180ft produced in 1941 as a strategic transport. Appropriately named Gigant, the great glider was towed by no fewer than three Me110 twin-engined fighters, or two Heinkel 111 bombers joined together with a fifth engine fitted at the joint. The Me321 was made of welded steel tube and plywood with a fabric covering and could carry 48,500lb of military stores or a company of infantry.

Later a variant powered by six engines was produced and although it was usually well armed with machine guns and cannon, it was an easy prey for Allied fighters. After the addition of bullet-proof glass and several tons of armour proved ineffective, it was flown only under the protection of fighter escort.

The Allies used gliders during the invasion of Sicily and later during the D-Day landings in France. Gliders were not expected to have a long service life as few would be usable after crash landing with their loads of assault troops. The wooden Airspeed Horsa was built mainly by furniture manufacturers and joiners, leaving aircraft manufacturers free to construct more complex aircraft. Over 3600 Horsas were built and they played a major role in the airborne attack on Arnhem and the later crossing of the Rhine.

The General Aircraft Hamilcar, also used in the D-Day landings, was a larger glider

which was capable of carrying a seven-ton tank. Another American glider, the Waco Hadrian, was used in the invasion of Sicily and in the Far East. It was of welded steel construction and featured a nose which could be swung up to allow direct access to the fuselage. The Waco was the first glider to be towed over the North Atlantic; one was towed by a C-47 in easy stages from Montreal to Britain.

The German equivalent of the DC-3 was, of course the Ju52/3m, not a noticeably pretty aeroplane with its three engines and customary corrugated sheet surfaces. Nonetheless, it was very reliable and capable of operating into small rough landing strips, though its slow speed brought heavy losses when supplying Rommel's Afrika Corps. When the larger Ju252 was proposed as a successor metal was getting scarce and the Nazi leaders decreed that wood should be used for a new transport aeroplane. Junkers therefore built the Ju352 which was similar in appearance to the all-metal Ju252. Its performance was not considered adequate, however, and it was decided to continue building the 'Auntie Ju' which was used on all fronts. Over 4800 were built.

Junkers also built strategic transport aircraft, notably the Junkers Ju90, first introduced before the war by Lufthansa, which in turn led to the larger Ju290. An interesting

German tactical transport was the Arado Ar232. Its high wing allowed vehicles to drive in close to the cabin, it had short take-off and landing (STOL) performance and the multi-wheel landing gear enabled it to cope with rough fields—and earned it the nickname of 'the millipede .

For carrying armaments to North Africa the Germans had the Blohm and Voss BV222 six-engined flying-boat originally conceived for Lufthansa, but the war had begun by the time the first prototype flew in 1940 and it was adapted for military use. About a dozen of the large flying-boats were built and they led to the even larger BV238, with a wingspan of 197ft and a length of 142ft. The development of the BV238 was delayed by some French prisoners who succeeded in 'losing' some of the blueprints of a flying scale model which was to be built in Czechoslovakia.

Air transport of small size was to prove important during the war for communications between military officers and government leaders and similar duties. In Germany, the little twin-engined Siebel 204 filled the requirement admirably and was produced in large numbers by Czech and French factories for the Luftwaffe. Of similar appearance, the French Caudron Goëland was produced during the war for the Luftwaffe as well as the Vichy government. It remained in

Above: *Also prominent in intercontinental passenger services during the war years was the famous Boeing 314 Clipper flying-boat of 1938, which was developed for Pan Am as the first airliner capable of commercial operation of services over the Atlantic and Pacific Oceans. The Clippers could carry up to 89 people at 184mph over a 5200-mile range. During the war years they were operated by PanAm and BOAC*

Facing page upper: *Most unlikely, and uncomfortable, passenger aeroplane during the war was the DH98 Mosquito fighter/bomber. Of the nearly 8000 built 10 were used by BOAC to maintain the important route between Britain and Sweden after Europe was overrun by Germany. Strategic and propaganda materials were the chief loads but occasional important passengers were carried in the bomb bay,*

The Focke-Wulf Fw200 Condor was a long-range four-engined airliner for 26 passengers ordered by several airlines other than Lufthansa just before the war. Most of those built as passenger aeroplanes became military transports during the war, including one sold to the Danish operator DDL which fell into British hands. Illustrated is one of two Condors delivered to Sindicato Condor of Brazil

production after the war and a total of 325 was built.

The American aircraft industry also produced light communications machines which were used in quantity in all theatres of war. The Beechcraft Model 18 was first produced in 1936 but was used extensively during the war. The type became a classic in the DC-3 tradition and remained in production for 32 years. Built as a trainer, the Cessna Bobcat also found wide use as a light personnel transport with the USAAF and US Navy.

British designers produced three aircraft in the light communications category although at the height of the war they were used mainly for pilot and navigational training. The popular DH Rapide biplane became the Dominie in military guise and it remained in production until 1946. It was generally regarded as a pretty aeroplane and nearly 700 were built. The Airspeed Oxford trainer was built in vast numbers totalling over 8000 when production ended in 1948. Both the Oxford and the even more numerous Avro Anson trainer served as communications aircraft. Over 11,000 Ansons were built and the type also remained in production after the war ended, providing transport for thousands of serviceman.

The Short Stirling was a four-engined bomber at the beginning of its career but was eventually superseded by the Halifax and Lancaster. However, rather than scrap the many Stirlings that remained in service the RAF converted them for use as glider tugs and troop transports. The Armstrong Whitworth Albemarle also began life as a bomber but was never used in that role. It was an unusual aircraft in that it was designed of wood and steel to enable subcontractors to build the components for eventual assembly by the aircraft manufacturers. This did not prove to be notably successful but as a glider tug the Albemarle gave good service in the latter part of the war.

Utilising the wings and tailplane of the famous Avro Lancaster bomber and with a third rudder added, the York transport aircraft first flew in 1942. Few were delivered before the end of the war although BOAC did employ the type on services to Tripoli and several aircraft were fitted out as VIP transports for Prime Minister Churchill, General Smuts, Lord Louis Mountbatten and others. Eventually over 250 were built and the York continued to give good service with the RAF after the war.

The various designs of communications aircraft that saw service during the war all had one thing in common—an ability to fly slowly which enabled them to land and take off from short rough fields as no other type of aircraft could. With few exceptions, the light aircraft used were fitted with a high wing and tail wheel, which seemed the best configuration for slow accurate flying.

Ilyushin Il-14
First flight 1953
Span 104ft (31.7m)
Length 69ft 11in/73ft 2¼in (21.31/22.31m)
Accommodation 18/28-32 passengers
Gross Weight 38,000lb (17,250kg)
Power two 1900hp
Cruising speed about 200mph (320km/h)
Range about 900 miles (1449km)

The German Fieseler Fi156 Storch was one of the most famous aircraft in this category. Aptly named, because its long undercarriage gave it a stork-like appearance, the Storch had an astonishing slow-flying ability which more than once saved it from destruction when attacked by Allied fighters. Stories of pilots flying around a tree to avoid getting into the gunsights of a Spitfire testify to the manoeuvrability of the Storch! It was produced in large numbers and was built in France and Czechoslovakia as well as Germany.

The American Piper Cub is probably the nearest Allied equivalent to the Storch. It was introduced in 1930 by the Taylor Aircraft Company and was later used to launch the Piper Company, which had produced 10,000 of the type by 1941, many for the United States forces. Like the German design, the Cub cruised at less than 100mph but could land almost anywhere. Taylor had a genius for designing this type of aircraft and later produced the Taylorcraft Auster, a machine which saw service with the RAF before the design was taken over by the Auster Aircraft company, which continued to develop the aircraft for some years.

Difficult operating conditions have often stimulated the design of aircraft with special flying qualities. Canada has bred several such aircraft and the Noorduyn Norseman was one of the type. The Norseman was a high-wing eight-seat general-purpose aircraft powered by a 600hp Pratt & Whitney Wasp Junior. It was not the quietest of aeroplanes but it was ideally suited to its tough military role.

Two other American designs saw widespread war service; the Stinson Sentinel and the Fairchild Argus. Just over 1700 Sentinels were built and it was used for all manner of transport purposes including casualty evacuation. Many soldiers owe their lives to air transport, for the ability to carry wounded men to proper hospital facilities enabled medical attention to be given with the minimum delay. Aviation has brought a horrible new dimension to modern warfare but it also bore the Red Cross to men stricken by disease or wounded in battle. The four-seat Fairchild Argus was used by United States and British forces to carry officers about their duties.

All the aircraft in the light-plane category so far mentioned are of high-wing design but the British used two low-wing aircraft for communications work. The Percival Proctor was developed from the famous Gull of the 1930s and was used extensively by the RAF both as a trainer and a light transport aircraft. The Miles M38 Messenger was developed from the earlier M28 of similar configuration. The generous flap area on the wing enabled the Messenger to land in short fields. Field-Marshal Montgomery used a Messenger as a personal transport after the Normandy landings.

A special and unusual organisation was set up in Britain at the beginning of the war. Called the Air Transport Auxiliary, it consisted of airmen who for one reason or another, could not become fighter or bomber pilots. The distinctive dark blue uniform was worn by both men and women of many nations who wanted to help the war effort: Americans, Europeans—including the former chief pilot of the Polish airline LOT—and, of course, Britons joined the ATA to fly aeroplanes. For the most part the pilots flew aircraft from the factories to service airfields but they also flew transport aircraft, freeing RAF pilots for more militant tasks.

The Japanese aircraft industry produced prodigious numbers of combat machines during the war but also designed and manufactured several transport types. Like the other protagonists, Japan saw the benefits of using gliders for assault purposes. The Kobusai Ku-8 was capable of carrying 20 troops and saw service in several campaigns. In addition to licence production of the DC-3, Japan was granted a licence to build the Lockheed 14 before the war. Kawasaki developed the design as the Ki-56 and nearly 120 were built as cargo transports.

Mitsubishi produced the twin-engined Ki-57, which could carry 11 soldiers and became the standard military transport; 500 were built and it was used for dropping paratroops as well as for communications duties. The Nakajima Ki-34 was a small eight-passenger communications aircraft and nearly 200 of them were built for service in the wide area occupied by Japanese forces.

The defeat of the Axis powers brought an end to the high status Germany had built up in air transport. Its position was strongly challenged by America during the 1930s but its influence was widespread and Germany had been an innovator in airliner design. By 1945 all this was in ashes and the great day of Junkers, Dornier and others were gone.

Technical innovation was by no means limited to the Germans and the Americans. Even during the war Britain made plans for the production of transport aircraft after the war. The Brabazon Committee was set up to consider postwar needs and it made several proposals designed to put Britain in the forefront of aircraft production.

The patient efforts of Frank Whittle and his team brought results towards the end of the war and the jet engine was to revolutionise aviation, civil as well as military. In the postwar reconstruction Britain brought a new sound to the skies of the world with the Vickers Viscount and added a new dimension to air transport with the de Havilland Comet. But, as in so much else, it was to fall largely to the Americans to exploit the full commercial potential of the new technology.

Virtually every civil and military role within its physical capability has been fulfilled by the Avro 652A Anson, or Avro 19. The Avro 652 breed, of which about 11,000 were built and served throughout the world, started life in March 1935 as a two-crew/four-passenger 165mph low-wing monoplane with manually retractable undercarriage. The two original machines flew the long Imperial Airways Croydon-Brindisi route with virtually absolute regularity from 1935 for several years before being impressed for war service. The military counterpart was the 652A Anson 1, which also first flew in March 1935 and differed mainly in having more-powerful engines, large cabin windows and a dorsal turret. It was to become the universal workhorse of WW2, known variously as the faithful 'Aggy' or 'Annie', and thereafter to many operators as a reliable and economical eight/nine-seat feederliner or easy-loading freighter. The aircraft shown is a Series 2 Anson, a variant which first appeared in 1944 and introduced a new tapered wing, more internal headroom and hydraulically operated undercarriage.

6. A Shrinking World

THE SIX YEARS of the Second World War changed the world considerably. The days of the European empires were clearly numbered, new nations were winning their independence and a new pattern of power blocs was taking shape.

As at the end of the 1914-18 war, air transport was to play a major role in rebuilding the nations' economies shattered by war. Hundreds of military transports became available to the airlines and thousands of skilled aviators were determined to become involved in the airline industry. There were other parallels; great advances had been made, not only in the design and construction of aircraft but also in the development of radar, radio communication and navigational aids. There, perhaps, the similarity ends, for the airlines of many countries sprang into action with quite remarkable speed. In contrast to the faltering steps of the early 1920s, the late 1940s saw strides in air transport.

North, Central and South America were the best placed areas for quick resumption of public air transport. Their airlines had continued to operate during the war, albeit under severe restraints, the nucleus of the trunk carriers had been maintained and DC-3s galore became available to the airlines. Changes had been made during the war in the administration of civil aviation in the United States. In 1940 the Civil Aeronautics Board took over from the Civil Aviation Authority and a Bureau of Air Safety was set up, responsible to the CAB. Airlines already holding licences to operate routes were granted what became known as ' Grandfather Rights '—that is to say the new authority would not withdraw existing licences. However, all new routes had to be certified by the CAB and an era of competition was ushered in by the new authority. Routes such as New York-Boston which had previously been the monopoly of American Airlines, were opened up to North East Airlines and Eastern Airlines, a liberalisation pattern to·be repeated in many areas.

Although America was ready for a dramatic increase in air transport, initially there were problems which took time to overcome. Such was the demand for air travel that the technical and operational facilities had great difficulty in keeping up; delays were commonplace, the terminals woefully overcrowded and untidy, and inadequately trained staff were unable to give efficient service. However, the men of the Military Air Transport Command who had organised the movement of 23,000 troops, 1200 vehicles and tons of supplies to Japan within 16 days of the end of the war were soon returned to the airlines which formerly employed them. The initial postwar difficulties were soon overcome.

The three main coast-to-coast trunk carriers, American, United and TWA, were joined by another, Northwest Airlines, and the overseas monopoly of Pan American was well and truly broken. Northwest Airlines was granted licences to serve cities in the Orient opening routes via Alaska. The Atlantic, for long the preserve of BOAC and Pan American, was opened to TWA and American Overseas Airlines. The latter was formed in 1945 by a merger of American Export Airlines with American Airlines and it was the first to operate a scheduled landplane service across the Atlantic. AOA flew DC-4 aircraft into Hurn (Bournemouth), which at that time was an international terminal pending the opening of London Heathrow to world traffic.

During the war American Export Airlines had served Lisbon and TWA operated Boeing

The explosion of air travel in the immediate postwar years was possible largely because of the vast numbers of demobilised service transports thrown onto the market, and chief of them was the C-47/DC-3, or Dakota. As traffic grew and bigger aircraft appeared, the DC-3 became a sort of reach-me-down, handed on successively to new airlines and new roles. This picture shows one such in the late 1970s, still smartly turned out and in the service of Southern International Air Transport.

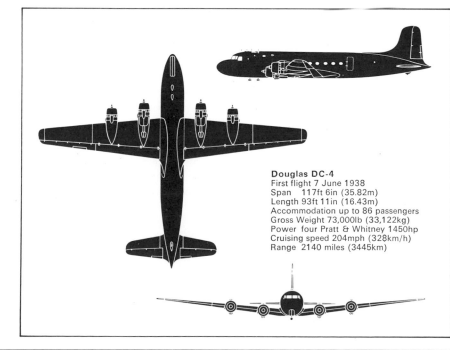

Douglas DC-4
First flight 7 June 1938
Span   117ft 6in (35.82m)
Length 93ft 11in (16.43m)
Accommodation up to 86 passengers
Gross Weight 73,000lb (33,122kg)
Power four Pratt & Whitney 1450hp
Cruising speed 204mph (328km/h)
Range 2140 miles (3445km)

307s over the Atlantic for the new military owners of the aircraft. At the end of the war TWA was given rights to serve several European cities as well as the Middle East and beyond to India and China.

For a brief period United States carriers enjoyed a monopoly of services to Europe after BOAC withdrew its Boeing 314 flying-boats. The monopoly did not last long, however, for KLM began DC-4 services to New York in May 1946. Plesman, with characteristic astuteness, had quickly negotiated the loan of 14 C-54 aircraft at the end of the war and his airline was soon back in business.

Pan American's firm hold on Latin America was broken by Braniff and Mexico was added to the network of Eastern, United and American. Air transport within Latin America grew apace during the war; the economies of the South American countries were stimulated by the war effort of industry in the United States and several national airlines became established during this period. Mexico, Brazil, Colombia and Argentina had emerged as leading aviation countries while the former 'sponsoring' nations—principally Germany and France—became embroiled in warfare. Colombia's AVIANCA, although closely associated with PanAm, nevertheless became an independent airline and the principal carrier of the nation. Argentine Airlines became the country's national carrier although several other airlines continued to thrive. In Mexico, PanAm had shares in both CMA and Aeronaves de Mexico but after the war the American airline was obliged to reduce its holdings to a minority. CMA had grown through its links with PanAm whereas Aeronaves had assumed its strength by gradually absorbing smaller carriers.

The Venezuelan government was not so much concerned with possessing a profitable airline as one which would forge links with neighbouring countries. The oil revenues earned by the country enabled LAV to be established without the need to produce capital from ticket sales or other sources.

Brazil has for long been the leading aviation country in South America. It is a vast country with poor surface communications—ideal conditions for the development of air transport—as the Condor Syndikat realised before the war. American experts replaced Germans in the early 1940s and Varig, Cruzeiro do Sul, VASP, and others flourished as the economy strengthened and isolated communities came to rely upon air transport. Of the Focke-Wulf Condors operated by the

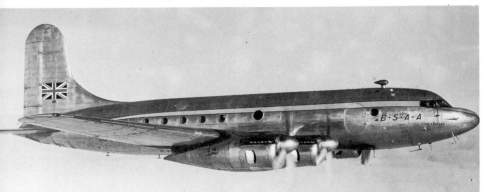

Germans in Brazil, two were fitted with Pratt & Whitney engines and remained in service until the end of the decade. In 1946 Panair do Brasil—an associate company of Pan American—began services to Europe using Lockheed Constellation aircraft, flying to London, Paris, Rome and later to Frankfurt and Istanbul.

During the 1940s many countries in Central America and the Caribbean established independent airlines. As early as 1931 an energetic New Zealander, Lowell Yerex, had formed TACA (Transportes Aereos Centro-Americanos) in Honduras. Gradually TACA-associated airlines were founded in many neighbouring countries but by 1946 the ' Yerex empire ' began to crumble. With the postwar abundance of DC-3s, DC-4s and C-46s, the Latin American airlines grew at a pace which nearly matched that of the United States.

Under the CAB policy of encouraging competition United Airlines was granted a licence to serve Hawaii and by the end of the 1940s the Hawaiian Airlines monopoly within the island group was broken by Trans-Pacific Airlines (later to become Aloha Airlines). Formed as Inter Island Airways in 1929, Hawaiian Airlines used Sikorsky S-38 flying-boats to link Honolulu with the outlying islands.

In continental USA four-engined airliners soon ousted the DC-3 from the trunk routes. A profitable airliner before the war, the DC-3 proved to be too small for major routes and the DC-4 took its place. Then TWA introduced serious competition to carriers operating the DC-4 with the elegant Lockheed Constellation, which had been designed to fulfil TWA's requirement for a fast pressurised airliner for its coast-to-coast routes.

The ' Connie ', as it became affectionately known, entered service on the New York-Los Angeles run in February 1946, three weeks before American and United introduced the slower and unpressurised DC-4. TWA suffered a setback, however, when a Constellation crashed, causing the type to be grounded for modifications to the fuel system. TWA had been denied benefit from its sponsorship of the Boeing 307, but in the Constellation the airline had an aircraft which brought a major advance in passenger comfort and was to spur Douglas to produce a competitive airliner a year later.

Above: *As soon as the war ended it became fashionable for western airlines to provide a transatlantic service, using one or more of the staging airports set up for wartime aircraft ferrying. Swedish Airlines opened a transatlantic service in 1945 using converted B-17 bombers impounded in Sweden during the war, but switched to the new DC-4, as pictured, as soon as Douglas was able to deliver.*

Left: *The Avro Tudor was as big a failure as its immediate predecessor, the Avro York, and the contemporary DC-4 and DC-6, were successful. The Tudor 1, which first flew in June 1945, was the first pressurised British airliner and was intended, but after a protracted modification programme was rejected, for BOAC North Atlantic routes. Six of the aircraft then taking shape were completed, with a 6ft fuselage extension and 32 seats, as Tudor 4s, for BSAAC's South Atlantic route and entered service in 1947; one of them, 'Star Leopard', is pictured. After the unexplained loss of 'Star Tiger' in January 1948 and the similar disappearance between Bermuda and Jamaica of 'Star Ariel' about a year later the class was withdrawn and relegated to freight and charter work.*

In April 1947 United Airlines introduced the DC-6, an enlarged and pressurised development of the DC-4. Alas, the DC-6 too had problems initially and, although it was flown without passengers for three months to ' iron out the bugs ', two crashes later led to its grounding in November 1947. The DC-6 did not re-enter service with American and United until March in the following year.

Stimulated by the sharp competition, both Douglas and Lockheed worked closely with their airline customers in the development of efficient and safe aircraft. Despite the efforts of Boeing and several European aircraft designers, the Constellation and DC-6 families enjoyed a position of primacy on the trunk routes of the world for many years.

Although ousted from the trunk routes, the DC-3 continued to be much in demand for the many feeder airlines that sprang into existence after the end of the war. Such was the reliability of the DC-3 that in 1944 some airlines had been managing to get a utilisation of over 10 hours a day and seat load factors of nearly 90 per cent were not uncommon.

For distances of over 200 or so miles in America air travel had become the norm and the railways were never again to enjoy the popularity which had been barely challenged before the war. By 1948 the five leading US trunk airlines were carrying over 10 million passengers a year and by the end of the decade the number of passengers carried each year had increased almost six-fold since 1943. The total of airline-served cities had risen to about 600 by 1950; every major city in the United States was ' on the air map ' and the nation's citizens became accustomed to using air travel with casual ease.

The war had shown that aircraft such as the C-47 and C-54 could be used to carry bulky freight and US airlines were the first to exploit the possibilities for great improvements in operating economics by setting up freight services. In 1944 American Airlines began a transcontinental cargo service using DC-3s and a year later Flying Tiger Airlines was formed as a cargo carrier; it too established transcontinental services using the larger C-54. The same type of aircraft was selected by Seaboard and Western Airlines to open a transatlantic service.

Although Pan American Airways had lost its monopoly as America's overseas airline, it continued to play a major role as the country's principal flag-carrier and it was the first airline to order the Boeing Stratocruiser. In the tradition of the Boeing 247 and 307 Stratoliner, the new aircraft was developed from a bomber—the B-29 Superfortress. To the wings and tail of the bomber was added a ' double-bubble ' two-deck fuselage which offered a high standard of comfort for the passengers, including a bar and lounge on the lower deck, which was connected to the upper by a spiral stairway. The Stratocruiser was first flown in 1947 and over 50 were built, not a large number but a portent of the Boeing company's coming domination of the airliner market.

As military flyers returned to civilian life in the United States it was perhaps inevitable that enterprising non-scheduled airlines should appear. With many military transport aircraft coming onto the market it was not difficult to set up in business. Many of the new charter carriers attempted to win business by undercutting scheduled airlines' rates and the resultant ' shoestring ' operation of many of the small carriers led to a lowering of safety standards; after several accidents new regulations demanded proper maintenance and flying standards. Matters were improved thereby and in due course some of the well-run charter companies were to play an important part in the development of air transport in the United States.

The rapid postwar resurgence of air transport in America led to a boom on the stock market. The value of American Airlines' shares, for example, soared to $84 in 1944 after having been valued at $2 in 1936 and $58 in 1942.

As the 1940s progressed, American industry responded to the demand for more efficient airliners for short- to medium-distance routes. They were often announced as DC-3 replacements and some were commercially successful, others less so. None could really be expected to replace the DC-3, for modern standards required cabin pressurisation and other expensive refinements and all were considerably more costly than the simpler airliners of the 1930s. One of the newcomers, in November 1946, was the Martin 2-0-2, a twin-engined machine with a capacity for 40 passengers. Only 31 of the original model were built, but a later development, the 4-0-4, was ordered by TWA and Eastern Airlines. A notable feature of the Martin design was a built-in stairway (integral air stairs) to the rear of the passenger cabin which made it independent of airport mobile stairs and considerably reduced turnround times at smaller airports.

Although the Martin machines remained in service for many years, they did not enjoy the success of a contemporary Convair design. The Convair 240 was also a twin-engined airliner capable of carrying 40 passengers and it was followed by Models 340 and 440, which had a lengthened fuselage and an integral stairway to the front of the cabin.

Restoration of air services in Europe took a rather different path; considerable wartime destruction often meant that air transport was the only means of communication during the early postwar years. In Holland, for example, the rail network had been shattered and the Netherlands Military Air Transport

Service employed a fleet of de Havilland DH89s to link five cities with the capital. KLM quickly acquired Douglas DC-4s and by November 1945 operated a twice-weekly service to Djakarta (formerly Batavia), followed in 1946 with services to New York and the Dutch West Indies. It was typical of the pattern in Europe with the colonial powers anxious to reopen links with their overseas territories. Although some European countries chose to change their prewar air transport policies, most maintained the monopoly situation established by their governments during the 1930s.

Britain ended the war with her Empire intact (although it was not long to remain so) and consequently BOAC's principal task was to maintain links with countries many thousands of miles from the United Kingdom, using mainly converted bombers in the early postwar period. Two British bombers converted for transport purposes were the Handley Page HP70 Halifax and the Avro 683 Lancaster. The Halton was a conversion of the Halifax produced for BOAC in 1946 while delivery of Avro Tudors was delayed. The Halton could carry 10 passengers, and 8000lb of mail, baggage or freight in a pannier fitted in the bomb bay. The 12 Haltons flew for a little over a year with BOAC before joining the considerable number of civil Halifaxes in use by charter airlines and ended their career in intensive service on the Berlin Airlift in 1948-9.

The main contribution to civil aviation of the Lancaster itself was its use as a testbed for Rolls-Royce engine developments for the Tudor airliner and as a training vehicle for Lancastrian crews. Several were also employed in the development of in-flight refuelling and Lancaster tankers played an important part in the Berlin Airlift.

The Lancastrian was an elegant conversion of the Lancaster initiated by Trans-Canada Air Lines for a transatlantic service, which it in fact opened in July 1943 with a record flight carrying Service mail. The TCA Lancastrian fleet numbered eight aircraft, and BOAC took a total of 20 during 1945 with which, among other things, it inaugurated an England-Australia (Kangaroo Route) service in May that year jointly with Qantas, the British and Australian crews exchanging at Karachi. The service lost money as the Lancastrian carried only nine passengers, in inward-facing seats along one side, but it established a Hurn-Sydney three-day schedule and guaranteed the final end of the old leisurely Empire Air Route schedules. The Lancastrian was also used to inaugurate a Hurn-Buenos Aires-Santiago-Lima service in 1946 with British South American Airways Corporation, which had six 13-passenger machines, and others were delivered to Alitalia (then a dependant of newly formed British European Airways Corporation), Silver City and Skyways.

The Lancaster bomber also partly sired the Avro 685 York transport aircraft, production of which finally got under way in 1945, although the prototype had been designed and built in only six months in 1942 and first flew in July that year, and three had been built in 1943. The York incorporated the Lancaster mainplane and Rolls-Royce four-Merlin power plant, and the tail unit with a third fin added. When production ended in 1948 over 250 Yorks had been delivered and operated with great frequency and reliability on most of the world's major air routes with BOAC, BSAAC, the joint BOAC/RAF Transport Command services and numerous other airlines and charter companies. The BSAAC York flagship

The Douglas series of transports appeared in increasing size and range throughout the late 1940s and early 1950s, the DC-6 first appearing in United Airlines service in April 1947 as an enlarged pressurised version of the DC-4. There were various development problems and two crashes led to the DC-6 being grounded until the troubles were eradicated and the type could be returned to service in March 1948. The DC-6 and the contemporary Lockheed L-049 Constellation then rapidly outstripped all competition on the long-range services of the world's airlines. These later Douglas machines also proved to be long-lived. The picture shows a DC-6A/B in service in 1977 with the Swiss airline Balair.

Star Leader in 1946 was the first aircraft to land at London Heathrow nonstop from North America, and others set up prodigious records on the Berlin Airlift.

The emergence from the war as the sole European country with intact industrial capacity and suitable aircraft presented Britain with an opportunity to establish a European network of air services. During and immediately after the war RAF Transport Command maintained air services to many parts of the world and until British European Airways became fully operational continued to fly civil air services. BEA was charged with building up a network of routes in Britain and to the Continent, taking over the European services of BOAC. The fledgeling airline began life with a motley collection of DH89s, DC-3s, Avro Nineteens (a later development of the Anson) and Junkers Ju52/3ms.

Of the several new aircraft designs ordered for and by BEA in its formative years from British industry, only the Vickers VC1 Viking saw regular airline service. It became a mainstay of the BEA fleet for nearly a decade, until replacement by the turboprop Viscount in the mid 1950s, and figured prominently in independent and charter fleets for many years thereafter.

The Viking was developed from the remarkable Wellington bomber, with a new stressed-skin metal body initially to take 21 passengers and a crew of four; capacity was increased to 36 passengers in the later 1B variant with longer fuselage. The prototype was first flown in June 1945, and a relatively troublefree development ensured that it was the first postwar British civil transport to enter airline service, which it did on BEA's Northolt-Stavanger-Oslo route in September 1946. The Viking retained the two Bristol Hercules radial engines of the Wellington, which gave it a cruising speed of 210mph with a range of up to 1875 miles. A Viking had the distinction of being the first-ever turbojet airliner in 1948; G-AJPH was fitted with two Rolls-Royce Nene jet engines and furnished as a 24-passenger transport, by which the 39th anniversary of Blériot's first Channel crossing was celebrated on 25 July that year when it flew from London to Paris in just over 34 minutes.

It took BEA until 1947 to absorb all the UK domestic carriers so that some independent airlines survived for a short time. In 1945 Channel Islands Airways resumed Jersey and Guernsey links with the mainland using DH89s and, later, DC-3s. This airline was one of the first to order the new Bristol 170, a twin Hercules-powered high-wing aircraft initially designed as a military transport capable of operating from jungle airstrips. The type first flew in 1945 and was adapted in 1946 for civil use, fitted with nose doors to admit road vehicles and heavy

freight, as the Series I Freighter. The Series II 34-seat passenger aircraft, type-named Wayfarer, first flew in 1946; it became the first postwar British passenger aircraft to gain an unrestricted Cerificate of Airworthiness in June that year and a few days later started a successful period of operation on Channel Islands' Jersey service.

The Bristol 170 was certainly not a pretty aeroplane but as the Freighter it achieved fame on the cross-Channel car ferry services originated by Silver City Airways in July 1948. Modified for Silver City to carry two cars forward and their occupants and a few additional passengers in seats in the rear, the Freighter 21 created a huge traffic across the English Channel, which led to the establishment of additional ferry routes and the introduction of the Freighter 32 with extended fuselage to take a third car and more passengers. In the service of Silver City, and later Channel Air Bridge and others, the Bristol Freighter carried hundreds of thousands of cars and millions of passengers on UK-Europe ferry routes, giving many people their first experience of flying. As the Freighters wore out and no other suitable aircraft emerged (save for a comparatively short success with the bigger Carvair DC-4 conversion), and the seaborne ferries were spurred by the competition to become more efficient the air ferries gradually petered out and an epoch in air transport ended.

With hindsight it can be said that the British aircraft industry tried to do too much too quickly after the war. Ingenious but sometimes impractical designs were built and some led to the demise of famous and respected companies. The Miles brother produced some splendid designs including the four-engined high-wing 20-passenger Marathon to Brabazon 5A Specification, limited production of which was undertaken by Handley Page after the Miles Company got into financial difficulties. A far-seeing company, Miles even proposed a supersonic research aircraft shortly after the war but it went no farther than a design study. One Miles design that did achieve a measure of success was the little M57 Aerovan, an unusual twin-engined aircraft with a useful box-like 530cu ft fuselage and tail carried on a boom. It could carry about a ton of freight or up to 10 passengers and nearly 50 were delivered mainly to charter companies and small airlines.

Far greater success was enjoyed by the small airliners from de Havilland, particularly the DH104 Dove, an eight-passenger twin-engined feeder liner built to the Brabazon 5B specification. The prototype flew in September 1945 and deliveries to airlines started in 1946 and eventually totalled more than 500. The Dove was the first British transport to employ reversing propellers for braking. It proved to be popular not only as a feeder liner but as an executive aircraft and (as the Devon) for military communications. An enlarged four-engined development was the DH114 Heron first flown in 1950, which could carry up to 17 passengers and was sold largely to operators using small airfields.

Carrying on the Short tradition of catering for waterborne aircraft, the SA6 Sealand amphibian introduced in 1948 had a similar capacity to that of the Dove and was also powered by two de Havilland Gipsy Queen engines. The need for amphibious versatility considerably diminished as new airfields appeared around the world, however, and only 24 Sealands were produced. Also first produced in 1948, the Percival P50 Prince was another British small airliner aimed at the medium-range market. It was a high-wing all-metal monoplane powered by two Alvis Leonides radial engines, and although neither the Prince nor the President final development found great success as a civil airliner, as the Pembroke the type was adopted by the RAF as a communications aircraft. As such it was still in service in the 1970s.

A grand design which came to nought was the Bristol 167 Brabazon, a very large airliner intended to carry 100 passengers in great comfort over the Atlantic. It had eight 2500hp Bristol Centaurus radial engines arranged to drive four pairs of contra-rotating propellers, a span of 230 feet and a length of 177 feet; with an all-up weight of nearly 130 long tons the Brabazon was an impressive if a rather noisy airliner. Much money was spent in its development, including the demolition of some houses and the diversion of a road to lengthen the runway at the Bristol airfield at which it was built. After four years of test flights the Brabazon project was abandoned in 1953 and a second machine intended as Brabazon 2 powered by Proteus turboprop engines was broken up when only half completed, having been overtaken effectively by the Britannia development.

In the postwar rehabilitation and development of air services in the British islands Aer Lingus and West Coast Air Services established links between Dublin, London and Liverpool using Avro Nineteens. Farther north, Scottish Airways had developed an extensive network of services to the Shetland and Western islands during the war and later opened a service to Rejkjavik in Iceland using a converted Liberator bomber. By 1947 these and other airlines had been swallowed up by BEA, it being government policy that only the three national carriers should enjoy the right to fly scheduled air services. Independent transport companies did manage to maintain a precarious existence and eventually some were permitted to operate services as associates of BEA or BOAC. Many small companies fell by the wayside during this period and it must be said that since the 1939-45 war Britain has rarely maintained a clear division between the private and public sectors in air transport.

As before the war, it became the custom for strong airlines to become involved in setting up carriers for other countries. Sometimes this took the form of technical assistance and

American manufacturers similarly assumed a dominating position in the medium-range airliner market and the twin-engined Convair-liner range particularly became as essential a tool to airlines around the world as the four-engined Douglas and Lockheed machines. The Convair line started with the 240, a 40-seat pressurised aircraft which began service with American Airlines in June 1948. The lengthened 44-seat 340 appeared around the turn of the decade and the 56-seat 440 Metropolitan a few years later. More than 1000 of the twin-engined Convair-liners were built and about 200 survived to be re-equipped with a variety of turboprop engines and a further lease of life. Illustrated is a Convair 440 in the service of the Norwegian charter operator Nor-Fly.

marketing advice but it often involved a financial holding in the infant airline too. With a 40 per cent holding in Aer Lingus, for example, BEA was content to let the Irish airline have a monopoly of services to the United Kingdom, until in due course, the Irish airline became totally independent of BEA. Airlines were also set up in Malta, Gibraltar and Cyprus with the aid of BEA, forming associations that lasted for many years.

By 1947 BOAC was in a similar position to some of the prewar airlines at the outset of their careers—it had a large fleet of many different types. Different factions within the airline championed the cause of the flying boat or landplane but it was clear that to operate a fleet of 175 aircraft of 18 different types was no way to become efficient. Quite apart from the early 'forced marriages' between airlines and manufacturers in the United States during the 1930s, it had long been accepted that a homogenised fleet makes sound economic sense. It is not from mere sentiment that such carriers as Swissair and KLM have always bought Douglas airliners, or United and Lufthansa have become regarded as 'Boeing' airlines.

Gradually it became clear to BOAC that the days of the flying-boat were numbered. Comfortable and splendid aircraft though they were, they proved no match for the economical new landplanes. Even so, although the Boeing 314 was withdrawn from the Atlantic run and the C-class and G-class flying-boats were retired in 1947, new flying-boats continued to be operated until the end of the decade. A fleet of 18 demilitarised and refurbished Short Sunderland patrol boats had been used by BOAC on reopened Empire Routes since January 1946; they were joined and partly replaced by 12 of the developed civilian version—the Sandringham —during 1947/8, and 18 Solents—a civil variant of the military Seaford flying-boat— during 1948/9. Sandringhams and Solents saw service with other airlines besides BOAC and two remain in operation to this day (in 1978) with an American airline, having first put in sterling service in Australia. The prospect of a new generation of airborne elegance was shortlived however, when all BOAC flying-boat operations ended in November 1950 and it was decided not to proceed with either the Short Shetland or the giant Saro Princess.

Charged by the government to support Britain's aircraft industry, BOAC has had a chequered history of success and failure in its choice of equipment. However, even the government of the day could see that the DC-4 and Constellation were sweeping the board with orders from the world's airlines as they emerged from the hiatus of war. It seemed inevitable that to remain competitive BOAC would have to buy airliners from the New World. Shortage of US dollars eventually dictated a compromise under which Constellations and Stratocruisers were bought from America while the Canadair Four would be supplied by Canada. The Canadian aircraft was a development of the Douglas DC-4, differing mainly in having a pressurised cabin and being powered by four Rolls-Royce Merlin inline engines in place of the Pratt & Whitney radials of the American airliner. Designated Argonaut by BOAC, the Canadair Four was also bought by Trans Canada Air Lines and Canadian Pacific Airlines.

One by one the aircraft left over from the wartime period of BOAC's operations were withdrawn, the Ensign in 1946 and in due course the Lancastrian, Halton and Liberator converted bombers. By 1950 the Solent was taken off the run to South Africa, finally ending an era of gentle and elegant British air transport. Their time was not quite over, however, for a dozen Hythe-class refurbished

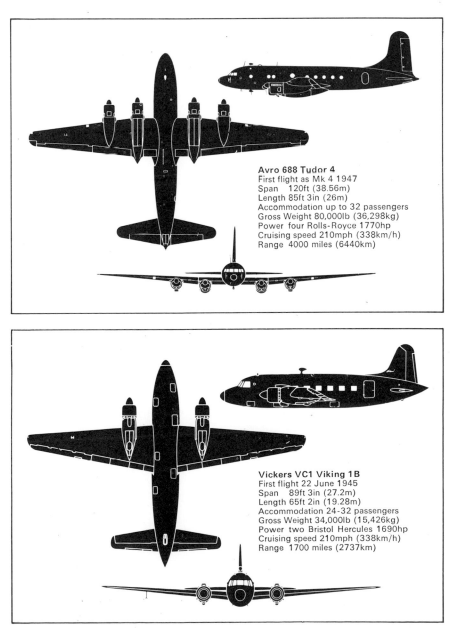

Avro 688 Tudor 4
First flight as Mk 4 1947
Span 120ft (38.56m)
Length 85ft 3in (26m)
Accommodation up to 32 passengers
Gross Weight 80,000lb (36,298kg)
Power four Rolls-Royce 1770hp
Cruising speed 210mph (338km/h)
Range 4000 miles (6440km)

Vickers VC1 Viking 1B
First flight 22 June 1945
Span 89ft 3in (27.2m)
Length 65ft 2in (19.28m)
Accommodation 24-32 passengers
Gross Weight 34,000lb (15,426kg)
Power two Bristol Hercules 1690hp
Cruising speed 210mph (338km/h)
Range 1700 miles (2737km)

By the end of the decade a new challenger to the Douglas Lockheed supremacy had appeared from Boeing in the Stratocruiser. This picture records the historic touchdown at London Airport of PanAm's first transatlantic crossing with Stratocruiser 'Flying Cloud' on 4 April 1949, with 60 people aboard.

Sunderlands, and some of the later boats, were bought by Aquila Airways from BOAC and put into service between Southampton and Madeira in 1949. Other destinations were later added to the airline's network but it did not stand the test of time.

BOAC did not lightly turn away from British products but some years elapsed before a successful design could match those from America. In June 1945 the Avro 688 Tudor 1 flew for the first time and BOAC ordered 21 of the type. The Tudor I was designed as a pressurised long-range airliner, with four Rolls-Royce Merlins and, surprisingly, with a tail-wheel undercarriage when most contemporary designs had changed to the nose-wheel arrangement.

After protracted development and considerable modification BOAC decided that the Tudor would not meet requirements for the North Atlantic route and cancelled its order. A batch of partly built aircraft was allotted to SBAAC after modification to Tudor 4 standard and six of them were delivered for use on the London-Bermuda service. Alas, two of them were lost without trace over the Atlantic, *Star Tiger* in January 1948 and *Star Ariel* a year later; the remainder were relegated to freight carrying or broken up, though three drastically modified by Aviation Traders gave good service on the UK-Africa Colonial Coach route in the 1950s.

The Avro 689 Tudor 2, and the later Mks 5 and 7, were designed with a bigger fuselage to carry up to 60 passengers on the relatively short stages of the Empire Air Routes, but they fared little better than the long-range

version. BOAC ordered 30 Tudor 2s in 1944 and after agreement with Qantas and South African Airways to use the type on all Empire Routes the order was increased to 79. But similar development difficulties were experienced and interest waned; Qantas bought Constellations and SAA turned to Skymasters and the BOAC order, reduced to 18 aircraft, was never executed as passenger liners, though seven of them made a major contribution to the Berlin Airlift.

Another early postwar British design that failed to realise the hopes of its designers was the four-engined Handley Page Hermes, the first British pressurised airliner, designed to take up to 50 passengers. The original HP74 Hermes 1 crashed on its first flight in December 1945, but the contemporary military transport version, the Hastings, gave rise to the HP74 Hermes 2 and later marks with nose-wheel undercarriages. The HP81 Hermes 4, of which 25 were ordered for BOAC, eventually became the first postwar British aircraft to enter BOAC service; they served as 50-seaters from 1950 on West and South African routes until replaced by Canadair C4s in 1952, and later saw extensive usage with provision for up to 78 passengers on trooping and charter work for many years. Normally powered by Bristol Hercules piston engines, the Hermes (Mk 5) served as a development type for the Bristol Theseus turboprop engine.

If BOAC had problems in finding the right equipment it did achieve the other national objective—that of establishing a worldwide network. Southeast Asia, Australasia, Africa

Above: *This picture shows two of the less widely used but nevertheless important British types to appear shortly after the end of WW2, a Bristol 170 Freighter of Silver City and a Morton Air Service de Havilland DH104 Dove. The Freighter first flew in December 1945 and, with nose doors, was the means by which Silver City Airways built up the remarkable car ferry service over the English Channel, starting in July 1948.*

Facing page upper: *Unlike the disastrous failure of its stable-mate, the Tudor, direct passenger descendant of the Avro Lancaster bomber, the Lancastrian, enjoyed a moderate success in airline service with Trans-Canada, BOAC, Qantas and Alitalia from 1945. Lancastrians were also used to open BSAAC's regular South Atlantic services in 1945-46 and after retirement from airline service 14 of them, fitted with fuselage tanks made an outstanding contribution to the Berlin airlift.*

Facing page lower: *A postwar Italian attempt to return to the airliner market was the Fiat G212 which first flew in January 1947. In fact the G212 was an enlarged version of the G12 built for ALI's international routes from 1940, of which several variants were built or proposed. Only nine civil G212s were produced, six for ALI and the Egyptian airline SAIDE.*

and North and South America were areas regularly served by BOAC and BSAAC by 1946. Moreover, BEA quickly became a major carrier within Europe, with rather fewer difficulties with equipment. In 1947 the first flight took place of the Airspeed AS57 Ambassador, an aircraft designed to conform to the Brabazon 2 specification for a medium-stage airliner and to the new international requirement for twin-engine airliners to be able to maintain height on only one engine. It was a high-wing design with nosewheel undercarriage and two Bristol Centaurus radial engines. The Ambassador, named the Elizabethan class in BEA service, had a wide pressurised cabin and offered a high standard of comfort. Although 21 were delivered to BEA between 1951 and 1953 it failed to find any other customers. Along with its Vikings and Ambassadors BEA retained numbers of DC-3s and to sustain its high rate of growth it embarked on the expansion and modernisation of its DC-3 fleet in 1950. All the aircraft were rebuilt by Scottish Aviation to provide a fleet of 32-seat Pionairs fitted with integral boarding stairs, finished in a neat new BEA livery and bearing the names of air pioneers. The fleet of Pionairs and Pionair/Leopard convertible freighters eventually reached 38.

France, like other Continental countries, had a major task in restoring air services and several small airlines flowered briefly before disappearing or being absorbed into larger companies. Having built aircraft for the occupying German forces, France ended the war with at least the nucleus of an aircraft industry. This enabled her to start services to London as early as October 1945, using Junkers Ju52/3ms built from parts manufactured in France. French leaders also could see that the new American airliners could play an important part in helping the country to regain its former position as a leader in aviation. Fifteen DC-4s and 13 Constellations were ordered from America and by the time they had begun to arrive, air transport had been nationalised once more and in 1946 Air France came into being again. As well as the American equipment, considerable numbers of indigenous designs were also ordered, including 40 Bloch/Sud-Est 161 Languedocs, 25 SO94 feeder liners and 30 SO30 Bretagne 30-seat airliners. These aircraft had some vintage, the Languedoc having first flown in 1939 and the Bretagne having been built in 1942. The Languedoc was a tail-wheel four-engined airliner with a range of about 1650 miles; it was produced for Air France, Iberia, LOT and Misrair, as well as for the French Air Force. With this aircraft the famous name of Bloch disappeared but Marcel Bloch, having survived the horrors of a Nazi concentration camp, later returned to France as Marcel Dassault and once more found a place of honour in French aviation.

As its new machines were delivered Air France set about restarting international services and in 1945 French African territories were linked once more to the mother country. A year later, in 1946, Air France airliners resumed services to Southeast Asia and South America, and opened a route to New York. Although the lion's share of overseas routes was allocated to Air France, several other airlines were also allowed to become established. Aigle Azur operated between France and North Africa, later using a small fleet of retired Boeing 307 Stratoliners. TAI and UAT were two airlines which had a close association with shipping interests and both served Africa and the Far East, initially with Ju52/3ms and later using Bristol 170s and DC-4s.

France has a long tradition of being an airminded nation and regardless of the political persuasion of its governments there has always been strong support for the country's aviation industry. French aviation policies have by no means been faultless but its industry has always shown a vigour and innovative spirit which is envied by many countries. As in Britain, some of her postwar airliners were a success while others failed. Manufacturers everywhere were having the greatest difficulty in matching, much less improving on, established American designs.

The prototypes of two very different French transport aircraft flew for the first time in 1949; the Breguet 761 Deux-Ponts, which became the 763 Provence in Air France service, and the Sud-Est SE2010 Armagnac.

The Armagnac was an elegant airliner, powered by four Pratt & Whitney engines, with a range of over 3000 miles as a 64-seater or a capacity of 107 passengers on short stages. The type was a commercial failure, although a few operated reliably with SAGETA in the 1950s. The far-from-elegant Breguet design was also powered by four Pratt & Whitney engines but differed in many other respects; it had a fat double-deck fuselage which enabled passengers to be carried on the top deck and cargo or passengers below. It did not enter service with Air France until March 1953 but was used with some success on routes between France and her territories in North Africa. The basic type name Deux-Ponts continued to be used colloquially; Air France charged a higher fare for *Pont Superieur* than for *Pont Inferieur* lower-deck passengers.

A moderately successful design was the Dassault MD313 Flamant, a general-purpose transport aircraft which was used extensively in French colonial territories. It was first flown in 1947 and over 270 were built and used mainly by the French Air Force. The prototype of the Nord N2500 Noratlas military/general-purpose transport flew for the first time in 1949. The Noratlas was a twin-boom machine with a capacious cabin and was normally powered by two French-built Bristol Hercules radial engines. The type was adopted by several air forces during the 1950s mainly for cargo but a civil passenger version for up to 47 passengers was bought by UAT and Air Algérie.

In neighbouring Belgium, Sabena was reinstalled as the national carrier and it soon set about building up a network which included Belgian territories in Africa. Two years later, in 1947, Sabena joined the growing number of European carriers serving New York.

Deprived of its role as a scheduled British airline under the postwar reconstruction, Scottish Aviation helped to set up a number of airlines, including COBETA in Belgium, SLNA in Luxembourg, and Hellenic Airlines in Greece. None of these ventures proved profitable, however, and all three ended services in 1950.

As its isolation was ended after the war Swissair resumed services in 1945 with DC-3s and embarked upon a period of steady but unspectacular growth. Lacking the stimulus of having to serve overseas territories and having no particular desire extravagantly to 'show the flag', Swissair has been notable for being a profitable airline with an acknowledged high standard of cabin service.

Left lower: No beauty by any standards, the Breguet 763 Provence, which first flew as the 761 Deux Ponts in February 1949 was nevertheless a serviceable airliner with accommodation for over 100 passengers on its two decks.

Left upper: As a practical and economical medium/long-range airliner for the early postwar period the idea was conceived of marrying the C-54/DC-4 airframe with Rolls-Royce Merlin engines. The result was the DC-4M, or Canadair C-4, first produced for Trans-Canada Air Lines, which put six on the North Atlantic route in 1947/8. With the failure of the Tudor, to conserve scarce US dollars, an improved version of the C-4, incorporating features developed for the DC-6, was adopted by BOAC, which bought 22 of the 40-passenger pressurised airliners to form the Argonaut class, the first of which was delivered in March 1949.

Below: As Europe was still fumbling for the right formula for a successful long-range airliner, by the end of the 1940s American manufacturers were poised to launch the next stage of development of their world-beating designs, one of which was the L-1049 Super Constellation.

It was not until 1949 that Swissair started services to New York, becoming the seventh European carrier to do so.

Spain and Portugal started international services in 1946 and 1947 respectively. Iberia soon joined the British, French and Dutch in opening services across the South Atlantic, beginning in 1946. Spain was unusual in permitting the establishment of an independent airline—AVIACO, formed in 1948. Using Bristol 170s this airline linked Spain with her colonies in Africa as well as operating some domestic routes. Following the pattern set by other European nations, TAP opened up services to Portugal's African colonies as soon as it was possible, beginning in 1947.

An interesting development took place in Scandinavia which, but for the war, might well have happened earlier, for discussions about pooling the air transport resources of Denmark, Norway and Sweden had started in 1938. After the war the impetus got under way again, leading to the formation of the Scandinavian Airlines System in July 1946. Having maintained services throughout the war, Sweden's ABA was in a good position to expand its network to the recently liberated Continental capitals. In neighbouring Denmark, DDL did not take long to resume services to Stockholm and London and in Norway DNL started international and domestic services, its fleet including Ju52/3m floatplanes which were used to link the remote coastal settlements with the capital. A Sandringham replaced the Junkers in 1947.

Initially the Swedish government decided not to invest in the new consortium and it fell to Marcus Wallenberg, a leading banker, to contribute Sweden's share in the enterprise. He founded Svensk Interkontinental Lufttrafik (SILA) and in June 1945 a converted B-17 bomber was used to open a route to New York. During the war several B-17s had landed in neutral Sweden and had been impounded; it was not difficult for SILA to convert some for passenger service. Before long though, a DC-4 ordered by SILA took over from the B-17.

The amalgamation of the Scandinavian air services did not take place all at once. The shareholding airlines continued to operate independently in Europe until SAS formed a European Division in 1948. When the three governments realised that the new enterprise was going to be a success they followed the example of other European countries and granted the carrier exclusive rights. Thus the long-distance services begun by Braathen's

South America and Far East Airlines (SAFE) were stopped at the behest of the Norwegian government. Other such international ventures have been tried but none has endured so long as SAS.

Sweden has long had a small independent aircraft industry, originally based on licence production of British and American designs, which has often been able to satisfy the nation's defence needs. In 1944 Saab began the design of a DC-3-size airliner. The result was the Saab 90 Scandia which first flew in 1946 and eventually emerged as a 36-seater. Ten were ordered by the national airline ABA, but the first four went instead to Aerovias Brasil (later to the Brazilian national carrier VASP), which ordered more. The Scandia did not sell elsewhere and eventually all 18 built (the final six aircraft produced in Holland by Fokker in 1954) went to VASP.

Farther north, in Finland, Aero O/Y began services with DC-3s and away out in the Atlantic Icelandair's Flugfelag Islands developed its valuable domestic services, providing remote communities with a vital link to the Icelandic capital Reykjavik. Journeys which could take many days by surface transport over the rugged terrain, would take no more than a few hours in the airline's DH89s and one Catalina flying-boat. Iceland's other airline, formed in 1944, later became the noted low-cost transatlantic operator Loftleidir.

In defeated Germany all aviation activity was forbidden and Lufthansa ceased to exist. As a 'non-belligerent' towards the end of the war, Italy was not subject to such restrictions and in 1947 Alitalia began with the support of BEA which took a shareholding in the new venture. At that time it was not the only Italian airline, for TWA helped the formation of LAI. Initially Alitalia used Lancastrians and such Italian transport aircraft as the three-engined Fiat G12 for up to 22 passengers, and the last and biggest of the Savoia Marchetti transport aircraft to enter regular airline service, four-engined SM95s furnished as 20-seaters. As they were joined in service by the DC-4 Alitalia spread its wings to more distant destinations, reaching Buenos Aires by 1948. Several smaller airlines began operations in Italy at the end of the war but none survived. Italy's aircraft industry made a number of attempts to produce marketable airliners; few however sold outside Italy and some ventures failed completely. The SM95 and the later SM102 twin-engined feeder liner were produced only in small numbers and only one prototype of the Breda Zappata BZ308, a handsome tricycle-undercarriage machine, was built before the company got into financial difficulties. Three six-seat Macchi MB320s, introduced in 1949 did sell to East African Airways but the type failed to achieve series production.

TWA helped the formation of several foreign airlines in much the same way as did BEA and BOAC. TAE was formed in Greece in 1946 and for a time ran in competition with the Scottish Aviation-supported Hellenic Airlines, until that venture came to an end. With the active participation of TWA, airlines were established in Iran, Saudi Arabia, the Philippines and Ethiopia. The availability of American aircraft and assistance did much to bring efficient airline services to many parts of the world.

Alas, far from heralding a period of peace, the end of the Second World War opened up an era of 'cold war' as East faced West over the Iron Curtain. Contact between the two blocs was minimal and aviation within the Soviet system owed little to the West. In Russia Aeroflot is a unique organisation in that it is very much more than the national airline. Crop spraying, border patrol and military transport have been the tasks of Aeroflot in addition to the basic role of

Upper: As well as serving BOAC and other airlines with exemplary reliability in the immediate postwar years, the Avro York, which made use of Lancaster bomber assemblies, went on to play a big part in the formation of various independents. Here a Dan-air York is seen soon after the company's formation in 1953.

Lower: An elegant medium-range airliner which provided an extremely pleasant ride for its passengers in a wide pressurised cabin and little noise disturbance to those on the ground was the Airspeed AS57 Ambassador, which first flew in July 1947. The Ambassador deserved a better fate than the procrastination that resulted in a belated BEA order for 20 aircraft, in late 1948, being the only one. BEA Ambassadors took the class name Elizabethan and were fitted to carry 47 passengers.

Lockheed L-049 Constellation
First Flight 9 January 1943
Span   123ft (37.5m)
Length 95ft 1in (28.97m)
Accommodation 43-65 passengers
Gross Weight up to 98,000lb (44,465kg)
Power four Wright Duplex Cyclone
　　　2200hp
Cruising speed 308mph (496km/h)
Range 3200 miles (5152km)

providing scheduled air services. The Soviet Union at the end of the war presented both a challenge and an opportunity for air transport. Never very extensive, the rail network lay in ruins, and the reconstruction plans for the country involved the development of underpopulated areas.

Air transport was to play—and still plays—an important role in developing the country. Many communities have come to rely on air transport as their principal contact with their neighbours and the outside world and an ability to land on rough grass or dirt airfields has been a feature of many Soviet air transport designs since the end of the war. Considering the immense task of reconstruction it is not surprising that Aeroflot concentrated initially on establishing domestic links and services to other Soviet-bloc countries, requiring machines of comparatively short range. The Li-2 (the designation applied to the Russian-built and US-supplied DC-3s and C-47s) bore the brunt of the initial expansion but indigenous designs soon followed. The Ilyushin Il-12, which first flew in 1946 and entered Aeroflot service in 1948, is perhaps most notable as a successful DC-3 replacement. It was an all-metal retractable-tricycle monoplane powered by two Pratt & Whitney-derived radial engines, with accommodation for up to 32 passengers at around 800 miles range or 27 passengers for about 1250 miles. Produced in considerable numbers, reported as more than 3000, the Il-12 not only formed the backbone of Aeroflot but also of several East European airlines too. The airlines of Hungary, Romania, Bulgaria and Jugoslavia were all set up with assistance from the Soviet Union but after the independent stance adopted by Marshal Tito, JAT went its own way and thereafter flew Western equipment.

Czechoslovakia did not fall into the Soviet camp until the coup in 1948. CSA had resumed operations in 1946 using Ju52/3ms and DC-3s and plans were in hand to open a transatlantic service with DC-4s when the country was drawn into the Soviet fold, to enter a period of uncertainty lasting several years before resuming its expansion programme.

A remarkable product of the Russian aircraft industry from 1947 was the Antonov An-2, a large biplane capable of carrying 12 passengers, powered by a single 1000hp Shvetsov radial engine. The An-2 has been produced in very large numbers; by 1960 5000 had been produced in Russia when the design was taken up by Poland, and it has also been produced under licence in China. It can be fitted with wheels, floats or skis and has had a long service life, several examples still operating scheduled services certainly until the late 1960s.

With the return of peace to South East Asia and the Pacific, air transport took root in several countries. Of course, Japan was not permitted to restart her airline, but Australia and New Zealand quickly got their airlines under way. Trans-Australian Airlines became the instrument favoured by the government to develop domestic air services. Gradually it took over the Qantas routes as that airline became more concerned with international services. TAA began life in 1946 using the ubiquitous DC-3 and later introduced DC-4s. 'Domestic' in the Australian context means serving cities separated by thousands of miles and aircraft with a suitable range for trans-Australian services were somewhat limited in the early postwar years. In 1948 TAA introduced the Convair 240—yet another 'DC-3 replacement'. Australian National Airlines had earlier become a major domestic carrier by amalgamating with smaller airlines. However it was hard hit by the government preference for TAA and had to struggle to remain a major force in Australian aviation. In common with many other countries in the early postwar years, Australia saw several small companies spring into existence. Wartime surplus aircraft were cheaply available and many ex-servicemen had got aviation into their blood. Alas, many failed in their endeavours but some—such as MacRobertson Miller Aviation in Western Australia and Connellan Airways in the heart of the country at Alice Springs, have thrived to this day.

Qantas, as the 'chosen instrument' of Australian aviation overseas, soon retired its converted bombers and in 1947 introduced the Lockheed Constellation onto the Kangaroo Route to London. Australia has never had a large aircraft industry but some indigenous designs have enjoyed a limited success in meeting the specific needs of the country. The de Havilland (Australia) DHA3 Drover was one such design. Based on the Dove feeder liner produced by the parent company in Britain, the Drover was fitted with a third engine, in the nose, and the tricycle undercarriage was replaced by a tail-wheel design. These modifications made the aircraft better suited to the harsh conditions of the Australian outback and as well as being operated by small local carriers such as Linderman Aerial Services, the Drover was used by many of the Flying Doctor services. Capable of carrying either nine passengers or two stretcher cases with attendants, the Drover was originally fitted with three 145hp Gipsy Major engines but several aircraft were later converted to take 180hp Lycomings.

The continued use of flying-boats reflected the island character of New Zealand. Tasman Empire Airways Limited (TEAL) flew Sandringham flying-boats between Auckland and Sydney, establishing a reputation for excellent service. Sunderlands were operated by the New Zealand National Airline Corporation to link Fiji, Samoa, Tonga and the Cook Islands with Auckland. In 1949 NZNAC replaced the Sunderlands with Solent flying-boats. British Commonwealth Pacific Airlines was formed in 1946 to link

Australia and New Zealand with the United States and Canada, starting services using DC-4s before taking the DC-6 in 1949. The airline was later taken over by Qantas.

Although KLM quickly resumed services to the Dutch East Indies after the war, the movement for independence prevented the re-formation of KNILM but in 1949 a compromise solution was found when Garuda Indonesian Airways was established under the joint ownership of KLM and the Indonesian government.

In 1946 Cathay Pacific Airways was formed by American and Australian interests. The British government was not entirely happy with this situation and two years later the major trading company of Butterfield and Swire took a majority holding in the airline.

Although Air India was formed in 1946, its antecedents go back to Tata Airlines of the 1930s. Tata remained the driving force of the new airline and must be counted among the great pioneer airline personalities. Air India eventually became concerned with international services, leaving domestic routes to be served by the Indian Airlines Corporation; once again the early postwar period saw the growth of several small airlines serving a number of cities in India but most were absorbed by IAC. After the great upheaval caused by Partition the new state of Pakistan was served by Orient Airways, linking the East and West sections of the country.

South African Airways soon resumed its services using six demobilised Lockheed Lodestars. In 1946 the Avro York was put onto the Sprinbok service to the UK, using five machines lent by BOAC pending receipt of SAA's own DC-4s in 1947. Farther north, perhaps inspired by the enterprising SAS venture in Scandinavia, Northern Rhodesia, Southern Rhodesia and Nyasaland formed Central African Airways in 1946. Initially Vikings and Doves and, later, Bristol 170s were used, but when the Central African Federation eventually broke up CAA disappeared.

As new nations were born in the years following the end of the war, so new airlines were established, often for several years using hired equipment and crews, and under the tutelage of big organisations in the business. An airline was looked upon as much an integral part of nation-building as the composition of a national anthem or the design of a flag. Middle East Airlines, El Al, Iraqi Airways, and others were established in the 1940s and have become mature and respected international carriers.

Canada had built up domestic and international networks during the war and although several successful 'bush' airlines became established, two carriers shared the dominating position in the country during the years of growth. Trans Canada Airlines was the government airline and seemed to be favoured when it came to allocating overseas routes. Using Lancastrians, TCA flew Atlantic services during the war and has since remained (lately as Air Canada) the only Canadian airline to fly scheduled services to the United Kingdom. However, Canadian Pacific Airlines also built up a major role as the country's flag carrier in several parts of the world.

To bring some order to the burgeoning airline world, the International Air Transport Association was founded in April 1945. Really a reformation of the prewar IATA, this body has become a controversial organisation which is often criticised. Nevertheless as the world's airlines gathered in Havana for the inaugural meeting of IATA, the foundations were laid for the efficient interchange between airlines which is taken for granted today.

For example, for £X one can fly by British Airways or Qantas from London to Sydney. For the same fare it is possible to stop en route at Rome, Bombay, Singapore and Djakarta, changing airlines at each point. To simplify the accounting after such a journey. the airlines agree on pro-rata rates so that when the various parts of the ticket finally return to an IATA clearing-house, each airline is paid according to an agreed formula. Such organisation is clearly to the benefit of the traveller, making his journey as trouble-free as possible and easing the transfer from airline to airline. The charge that IATA is apt to encourage high fare levels is less easy to defend and later developments in air transport have resulted in considerable variation in available air fares.

A year before the airlines set up IATA, several governments met to set up the International Civil Aviation Organisation. This body was concerned with the safety and technical aspects of air travel. ICAO has set standards which aircraft manufacturers must reach if their products are to be accepted in world markets. Airfields, navigational facilities, communications—these and many more subjects have become standardised as a result of ICAO's efforts.

Although IATA and ICAO helped to bring order and a common standard to air transport significant differences remained. For example, most European airlines entered pool agreements which resulted in shared revenues. This took some of the heat out of competition and congestion at popular travelling times, and allowed more sensible schedules of flights, spread throughout the day. Competition between airlines remained but was generally limited to such things as cabin service, type of aircraft and so on. In the United States, on the other hand, the American ideal of free competition simply had no place for the European policy of pooling.

Most successful of the postwar British piston-engined airliners was the Vickers VC1 Viking. Over 160 were built from June 1945 onwards for BEA and about 10 other scheduled airlines and the type became a mainstay of British aviation for well over a decade. Most of them were snapped up by charter companies as they were replaced by Viscounts in front-line service. The aircraft pictured in the service of Independent Air Travel in the mid-1950's is a long-nosed Viking 1B, a variant with fuselage extension that increased the passenger complement from 21 to 24 in original schedule airline service. They were, however, generally equipped as 32-seaters for subsequent tourist and charter work.

7. The Second Revolution

THE ADVENT OF the practical gas turbine led to a revolution in air transport which was every bit as crucial as the introduction of the DC-3. Research into alternative sources of power is as old as aviation itself, and as early as 1910 a jet-propelled aircraft had been produced. A Romanian living in Paris, Henri Coanda, designed and built a sesqui-plane—a biplane with the lower wing shorter than the upper—and showed it at the second Salon Aeronautique held in the city in 1910.

Coanda was an engineer who has come to be recognised as one of the important pioneers in aviation. His 'jet engine' was based on a 50hp water-cooled Clerget piston engine which drove a ducted fan, or ' turbo-propulseur ', to provide thrust. Alas, Coanda was no pilot and when testing his device in, as he thought, a stationary aircraft, so concerned was he with adjustment of the jet that he failed to notice that the aircraft was moving and gathering speed. So he suddenly found himself airborne and it was patently not the best moment to learn to fly! The aircraft crashed to the ground but fortunately Coanda was thrown out of the burning machine and did not suffer injury.

In Italy the Caproni-Campini CC2 (officially N1) flew briefly in 1940 using an updated Coanda jet system incorporating an afterburner, but the experiment was dropped. In the meantime Frank Whittle, a young cadet at the Royal Air Force College, had already sown the seeds of the world's first successful turbojet engine. In 1928 his thesis on future developments in aircraft design outlined his ideas on jet or rocket propulsion in which hot gases ejected through pipes would produce a reactive force on the walls of the containing vessel. Whittle planned to draw air into a compressor and feed it into a combustion chamber where it would be turned into hot gases of considerable energy. The gases would be passed

Herald of the jet transport era, de Havilland Comet 1 prototype G-ALVG, which flew for the first time on 27 July 1949. Initially a 36/44-seater for stage lengths up to 1750 miles, the Comet 1 cruised at 490mph and set up records on many BOAC routes before the crashes of 1953 and 1954 grounded the Comet 1 for good.

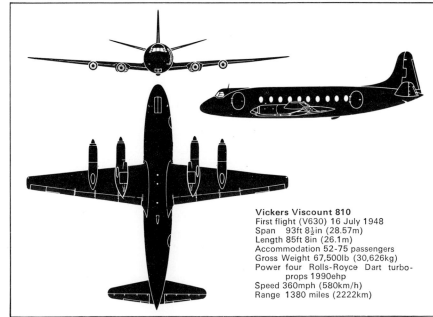

Vickers Viscount 810
First flight (V630) 16 July 1948
Span   93ft 8½in (28.57m)
Length 85ft 8in (26.1m)
Accommodation 52-75 passengers
Gross Weight 67,500lb (30,626kg)
Power four Rolls-Royce Dart turbo-
        props 1990ehp
Speed 360mph (580km/h)
Range 1380 miles (2222km)

first through a turbine, using some of the energy to drive a compressor by means of a shaft, the balance of the energy providing jet thrust for propulsion.

Few at the time shared Whittle's interest and neither the Air Ministry nor industry were prepared to back him. However, in 1930 he patented his ideas and six years later formed Power Jets Ltd and set about building his first jet engine. A year later, in 1937, his turbojet began bench tests and although Whittle encountered considerable difficulties, particularly as war threatened and then became an actuality, he overcame them and built a second and more successful engine. By then the authorities had begun to see the potential of the new method of propulsion and in 1941 Britain's first jet-propelled aircraft, the little Gloster E28/39, took to the air.

Meanwhile, in Germany Pabst von Ohain had also been working to produce a jet engine. His design was run for the first time in 1937 and an improved version was flown in the Heinkel He178 in August 1939. Thus, to Germany goes the credit for the world's first successful jet aircraft but fortunately for the Allies it was not until the spring of 1942 that an operational aircraft, the Messerschmitt Me262, entered service.

The Americans eventually realised the potential of the jet engine and, in April 1942, imported a Whittle turbojet; General Electric swiftly Americanised Whittle's design and two of the new engines were installed in the Bell XP-59A Airacomet, which flew for the first time in 1942. Jet propulsion was well and truly launched but, as in so much else, it was the needs of war that speeded its development. It was to take a further decade before the first turbojet airliner, the de Havilland DH106 Comet 1, entered commercial service, and another two decades beyond that for the turbofan to transform the aeroplane into the fantastically efficient mass transport tool it is today.

Within two years of the first flight of the experimental E28/39, the Brabazon Committee in considering Britain's postwar air transport needs, had recommended the design of a jet airliner. As the war drew to a close designers everywhere, well aware of the propeller's limitation of aircraft speed, were studying the possibilities of jet propulsion, but it is doubtful whether even the most farseeing of them imagined how soon gas-turbine-powered airliners would oust the majority of piston-engined machines. Gas turbines presented formidable difficulties. Very high temperatures were generated and components turned at speeds of up to 100,000rpm; until new metals were developed to withstand the harsh conditions turbine blades were apt to fly off under the high centrifugal forces and the expansion caused by fierce heating (creep) resulted in blades fouling the turbine casing unless clearances were made so great that the engine was hopelessly inefficient. The limitations on design so caused meant that early gas turbines had comparatively high fuel consumptions and short TBOs (time between overhauls). But gradually the difficulties were overcome and early doubts that the jet would ever be an economic civil transport engine, strongly expressed by a significant number of eminent men in the business, were eventually dispelled.

With Germany out of the running, much of the effective jet engine research in the early postwar years was British, with Rover, Rolls-Royce, Metropolitan Vickers, de Havilland, Armstrong Siddeley and Bristol, and metallurgical concerns, all playing a part. After a start towards the end of the war with imported British engines and licence manufacture of British designs, numbers of American companies, including General Motors, Pratt & Whitney and General Electric, were soon bringing their own prodigious technological resources to bear and the resultant competition brought rapid progress. Russia too entered the fray, working first from captured German engines and then much more effectively from drawings and examples naively supplied to them in 1947 by the British government of the latest Rolls-Royce Derwent and Nene jet engines, which were promptly stripped down and copied without bothering about the normal licence formalities or fees.

Everywhere jet propulsion was applied first to military designs, but transport aircraft were soon flying under the power of the new engines. In 1948 a Vickers Viking was experimentally fitted with two Rolls-Royce Nene engines, to become the first British turbojet airliner; others followed quickly, including the Tudor 8 and 9 (later named Ashton), and were used to investigate the many aspects of the civil use of gas turbines. It became evident that the pure jet engine was most efficient at high altitudes and many in the industry considered that propeller-driven aircraft would still prove to be most economical over shorter distances where it was impractical for airliners to climb to 30,000ft or more. Not only that, there were various other problems in propelling aircraft at high speeds, particularly compressibility as the speed of sound is approached, still to be overcome in the late 1940s. The combination of the smooth efficiency of the gas turbine with a propeller seemed to offer an

First of the long-range turboprop Bristol Britannia 100s flew in August 1952 but development troubles with the Proteus engines delayed entry into scheduled service until February 1957. The developed 300 series followed in December 1957 and inaugurated the first turbine-powered nonstop North Atlantic service. Here an ex-BOAC Britannia 312 is pictured at London Gatwick, in British Eagle service before its sale to an Argentinian operator in 1969.

attractive solution and development of turboprop engines was undertaken by several companies contemporaneously with that of turbojets.

Initially as a development of the Viking, in 1945 Vickers set about designing an airliner powered by turboprop engines. The original Viscount design was brought into line with the Brabazon 2B specification and after consideration of Napier, Armstrong Siddeley and Rolls-Royce engines the Vickers V630 Viscount powered by four Rolls-Royce Darts appeared, to make its maiden flight in July 1948 as the world's first turboprop airliner. Unusually for so new and advanced a concept, the prototype had a virtually troublefree development to gain a restricted C of A in August 1949 and full passenger clearance as a 32-seater for a month's scheduled operation with BEA in July/August 1950. A second V630 Viscount prototype was fitted with two Rolls-Royce Tay turbojet engines and used for research purposes.

Continued development of the Dart led to increases in power, so that the third Viscount appeared with an enlarged fuselage as the V700 and after its first flight in April 1950 an order for 20, later increased to 27, was placed by BEA for a slightly modified 53-seat version, the Viscount 701. Development and certification were again troublefree and the Viscount entered regular scheduled service with BEA as the Discovery Class in April

First production gas turbine-powered airliner in the world was the Vickers Viscount, which entered passenger service with BEA in July 1950 and was soon being supplied to many other airlines. The picture shows the first of the enlarged Viscount V810 series, which first flew in December 1957, in American Continental Airlines livery.

1953. In October the same year the prototype, named *Endeavour*, won the England-New Zealand Air Race, covering the 11,795 miles at an average speed of 290mph. Viscounts certainly opened a new era of faster, smoother, quieter and more comfortable air travel. It did not take other airlines long to get the message and orders materialised from all over the world—even the United States, the very fount of the modern airliner. Well over 400 Viscounts had been built when production ended.

An even greater furore was caused in air transport when the de Havilland Comet entered BOAC scheduled service in May 1952. The Brabazon 4 specification formulated during the war for a fast mail carrier/transport for the Empire Routes was the basis for the DH106 multi-jet proposal, the calculated performance of which interested BOAC to the point where the airline encouraged its development and, in December 1945, agreed to buy 10 aircraft. After considering several configurations, including one using three engines at the rear similar to the layout adopted about 15 years later for the Trident, de Havilland settled on a conventional arrangement with four de Havilland Ghost turbojets installed in the wing roots and a round-section fuselage with seats for up to 40 passengers and ability to cruise at 490mph.

The prototype Comet I flew for the first time in July 1949 and again, for an aircraft which was to herald a revolution in air transport, development was remarkably troublefree and production and route proving proceeded swiftly, with flight times more than halved on route after route. The world's first jet flight carrying fare-paying passengers

was BOAC's Comet 1 G-ALYP from London to Johannesburg on 2 May 1952 and as the aircraft took over the other Empire routes, the full extent of the revolution became apparent. The Comets operated consistently at load factors well above 80 per cent and by the end of their first year of operation about 27,700 passengers had been carried. The Comet cruised mainly above the weather at altitudes previously beyond the reach of airliners. The absence of vibration and exceptional comfort of the aircraft, coupled with halved flight times and high loadings, were just reason for the almost frenetic energy put in by the aircraft industry around the world to catch up.

Encouraged by the success of the Comet I, de Havilland went ahead with the Series II—a developed version fitted with four Rolls-Royce Avon engines giving more power than the Ghosts and so an improvement in performance. By the end of 1953 35 Comet IIs and 11 Comet IIIs (a further development with a longer fuselage) had been ordered. Although of the 21 Comet Is and IAs built three had met with accidents, none was attributed to the integrity of the engines or airframe.

The future for the Comet seemed bright but a devastating blow was to come, with the mysterious loss in January 1954 of a BOAC aircraft near the island of Elba in the Mediterranean soon after take-off from Rome. Expert examination of other Comets failed to reveal any mechanical defects and, after a short grounding while various precautionary modifications were made, the Comets flew again. Alas, barely a fortnight after the resumption of services, in April 1954 a

Above: The aircraft that started the massive swing to jet power, the Boeing 707, here seen in its early development stages in 1954. PanAm started its 707 transatlantic service in 1958 a few days after BOAC's Comet 4s had opened the route to jets.

Right: Although overtaken by the big American jets in capacity and range, the Comet 4 served BOAC well and the shorter-range high-capacity 4B version provided BEA with jet competition for Caravelle-equipped European airlines. A BEA Comet 4B is shown at Gatwick in 1968.

Comet bound for Johannesburg crashed into the sea near Naples, again shortly after taking off from Rome. The aircraft's Certificate of Airworthiness was withdrawn and all Comets were grounded.

The experts were baffled by the crashes and, until the wreckage of one of the Comets was recovered, could only speculate on the cause. The Royal Navy conducted a major salvage operation and using underwater television managed to locate most of the wreckage of the aircraft which had crashed near Elba. The pieces were returned to England where the technicians of the Royal Aircraft Establishment, Farnborough, conducted a minute investigation, backed by flight trials with a fully instrumented Comet and the now famous tank test, mentioned later. As far as possible, the aircraft was reassembled and the battered pieces of metal gradually told their story; the cabin had burst and failure had started at the corner of a window from a crack caused by metal fatigue resulting from repeated pressurisations of the cabin.

The phenomenon of metal fatigue was not unknown to aircraft designers and, because the Comet would be operating in a virtually previously unknown environment, de Havilland had worked closely with air safety authorities in devising methods of testing the structure so that it would withstand the higher cabin pressures required for high-altitude operation. It was believed that a cabin which would survive testing to double its expected working pressure would not give any problems in routine service. Although so tested, the cabin of the Comet did fail and it was clear that new criteria for fatigue

testing would have to be established, giving rise to the tank test. A complete Comet fuselage was placed in a huge tank of water and subjected to pressurisation-depressurisation cycles while at the same time the wings were flexed in a hydraulic rig, to simulate all the stresses experienced in repeated flights from take-off to landing.

The court of inquiry set up to investigate the Comet disasters concluded that in the knowledge existing at the time de Havilland could not have foreseen the failure of the cabin. The report and the experience of the British pioneering venture into jet travel and in devising new techniques was made available to the world's aircraft manufacturers, including the American, setting aside commercial considerations.

Thus the first Comet venture died and the long lead which Britain had enjoyed was lost. However, the new knowledge gained from the

disasters and their investigation was embodied in the bigger and faster Comet 4 and 4B, which served BOAC and BEA well from 1958 onward, and in the Comet 2s which went to RAF Transport Command. BOAC's Comet 4s entered service on the London-New York run in October 1958, beating Pan American's new Boeing 707 by a few days. So, despite all, to the Comet went the honour of opening the first transatlantic jet service, but the bigger Boeing 707 and DC-8 were about to bring the jet revolution to its full flood.

The first jet airliner in North America was not produced by the United States, however, but by Canada. In 1946 Avro Canada began the design of the C102, a four-engined jet airliner powered by Rolls-Royce Derwent engines, which flew for the first time in 1949 only two weeks after the Comet. The C102 was designed to carry 50 passengers at just over 400mph over stage lengths of 1100 miles. It did not attract any customers, perhaps because the design was not a sufficient advance over the latest piston-engined airliners. Indeed, with its straight wing it

looked like a piston-engined aircraft fitted with jets, rather resembling the Tudor 8. Avro Canada's military commitments obliged the company to abandon any further development of its civil jet project.

In the United States, too, the aircraft industry was heavily engaged in applying jet power to military aircraft. The Boeing company produced a bomber of radical design as early as 1947. Its sharply swept wings were long and slender and the six engines were suspended in pods beneath the wings. Originally, the new bomber was to have been a jet version of the B-29 with the engines buried in the wings, but visits by Boeing engineers to captured German aircraft factories drew attention to the work which had been carried out on swept-wing designs. Studies in the United States confirmed the German findings that much greater speeds were possible by employing swept wings. Thus the revolutionary B-47 beat other design submissions and was produced in large quantities, 2000 being built over a period of nine years. It was followed in 1952 by the larger but similar eight-engined B52, which

was also produced in large numbers for the next 10 years.

While it would not be true to say that the Boeing 707 was developed directly from the B-47 and B-52 bombers, they clearly influenced the design. Boeing's first thoughts on a jet transport were based on the Stratocruiser and design studies were given the number 367 (the military design on which the Stratocruiser was based). Many studies were made and the design finally chosen (the 80th study) bore little resemblance to the original aircraft. Although Boeing adopted a radical new design, it decided to retain the former designation, in order to avoid unwelcome curiosity. As far as competitors were concerned, the Model 367-80 was simply a development of an old aeroplane. When the type was given the new designation 707, the world was made aware that a revolutionary new airliner was about to be launched. The 707 first flew in July 1954.

The Boeing company, which for many years has been behind Douglas and Lockheed in the airliner business, overnight presented a serious challenge for which its competitors were ill-prepared. Boeing's experience in producing large jet aircraft was at last given a commercial direction and the company quickly established itself as a major supplier to the world's airlines.

Two years before the 707 prototype made its maiden flight, Pan American Airways ordered 20 Boeing 707s and 25 of the projected Douglas contender in the jet transport field—the DC-8. The move caused a considerable stir in airline circles, for the new airliners would be twice as big as then current types, and about twice as fast with a cruising speed of nearly 600mph. Fearful of being left behind, airlines flocked to buy the new Boeing and Douglas jets. The tragic interruption in the development of the Comet had allowed American industry to catch up with, and to overtake, the British lead. Introducing the Boeing 707 into service over the Atlantic in 1958, only three weeks after BOAC started Comet flights, Pan American quickly built up a lead as the major carrier on North American routes. TWA's piston-engined Lockheed 1649A airliners were no match for PanAm's Boeings and BOAC's Comets, and TWA had to be content with third place on the North Atlantic. .

Lacking the background of a big military jet aircraft project the Douglas Company had to put all its efforts into speeding the production of the DC-8 airliner or see the successful 707 swamp the market. The prototype DC-8, turning out to be very similar in appearance to the 707, flew for the first time in May 1958 and entered service the following year.

Jet airliners were to revolutionise travel within the United States as quickly as they did on international routes. In January 1959

American Airlines introduced the Boeing 707 onto the highly competitive New York-Los Angeles run. For a couple of months American had the edge until TWA took delivery of its first 707 in March and risking a setback if anything went wrong, immediately put its sole 707 into service without waiting for further deliveries. The gamble paid off as the 707 behaved perfectly. United and Delta, having opted for the DC-8 were unable to introduce their new airliners into service until September 1959.

Although the new American and British airliners enjoyed the limelight at the time, it is a fact that the Soviet Union already had a considerable network of jet services by the time Pan American started its first Boeing 707 service. Aeroflot had leapt from the little slow Il-12 and Il-14 aircraft into the jet age with the twin-engined Tupolev 104. Based on the Tu-16 jet bomber design, the Tu-104 was a crude machine by Western standards; the cabin interior was fussy and old-fashioned, and although performance was impressive, the engines were a lot less economical than their Western counterparts. Be that as it may, the Tu-104 brought great advances to air travel in the Soviet Union. First flown in June 1955, the Tu-104 entered service in September the following year and for a time it was the only jet airliner in service anywhere in the world. The original Tu-104 could carry 50 passengers but the Model A of 1957 had accommodation for 70 passengers and was followed two years later by the 100-seat Tu-104B.

As a nation which had been devastated by war and which was intent on closing the gap between themselves and the advanced industrial nations of the West, the Soviet Union was more concerned with improving its domestic network than forging links with foreign capitals. Consequently the West little noticed the rapid growth of Aeroflot's fleet of jet airliners. More concerned with maintaining services than making a profit, Aeroflot was not too worried about the poor economics of the Tu-104 but it did result in sales of the type being restricted to Eastern-bloc countries. Indeed, Russia has yet to produce an airliner which has sold in any quantity on the world's markets. Spurred on by the profit motive and a competitive environment, the West quickly developed jet engines which are very economical both in terms of fuel and in the amount of maintenance which they require.

The maintenance efficiency of early jet engines was measured in time between overhauls (TBO). An engine which could be run for 1000 hours of flight before a major inspection was obviously less expensive to operate than one which had to be inspected after only 400 hours or so. The few Russian airliners which have found their way into the hands of foreign operators (often as gifts to

Above: *Convair piston-engined airliners were given a new lease of life fitted with a variety of turboprop engines. This picture shows a Convair 640 powered by two Rolls-Royce Darts, one of three in service with the Canadian operator Pacific Western Airlines.*

Right: *Lockheed missed the first-generation turbojet market entirely but did get into turboprops with the L-188 Electra, which first flew in December 1957 and entered service with Eastern Airlines early in 1959, three months after the Boeing 707. Here an Eastern Electra is seen over Dulles in May 1972.*

I-SARO

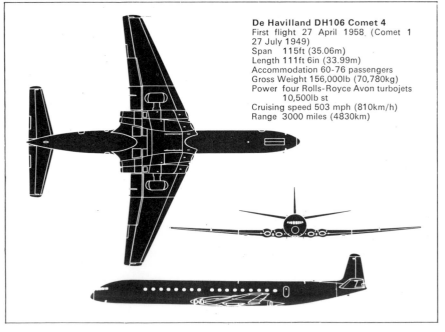

De Havilland DH106 Comet 4
First flight 27 April 1958 (Comet 1
27 July 1949)
Span 115ft (35.06m)
Length 111ft 6in (33.99m)
Accommodation 60-76 passengers
Gross Weight 156,000lb (70,780kg)
Power four Rolls-Royce Avon turbojets
 10,500lb st
Cruising speed 503 mph (810km/h)
Range 3000 miles (4830km)

newly independent nations) have usually had a poor maintenance record. Economical or not, the fact remains that the Tu-104 could fly from Moscow to Irkutsk, for example, with only one stop in a total of seven hours. The same journey in an Il-14 had taken 20 hours and involved five stops.

Russia, too, considered that a combination of the gas turbine with propellers would provide an efficient means of propulsion for airliners and produced the four-engined turboprop Ilyushin Il-18 in some quantity. Carrying up to 98 passengers, the Il-18 first flew in 1957 and entered service with Aeroflot two years later. The powerful Ivchenko engines of the Il-18 provided 4000shp and put the aircraft in the same category as the Lockheed Electra and Vickers Vanguard built in the West.

The Russians need for tough cargo transport aircraft led to the design of the Antonov An-10, a four-engined high-wing turboprop

aircraft, which made its maiden flight in 1957. The voluminous fuselage could accommodate 126 passengers but it is as a cargo carrier that the An-10 excelled. The An-10 also had a counterpart in the West in the Lockheed Hercules military transport.

Russia has a long history of building big aeroplanes, starting in 1913 with Igor Sikorsky's four-engined machine—the world's first—and followed by Tupolev's five-engined ANT-14 and eight-engined ANT-20 *Maxim Gorki* of the 1930s. The tendency has continued into the turbine-powered era with the four-turboprop Tu-114, developed from the Tu-20 bomber and first seen in 1957-8. The giant airliner, class-named Rossiya (Russia), was designed to carry 220 passengers on short hauls but was more notable for its high speed for a propeller-driven machine, reported as nearly 600mph maximum and just under 500mph maximum cruising, and for capturing various international range and

height-with-load records in the 1960s. Longer range versions of the Tu-114 had a restaurant amidships, a very civilised way of taking refreshments aloft, and was used by Aeroflot to introduce a nonstop service between Moscow and Khabarovsk in 1961, before introduction on several long-distance international services.

Few other East-bloc countries produced jet transport aircraft, although East Germany did build a four-engined airliner, the Baade BB152. It was a rather ugly aircraft designed to carry 57 passengers and flew in 1958, but did not enter production.

French enterprise in jet airliner design was more successful. The flair and inventiveness of France took shape in the Sud-Aviation SE210 Caravelle, an elegant airliner with engines mounted on the rear fuselage. This design feature, which had been proposed for the Comet as mentioned earlier, was later copied by other aircraft manufacturers in

After toying with a twin-engined turbojet design in the early postwar years, Fokker opted instead for a twin-Dart turboprop 32-seat airliner, which became the F27 Friendship and went on to become a world best-seller. The picture shows a Series 100 Friendship soon after delivery to the Italian (Sardinia) regional operator in 1964.

Britain, the USA and the USSR, for although it results in some weight penalty, a rear-engine layout makes for a very quiet cabin. The Caravelle was first flown in May 1955 and its development was accelerated by the adoption of the de Havilland Comet nose and two Rolls-Royce Avon turbojets, no French gas turbines being sufficiently advanced or powerful. Early Caravelles, of which Air France ordered 12 in February 1956 and later took up an option on 12 more, could carry up to 80 passengers on stages of about 1000 miles cruising at around 560mph. As the only short-to-medium range jet, as soon as it proved itself, foreign orders started to come in and by the time the first passenger service was flown, in May 1959, on the Air France Paris-Rome-Istanbul route, over 50 aircraft had been ordered. Including later developed types of increased speed and range, some of which had Pratt & Whitney engines and

could carry 109 passengers in high-density arrangement, well over 200 Caravelles have been sold.

The Caravelle undoubtedly helped France to regain her position as a major supplier to the airlines. Holland, too, regained her place as an aeroplane builder with the Fokker F27 Friendship which flew for the first time in November 1955. In true Fokker tradition, a high-wing design was adopted and, sensing the historic significance of the Vickers Viscount across the water, the decision was made to power it with two Rolls-Royce Dart turboprop engines. The F27 was another in a long line of intended DC-3 replacements and it has perhaps come closer than any other Western design to achievement of that position. With accommodation for up to 36 passengers and a cruising speed of nearly 270mph initially over 1250-mile or so stages, it soon established a strong position in the

short-haul market and was to join the Caravelle and Viscount in penetrating the fiercely competitive American market, and to overtake them by being selected for production in the United States by the Fairchild concern. Several versions of the Friendship have been produced, including various executive and military types, and with over 650 sold, the Friendship continues to win orders. British and Russian aircraft have been produced in the Friendship class but none has enjoyed the worldwide success of the Dutch machine.

Not all the new turbine-powered airliners met with commercial success. Armstrong Whitworth designed a four-engined airliner to Brabazon specification 2B and produced two prototypes which were successfully test-flown from April 1949. Powered by four Armstrong-Siddeley Mamba turboprops, the AW55 Apollo was designed to carry up to 41 passengers on medium stages at 280mph. It performed an impressive party trick when demonstrated lightly loaded at the Farnborough Air Display by flying on one engine. Although dismissed by some as showmanship, it nevertheless was an indication of the improved air safety standards of the new generation of airliners. The Apollo prototypes performed useful research service for the Ministry of Supply but the project was overshadowed by the Viscount and the AW55 did not enter production.

Apart from the Tu-114 already mentioned few turboprop airliners have been produced for long-distance routes; most manufacturers have moved from piston-engined designs straight into jet power. Bristol considered the design of a long-haul airliner powered by four Bristol Centaurus piston engines but later decided to fit its Proteus turboprop engines. The Series 100 Bristol 175 Britannia was originally designed to carry up to 64 passengers but when the first production model flew in September 1954 it could carry a maximum of 92 passengers at 335mph over nearly 4000-mile ranges. BOAC ordered 25 Britannias in 1949 and took delivery of the first for crew training in December 1955. Unfortunately, the Proteus encountered difficulties which led to a delay in the introduction of the Britannia into airline service until February 1957. However, it was still the first long-range turboprop airliner in scheduled service and some had been used on trooping and Hungarian refugee services for some months before that.

In 1955 BOAC ordered a batch of bigger longer-range Britannias, which became the 300 series and totalled 18 in BOAC service as the Britannia 312. On 19 December 1957 BOAC started the first London–New York nonstop service by turbine aircraft with its Britannias but that event was soon overshadowed by the advances made with pure jet travel.

Although the revolution brought about by Whittle's inventiveness was decisive, some manufacturers were slow to appreciate that the piston engine had had its day; they paid a heavy price for their conservatism. The Lockheed Company, for example, took many years to produce a turbojet airliner and although its Electra turboprop design sold in some numbers, mainly in the US, the company was largely edged out of the market by Boeing and Douglas.

Handley Page, too, made a blunder in producing in 1958 a 44-seat short-haul airliner powered by four piston engines. It was similar in layout to the Fokker Friendship but the Dutch selection at the outset of turboprop power proved a wise decision, for it soaked up most of the orders for airliners in its category. Although the Handley Page Herald was eventually rejigged with two Rolls-Royce Darts and was quickly in production its sales failed to reach three figures.

Towards the end of the 1950s Viscounts made up about a third of European airliners. Here Lufthansa and BEA Viscounts are seen at London Airport in 1959.

8. Postwar Boom

For long regarded as the world leader in air transport America in the 1950s sought for the most efficient path to profitability. Transatlantic air travel had grown apace and New York's La Guardia airport could no longer cope with the increasing volume of traffic. The decade opened with Idlewild (later renamed John F. Kennedy) as the main international terminal. By the end of the decade the whine of jets had replaced the growl of piston engines, ending one of the fastest and most complete revolutions in air transport history.

Perhaps as a reaction to the rigged monopolies of the 1930s, the CAB was determined to maintain an element of competition in air transport, and needless to say, its policy of licensing several carriers on routes previously allocated to only one airline drew strong criticism. It was argued by some that services such as the electricity supply and the telephone system were not subjected to the cold draughts of competition and only one gas main supplied a city's needs; so why should more than one airline be necessary? Severe competition between the railways had resulted in weakened if not exhausted companies which could survive only by a series of mergers; would the airline business be any different?

Although it could be argued that the CAB was overenthusiastic in encouraging competition, fortunately for the consumer, the objections to its policies were largely disregarded. Certainly there were cases where a third airline was allowed to operate on a route previously served—profitably—by two, leading to a position where all three ran at a loss. The enormous and generally profitable expansion of the airlines, however, pointed to the wisdom of the CAB's policies.

The free-enterprise 'pirate' airlines which burgeoned after the war flying bargain government-surplus aircraft survived only if they could operate safely and efficiently; most could not, and the established scheduled carriers were left to compete against each other. For the splendid DC-3s and DC-4s used by the pirate airlines soon began to feel the competition of the new designs which the manufacturers produced to meet the demands of the trunk carriers. Competition indeed demanded the very best both in terms of passenger comfort and economy of operation. At the very least passengers expected pressurised comfort and Lockheed and Douglas saw that they got it.

The pattern established in the late 1930s was repeated in the postwar boom; American industry, responding to the urgent

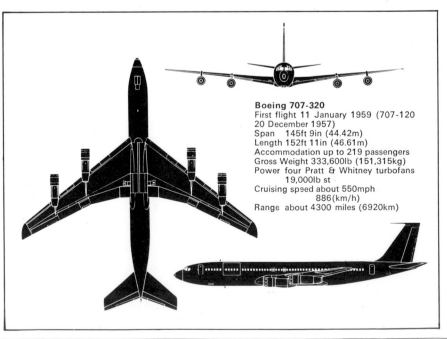

Boeing 707-320
First flight 11 January 1959 (707-120 20 December 1957)
Span 145ft 9in (44.42m)
Length 152ft 11in (46.61m)
Accommodation up to 219 passengers
Gross Weight 333,600lb (151,315kg)
Power four Pratt & Whitney turbofans 19,000lb st
Cruising speed about 550mph 886(km/h)
Range about 4300 miles (6920km)

These two aircraft span the decade of the 1950s; A China Airlines DC-4 Skymaster stands at Hong Kong Kai-Tak Airport as a Korean Airlines Boeing 707 is about to touch down.

demands of the nation's domestic carriers, produced efficient airliners in large quantities. The long production runs led to low unit costs and the airlines of the world flocked to by such aircraft as the DC-6B and Constellation. An improved and stretched variant of the DC-6, the DC-6B has come to be regarded as one of the most efficient airliners ever built. Introduced into service in 1951 by American Airlines, the DC-6B was five feet longer than the original DC-6 enabling it to accommodate a maximum of 102 passengers. It cruised at 315mph and had a range of 3000 miles; the DC-6B was both comfortable and profitable. Although only 286 DC-6Bs were built, many remain in service over 25 years later and it has earned the right to be called a classic of its day.

Meanwhile Lockheed stretched the Constellation's fuselage by no less than 18ft to produce the L-1049 Super Constellation which entered service with Eastern Airlines in late 1951. Originally powered by 2700hp Curtiss-Wright Cyclone engines, the Super Constellation was later fitted with the 3400hp Curtiss-Wright Turbo-Compound engine and produced in C, D, E, F and H variants of improved performance.

To meet the challenge provided by the Super-Constellation, Douglas made a further stretch of the DC-6B fuselage, fitted the Turbo-Compound engines and called the new aircraft the DC-7. Adopted by American Airlines, the DC-7 in 1953 achieved a breakthrough long awaited by the American airline industry; it could fly nonstop between New York and Los Angeles in both directions. The Super Constellations operated by TWA could fly the transcontinental route nonstop in an easterly direction but were obliged to stop to refuel at Chicago on the return journey against the prevailing winds. Lockheed solved the problem by producing the L-1049G version with extra fuel tanks at the wing-tips. The extra tankage permitted TWA to compete with American Airlines on an equal footing.

By the end of the 1950s the rise of domestic air transport in the United States had completely changed the pattern of travel. Rail traffic continued its steady decline and even the indispensable motorcar declined in popularity as a means of getting from city to city.

Another route for which the airlines had long wanted an aircraft with a nonstop capability was the North Atlantic. Most operators had to put down at Goose Bay, Labrador, Gander, Newfoundland or Shannon, Ireland, to refuel and the first manu-

facturer to produce an airliner which could cut out these stops would be assured of a ready market. Needless to say, both Lockheed and Douglas put every effort into giving the Super Constellation and DC-7 the necessary range. Douglas was first in the field with the DC-7C Seven Seas, which featured a 10-foot addition to the wing span and an increased fuel capacity which gave it a range of about 4600 miles. For this machine those tiresome refuelling stops were over and Pan American Airways started North Atlantic services with the DC-7C in 1956.

It took PanAm's main competitor, TWA, a year to catch up but once again Lockheed found a solution to the challenge. It completely redesigned the wing of the Super Constellation, substituting one of high-aspect ratio for the original, in the L-1649A Starliner. It represented the ultimate in piston-engined airliner development, having a range of over 6000 miles. Only 43 Starliners were built, for in the year of its introduction into service turbine-powered aircraft were also put onto the Atlantic run. The small Israeli airline El Al made a big impact on the market when, with the turboprop Bristol Britannia, it offered a big step forward in airliner comfort. 'No Goose No Gander' ran its advertisement announcing its ability to operate nonstop transatlantic services; within a year El Al had doubled its share of the market.

Some airlines, such as Air France, operated the Super G version of the Super Constellation on their Atlantic services, offering sleeping accommodation to those who could afford such luxury. Air France and Lufthansa also operated the Starliner and its long range permitted the French carrier to follow SAS in opening one-stop services to Tokyo via the polar route.

It was the DC-7C which pioneered the Polar route, however, when SAS opened a service between Copenhagen and Tokyo via Anchorage in February 1957. A new experience for aircrews and passengers alike, the polar services introduced one of the natural wonders of the world to the travelling public. The majestic beauty of the ice fields and sometimes the Aurora Borealis were a magnificent sight. New safety precautions had to be introduced, however; survival equipment was carried in case of an emergency landing in the northern wastes including a shot-gun for protection against polar bears. Passengers were called upon to have considerable stamina for the journey which involved a flying time in excess of 30 hours. The noise and vibration levels of

piston-engined airliners made sleep difficult on such a journey and in those days the first-class cabin was located at the rear of the aircraft, as far away as possible from the source of noise and vibration. Those few feet did make a difference, too, for with the engines no more than a distant rumble, sleep in the comfortable first-class cabin was indeed possible, at least for some.

When Lufthansa restarted North Atlantic services in 1955 it used Super Constellations to open routes from Frankfurt and Dusseldorf to New York. TWA loaned captains to help the new airline to become established, as many as 20 captains being seconded at one time. Anxious to make up for lost time, Lufthansa took a gamble with one of its new Lockheed L-1649As (Super Stars as the airline called them). Although it was capable of carrying 86 passengers, the cabin of the L-1649A was adapted luxuriously to take

eight first-class seats, 18 de luxe seats and four beds. It was called the Senator service and operated twice a week over the Atlantic, helping to re-establish the name of the airline with transatlantic passengers.

Although the DC-7 and Super Constellation series were the means by which many airlines expanded their international services, they were nevertheless the end of a breed soon to be overshadowed by the advent of the jet age. Although the Comet 1 proved to be a false start to the jet revolution, it is surprising that Lockheed apparently ignored the portent. For, with the L-1649A, the company effectively bowed out of the long-haul airliner market for many years. Douglas was better prepared with its DC-8 and was able to 'stay in the ring' with Boeing, battling for orders worldwide. Lockheed turned to turbine power for its next design, the turboprop L-188 Electra powered by four

The DC-6B was introduced into service in 1951 by American Airlines; it was 5ft longer than the standard DC-6 and could carry up to 102 passengers for 3000 miles at 315mph. The DC-6B helped to found many of the new postwar airlines and contributed to the profitability of others. As it was replaced in front-line service by later aircraft it provided efficient starting equipment for more new airlines, including specialist freight carriers.
The DC-6B is operated by International Freight Airways of Belgium on passenger and freight charters and is seen here at Jersey.

Left: *First of the piston-engined airliners to have nonstop transatlantic capability with a profitable load was the DC-7C Seven Seas, which had a fully loaded range of over 4500 miles. PanAm introduced Seven Seas such as this 'Clipper Bald Eagle' on the North Atlantic in 1956.*

Allison 501 engines. It was first flown in December 1957 and entered service with American Airlines and Eastern Airlines just over a year later, three months after the Boeing 707.

The Electra could carry nearly 100 passengers and did sell to a number of carriers throughout the world, but it was used mainly for short and medium-range routes. Confidence in the aircraft was momentarily lost when three early crashes were attributed to wing spar failure caused by local vibrations set up by an engine. Suitably modified, about 170 Electras went on to give good service for a number of years. Effectively, however, Lockheed was no longer a major supplier to the world's airlines and with the L-1649A a chapter closed, not only in air transport history but in the history of Lockheed.

The third jet airliner to enter production in the United States was the Convair CV-880 which was flown for the first time in 1959. It turned out little short of a disaster and cost the manufacturers a lot of money. The later Convair jet airliners which did find a limited place with airlines will be described in the next chapter. Medium-haul piston-engined Convairliners had enjoyed quite good success and, in an endeavour to meet the competition provided by the Viscount, various turboprop conversions of the Convair 440 took place. The Napier Eland, Rolls-Royce Dart and Allison turboprops were tried but the CV-580 as it became known, was not widely adopted.

While domestic air travel in America grew rapidly in the 1950s, many countries in other parts of the world were hardly less active in expanding air travel. South America, for long an area of rapid airline growth, continued apace with new routes being opened and further developments in the airline business. Venezuela's LAV continued to operate modern equipment starting with the Lockheed Constellation and Martin 202, followed later by the Super Constellation which was used to open new routes.

In Brazil Varig grew by absorbing some smaller airlines and in 1955 opened a service from Rio de Janeiro to New York using Super Constellation aircraft. One of Brazil's other airlines, Panair do Brazil, opened what was then the world's longest non-stop service from Rio to Lisbon, a distance of 4837 miles which took over 21 hours, initially with a Constellation and later a DC-7C.

The decision to establish a new capital in the middle of the jungle gave a further fillip to the air transport industry in Brazil, for no road links existed with Brasilia when the capital was founded in 1957. REAL became the first airline to begin services to the new city, quickly followed by Cruzeiro do Sul and VASP. Ultimately an ' air bridge' from Brasilia to both Rio de Janeiro and Sao

Paulo was opened by the principal regional carriers. Brazil's airlines were quick to take advantage of the latest advance in aviation, ordering new equipment when it became available. The Convair 240 was widely used for domestic services within Brazil but in 1958 VASP ordered the new Vickers Viscount and a year later Varig introduced jet travel to the region by opening a Caravelle service to New York.

A somewhat confused picture emerged in the Argentine where a number of carriers operated scheduled services. As in Brazil, the Convair 240 became the principal airliner for the many domestic routes. In 1950 Aerolinas Agentinas was granted a monopoly as the country's overseas airline and opened a DC-6 service to New York. However, with the collapse of the Peron administration five years later, private airlines were once again permitted to serve international routes although few survived.

In Central America, Aeronaves de Mexico, one of the airlines which quickly recognised the advantages of the gas turbine, introduced the Bristol Britannia on its services to New York in late 1957. Mexico, too, clearly intended to be one of the leading air transport countries in the Americas and was later to become one of the first operators of the Comet 4.

In Canada the conflict of interests between publicly owned Trans Canada Airlines (now Air Canada) and privately owned Canadian Pacific Airlines took some time to resolve. From its base in Vancouver CPA had gradually built up an international network, especially over the Pacific area but TCA's monopoly of the domestic transcontinental services was not broken until 1959, when CPA was granted a daily frequency and introduced the turboprop Britannia onto the service to compete with TCA's Super Constellations. It was CPA's second attempt to get turbine aircraft into service; in the early 1950s the airline ordered the Comet but after the Comet failure it was obliged to operate the DC-6 on its international routes.

In the meantime TCA had gone turbine-powered on many of its routes with the Vickers Viscounts, of which it built up a fleet of 50. In 1955 CPA opened a polar route from Vancouver to Amsterdam, being barred from using London as its European terminal because TCA was the only Canadian carrier designated to serve the UK capital. CPA started a service to Lima and Buenos Aires in 1957 and later extended its network over the Central Atlantic to Lisbon.

Conflict between major domestic carriers was a feature of the airline industry in Australia until a compromise was reached in 1952. In that year the government decided to give privately owned Australian National Airways equal rights with publicly owned Trans Australian Airlines. The earlier

mixed fortunes of ANA had taken its toll and its fortunes were stabilised in 1957 when the airline was bought by Reg Ansett, who began his airline career operating flying-boats in the late 1940s. The government refused TAA's application to operate Caravelles but allowed it to buy Viscounts, while Ansett-ANA continued to use DC-6s until the turbo-prop Lockheed Electra became available in 1959. Since the late 1950s the two carriers have generally operated similar equipment.

Free from political conflicts which beset the two domestic carriers, Qantas grew in influence overseas, using successively Super Constellations and Electras before starting Boeing 707 services in 1959. On the Austra-lia-New Zealand service Tasman Empire Airways (TEAL) enjoyed a virtual monopoly; it gradually phased out its Solent flying-boats, replacing them with DC-6s and then turboprop Electras; after Qantas disposed of its holdings in TEAL in 1961, the two airlines shared the service.

Air transport helped in the development of other countries in the British Common-wealth and the 1950s saw the establishment of airlines which have since become world leaders. The domestic airline scene in India was one of confusion until the Indian Airlines Corporation was given a virtual monopoly in 1955. Two years later Viscounts were acquired by the airline to become the main-stay of its routes for some years. Services in the more remote areas were provided by de Havilland Herons and DC-3s. Having be-come Air India International in 1948 in recognition of its status as the national

overseas carrier, the airline became a state corporation in 1953. As a nation India has always steered an independent political course and has helped to polarise the power of 'third world' nations. Its overseas airline has played an important role in projecting India's image and quickly built up a network to include the Far East, Australia, East Africa, Europe and the United States. Equipped with Super Constellations, Air India established a reputation for excellence in cabin service which set a standard by which other airlines were judged. Maintaining its position as a leading airline, Air India (the International was later dropped) was the first airline to operate the Rolls-Royce Conway-powered Boeing 707.

India's neighbour also operated Lockheed Super Constellations when Pakistan Inter-national Airlines introduced the type in 1954. Formed in 1951, PIA was of immediate importance to Pakistan, maintaining links between the separated east and west parts of the country. Convair 240s were preceded by DC-3s, the faithful machine which was still being used to launch new airlines in the 1970s. Viscounts in turn replaced the Convairs and Fokker F-27s were introduced to serve regional airports, leaving the DC-3s to operate coach-class services to remote towns from Dacca in East Pakistan. PIA established close relations with neighbouring Moslem carriers but actual mergers never took place.

With the help of Pan American Airways, an airline was established in Afghanistan in 1955. Ariana Afghan Airlines did not grow into more than a regional carrier although even-

The Lockheed Model 49 (later 049) Constellation was the basis of much airline expansion in the late 1940s and early 1950s. The Mk6, or 649, introduced improved performance and capacity and the 749, as this one pictured still in charter service in the 1970s, provided extended range through wingtip petrol tanks.

tually services to Europe were opened. India's northern neighbour, Nepal, formed an airline in 1958. The deep valleys in the country make surface communications difficult and sometimes impossible; Royal Nepal Airlines soon became a contributor to the national economy by bringing tourists and businessmen from Delhi and Calcutta. Katmandu was the centre of the Royal Nepal Airlines network and once again it was the DC-3 which gave sterling service in the formative years of the airline.

Air Ceylon has had a chequered history which began in 1948. A series of management contracts have involved Australian National Airways, KLM, BOAC and UTA. Although a popular tourist destination for German and Swiss, in particular, the country has had difficulty in supporting long-distance scheduled air services; hence the chain of attempts to work with established international carriers.

Union of Burma Airways has also never grown beyond being a regional carrier although its domestic network has long been important in the country. In 1953 UBA operated Handley Page-built Miles Marathon airliners but the type was not a success and two years later the airline ordered the Viscount, a machine by which many airlines were to become modern and efficient. Burma has encountered a series of economic and political difficulties but has tended to hold itself aloof from internatonal affairs. The fact that UBA only serves neighbouring countries is a reflection of the country's foreign policy.

If any country has a natural need for air transport, it is the Philippines. Consisting of thousands of islands, the country has come to rely on aviation as a means of linking its scattered communities. However, political difficulties resulted in the suspension of Philippine Airlines international services in 1954. PAL had expanded rapidly but Manila was clearly not so important a commercial centre as Tokyo or Singapore. Concentrating on domestic services, Philippine Airlines used modern airliners such as Viscounts and Friendships to maintain its network. For the more remote areas where airfields were mostly little more than airstrips carved out of the jungle, de Havilland Otters and Scottish Aviation Twin Pioneers were used.

Both these aircraft could be described as bush machines designed to be able to fly into the smallest grass airstrip, even if it was surrounded by steep hills. The de Havilland (Canada) Otter first flew in 1951, powered by a single 600hp Pratt & Whitney Wasp engine and able to carry up to 14 passengers at 139mph. The Scottish Aviation Prestwick Pioneer, which first flew in 1950, had a single 560hp Alvis Leonides engine and a high wing and generous flap area which enabled it to be flown very slowly and safely into tiny airstrips. The twin-engined Twin Pioneer first flew in 1955; as a 16-seater it has been used by several remote airlines needing a machine to serve 'impossible' airfields.

Garuda Indonesian Airways was established in 1956 with the assistance of KLM, but anti-colonialism led to the eventual withdrawal of all Dutch personnel. Later, when

political tempers had cooled, a special relationship with KLM was re-established but in the main the Indonesian carrier has continued to go its own way, at first using Convair 240s and then turboprop Electras to expand its regional services.

Torn by civil war, China had two main airlines but as Chiang Kai-Shek retreated, China Air Lines was finally holed up in Formosa (Taiwan) and has been that island's carrier ever since. Having expelled the Chinese Nationalists from the mainland the Communist forces in 1952 set up the People's Aviation Corporation of China. At that time Russia was a firm ally and helped the formation of the airline by supplying Li-2s (DC-3s in all but name). Two years later the carrier became the responsibility of the Civil Aviation Administration of China and

has since been known as CAAC. Ilyushin 14 and then Il-18 airliners were later supplied by Russia but, to the surprise of many who considered China to be basically antagonistic to the West, CAAC ordered Vickers Viscounts from Britain. Considering the size and density of population of China, its air transport fleet has remained relatively small.

When restrictions on operating airlines were eased by the occupying powers in 1951, Japan quickly established domestic services using DC-4s and Martin 202s. All Nippon Airways grew from a collection of smaller carriers. In the 1950s it operated Convair 440s on its trunk routes and used de Havilland Herons to serve smaller towns. With international services in mind, Japanese Air Lines ordered the Comet in 1952, but had to be

Above: Boeing's return to the passenger aircraft field after WW2 was with the Model 377 Stratocruiser, based partly on the 1942-designed Model 367 C-97 Stratofreighter and partly on wartime developments in the B-29 Superfortress bomber. Here a night-time scene at London Airport North highlights some of BOAC's fleet of 10 Stratocruisers operated virtually throughout the 1950s.

Below: The Lockheed 049 stretched to the Super Constellation and finally to the L-1649 Starliner with a range of over 6000 miles, but these latest piston airliners were already in the shadow of the gas turbine. An ex-Air France Super Constellation in Catair service is pictured here at Le Bourget in 1972.

content with using DC-6 aircraft leased from Flying Tiger and Slick Airways to inaugurate services from Tokyo to San Francisco. The name was shortened to Japan Air Lines in 1954. JAL's rate of growth has been as astonishing as the economic growth of Japan itself, its network and fleet rapidly becoming one of the world's largest. To maintain its new-found position as a leading airline, JAL ordered DC-8s in 1955.

The tiny British colony of Hong Kong may be regarded today as an anachronism. The European empires have long since passed away even though European influence may remain, but in Hong Kong Britain has an important trading centre in the Orient as well as a useful bargaining counter when it comes to negotiating traffic rights with other countries' airlines. As it was not associated with the original Cathay Pacific Airways formed by Australian and American interests, BOAC encouraged the establishment of Hong Kong Airways. It did not flourish although, equipped with Viscounts, it did serve Tokyo and Seoul. For such a small 'country' it seemed sensible to have only one airline and in 1959 Hong Kong Airways merged with Cathay Pacific Airlines. It was the first carrier in the region to buy Lockheed Electras and has become a major carrier in the Pacific region, reflecting the commercial importance of the densely populated colony, particularly as a gateway to Communist China.

Thailand, is also an important link between East and West, Bangkok having become a much used stop on the airlines' eastern routes. Pan American was involved in early attempts to establish an international airline in Thailand but eventually it was SAS in 1959 which concluded a managerial agreement. The arrangement was of great benefit to both partners; Thailand was able to draw on the technical and marketing experience of the Scandinavian carrier as well as having

immediate access to modern equipment. By its new close ties with Thai International, SAS could expand its Far East network. Certainly the new airline began life vigorously for, within a week of its formation its network stretched from Calcutta to Singapore.

One of the exciting areas of development in air transport during the 1950s was the Near East. Oil exploration and extraction led to a rapid increase in air transport in the Arab world. Several airlines were formed with outside help but most eventually became completely independent. Although sudden riches brought wealth to some Arab countries, few had the expertise to run their own airlines. Saudi Arabia turned to TWA to establish its national airline, beginning with a fleet of 10 Convair 340s. A very rich country, but fiercely traditionalist in upholding the Moslem faith, Saudi Arabia encouraged the growth of its airline but would not permit alcoholic drinks to be served on board its aircraft.

With the aid of Sabena, Persian Air Services was formed and used DC-7C aircraft leased from the Belgian airline. Beset with

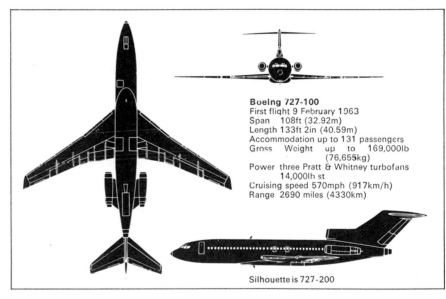

Boeing 727-100
First flight 9 February 1963
Span   108ft (32.92m)
Length 133ft 2in (40.59m)
Accommodation up to 131 passengers
Gross   Weight   up   to   169,000lb
(76,655kg)
Power three Pratt & Whitney turbofans 14,000lh st
Cruising speed 570mph (917km/h)
Range 2690 miles (4330km)

Silhouette is 727-200

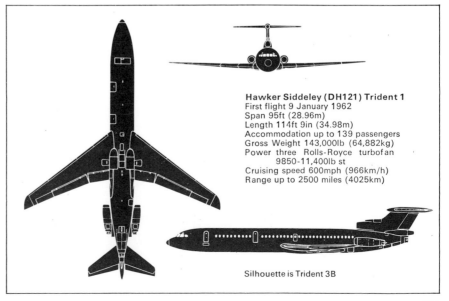

Hawker Siddeley (DH121) Trident 1
First flight 9 January 1962
Span 95ft (28.96m)
Length 114ft 9in (34.98m)
Accommodation up to 139 passengers
Gross Weight 143,000lb (64,882kg)
Power three Rolls-Royce turbofan
9850-11,400lb st
Cruising speed 600mph (966km/h)
Range up to 2500 miles (4025km)

Silhouette is Trident 3B

government interference and other difficulties, the airline was later to merge with Iranian Airways to become Iran Air.

For many years, and especially in the 1950s, the leading air transport nations in the area were Egypt and the Lebanon. Strongly nationalistic and determined to become the political leader of the Arab world, Egypt needed to have a vigorous airline. In 1949 the government nationalised Misr, an airline formed before the war by the British Airwork company and changed the name to Misrair. In 1955 Viscounts took the place of the older Vikings and Languedocs and by the beginning of the next decade Comet 4Cs were acquired.

Less concerned with political leadership, the Lebanon assumed the important role of link between the Arab world and the West. Politically stable, it attracted investment from many quarters and became an important banking centre. All these elements were conducive to the growth of air transport and indeed this tiny country at one time boasted four international airlines. Later to be recognised as a leading figure in air transport, Sheik Najib Alamuddin led Middle East Airlines. With the assistance of Air France, Air Liban was formed in 1951 and equipped with Languedoc airliners. Three years later DC-4s were added to the fleet and by 1959 they in turn gave way to DC-6Cs. Formed in 1956, Lebanese International Airlines later received assistance from Sabena which also took a holding in the company. Last but not least, Trans-Mediterranean Airways was established in 1953 as an all-cargo carrier using a fleet of five Avro Yorks. Clearly some order had to be brought to this situation for even the booming Lebanese economy could not support so many airlines; by 1963 MEA had absorbed Air Liban and LIA, leaving TMA to become a major all-cargo carrier.

The establishment of Arab carriers grew apace and by 1961 17 airlines had been formed in the area. Unhappily the enmity between the Arab nations and the new state of Israel prevented co-operation between their airlines. Nevertheless Israel's El Al quickly became the means by which the besieged country maintained links with more friendly nations. In 1951 El Al became the first non-European airline to begin a scheduled service over the Atlantic, using Constellations. Many small carriers conducted business in Israel but the principal domestic airline was Arkia; a 'daughter' of El Al which provided fast services between Tel Aviv and Eilat on the Red Sea.

The burgeoning airlines of the Near East equipped themselves with modern aircraft as soon as possible, the Viscount becoming popular with MEA, Kuwait Airways, UAA, Iraq Airways and THF, the Turkish airline. Eventually Arkia too operated a small fleet of Viscounts.

The political wind of change which blew through Africa in the 1950s brought with it

Although its entry into service was delayed, the Bristol Britannia became the first long-range turboprop airliner and earned a reputation for quiet comfortable travel. This Britannia Airways Britannia 102, pictured at Birmingham in 1970, was acquired from BOAC in 1965.

new airlines in its wake. The West African Airways Corporation for example, was formed to serve Nigeria and the Gold Coast. Marathons, Bristol Freighters, Doves and DC-3s made up the fleet initially but by 1957 the airline had 'grown up' to lease Argonauts and Stratocruisers from BOAC. A year later, however, Ghana and Nigeria gained their independence; WAAC became Nigerian Airways and Ghana formed its own airline. As a symbol of national pride and identity an airline had become as important as a seat in the United Nations.

The airlines of North Africa grew steadily, even before the various countries gained their independence. Traffic to and from metropolitan France boomed as the economies of the North African countries were closely bound up with that of France. Tunis Air was the first to be formed in the area in 1948 and was followed by Royal Air Maroc and Air Algerie; each thrived but they remained little more than regional carriers.

Ethiopian Airlines was formed with the assistance of TWA as early as 1945 but it did not begin a programme of expansion until the 1950s. Using DC-6Bs the Lion of Judah symbol on the tail of the airliners began to fly beyond Africa and in 1958 a service to Europe was opened, terminating at Frankfurt.

East African Airways opened a weekly service to London in 1957 using Argonauts leased from BOAC. The thriving Asian community in the area encouraged the establishment of a service to Bombay, too. EAA was determined to become a modern airline and introduced a small fleet of Comet 4Cs as soon as possible, working the aircraft hard to keep the three 'parent' nations content with the operation.

South African Airways maintained a policy of updating its fleet regularly, exchanging its DC-4s for Constellations in 1950 and in turn introducing the DC-7B in 1956. To improve the service on its domestic network, SAA took delivery of Viscounts in 1958. As more and more black African nations became independent, South Africa found itself increasingly isolated and but for air transport, the country would surely have been cut off from the rest of the world. By ordering Boeing 707s in 1958, SAA was to be able to continue operating to Europe despite its inability to overfly many African countries. The new jets entered service in 1960 and provided a lifeline with industrial nations with whom South Africa had long traditional ties.

Central African Airways did not receive modern equipment until the delivery of Viscounts in 1956. Operating Viking aircraft to Johannesburg from Salisbury, the airline managed to generate good traffic on the route, later pioneering low-cost night flights between the two cities. In 1953 CAA opened the Zambesi coach-class services to London, a very slow and doubtless tedious journey which nevertheless attracted passengers by offering low fares. The South African charter airline Trek Airways was another pioneer in low-cost air travel, initially with a service to Europe with Vikings which were later replaced by DC-4 aircraft.

And so to Europe, where the 1950s were no less important in marking a period of rapid expansion and development. A curious situation existed in Austria which was once more permitted to operate air services. The main political parties vied with one another to establish a national airline encouraged by various other European airlines. The Austrian Peoples Party formed Air Austria with the aid of KLM and later the Fred Olsen company. Meanwhile, the Austrian Socialist Party enlisted the aid of SAS in forming Austrian Airways. These airlines were largely 'paper' companies and in 1957 the two factions resolved their differences to enable Austrian Airlines to begin operations the following year, initially using Viscounts leased from Fred Olsen, the Norwegian charter operator.

In Germany the old Lufthansa was buried beneath the ashes of the Third Reich and for some years any form of aviation activity was forbidden by the occupying powers. In 1951 the transport ministry, with the approval of the Allies, set up a working group to study the steps which should be taken to re-establish a national airline. Headed by the traffic manager of the old Lufthansa, the 'Buro Bongers' eventually led to the formation of the new Deutsche Lufthansa in August 1954. For long-distance services Lockheed Super Constellations were ordered and Convair 340s were selected to open European routes. In April the following year the Convairs began services with BEA pilots in the captain's seat and German co-pilots by their sides; similarly, when the New York services opened they were captained by TWA pilots. The first pilots of the new airline were trained at the Air Services Training school in England but in 1955 Lufthansa opened its own school in anticipation of a rapid demand for aircrews. Throughout the 1950s the airline expanded its network and in 1958 introduced the Viscount onto European routes. To hasten the developments of international services, a series of pool and co-operation agreements were concluded, including one with Air France regarding South Atlantic flights, resuming a collaboration which began before the war.

In 1959 Lufthansa joined with Air France and Sabena in discussions which were to have led to the formation of Air Union the following year. The enterprise failed, however, because the respective governments could not agree on an administration formula. By the end of the decade the Lufthansa

network stretched to North and South America and the Far East. For Lufthansa, the piston-engined airliner era was shorter than most, for within five years of reopening services, the Super Constellations began to take second place to Boeing 707s.

Already welcomed back into the fold of civil airline operators, Italy's two airlines continued to operate independently until 1956 when LAI was finally absorbed into Alitalia. Convair 340 and DC-6B aircraft were followed by Convair 440 and DC-7C machines as Alitalia continued its steady growth. The airline took over the order for Viscounts placed by LAI and in 1958 joined the growing queue for the new DC-8 jet airliner. As with many carriers, the jet era was to open a period of rapid expansion for Alitalia.

Italy's aircraft industry has grown steadily since the war and has been mainly concerned with the production of military machines. Piaggio is a famous name in aviation as well as the world of mopeds and in 1948 the company's P136 amphibian flew for the first time. The high 'gull' wing kept the two Lycoming engines well clear of the water but the growing number of airfields throughout the world diminished the market for flying-

boats. Piaggio therefore set about developing the design as a landplane for use as a third-level airliner or executive transport. The P166 bore a close resemblance to the earlier machine but was designed for operation from land only. The pusher engine layout was unusual but the P166 had a sprightly performance which gave it an appeal to bush operators. Airline users of the Piaggio P166 included Ansett in Australia.

Yugoslavia's JAT demonstrated its independence of the Soviet camp by buying Convair 340s and DC-6Bs from the United States. In an attempt to form a consortium of airlines in the Balkans, JAT held discussions in 1953 with neighbouring airlines, in particular those of Greece and Turkey. However, a Balkan grouping along the lines of SAS was not to be; the temperament of the different nations was not conducive to the close collaboration necessary for such a venture.

In Greece TAE grew in stature by absorbing other carriers but the airline failed to operate profitably. When the shipping magnate Aristotle Onassis approached the Greek Government with an offer to take over the airline the move was accepted with alacrity. Guaranteed a monopoly as the national carrier, Onassis changed the airline's name to Olympic Airways and operations began in 1957 under the new banner. The old DC-4s were not competitive with the equipment flown by neighbouring countries and DC-6Bs were leased from UAT until new aircraft could be obtained from the United States. The main aim of the new management was to strengthen the airline's European and Mediterranean network. Some years were to elapse before longer distance routes were to be opened.

In 1954 the airlines of Hungary, Romania and Bulgaria were freed of their dependence upon Russia but tended to continue operating Soviet equipment. LOT too demonstrated the Polish airline's independence by purchasing Convair 240s from America in 1957. The Vickers Viscount was later to become the airline's front-line airliner on European routes. The Czechoslovakian airline CSA made only moderate progress in the early 1950s operating Il-14 airliners. In 1957, however, the airline joined the ranks of jet operators by taking the Tupolev Tu-104A, with which CSA spread its wings to Paris and Brussels, later adding Cairo to its network. CSA became quite adventurous in opening new routes, often operating to countries not served by Aeroflot.

Czechoslovakia has never had a large aircraft industry but its designs have won a wide respect, especially in the field of competition aerobatic aircraft. In the transport category, however, Czecholsovakia has made a significant contribution to East European aviation. The Aero 45 four-seat aircraft

Left: *The Washington operator Allegheny Airlines was the first to take up the turboprop Convairliner and chose the Napier Eland-powered version, the 540 pictured here, for scheduled services between Washington, Pittsburgh, Philadelphia, Boston, New York and Providence.*

Below: *Caravelle deliveries got under way by March 1959 and SAS was among the first airlines to receive them. Here a group of the early arrivals is seen at Copenhagen Airport in July 1964.*

first flew in 1947 and led to the slightly larger Aero 145. Successful though the air taxis were, the L-200A Morava, first flown in 1957, was an even greater success, being adopted as the standard communications and small feeder aircraft throughout the Soviet bloc.

The Russian airline was principally concerned with building up its domestic network, for the Soviet Union covers a vast area in which surface transport facilities were, for the most part, poor. The Il-14 remained the principal airliner in the Aeroflot fleet until the advent of the Tu-104 jet aircraft in 1956. With a domestic network stretching from Europe to the Pacific, Aeroflot was content to leave the development of international services to the Soviet satellite countries. The Moscow to Vladivostok run is twice the distance of the New York-San Francisco route, a fact which puts the task of Aeroflot into perspective. By the end of the 1950s Aeroflot was carrying 20 million passengers annually.

Finland has managed to retain its independence since the end of the war even if obliged to treat its mighty neighbour with due deference. Never obliged to operate Russian aircraft, Finnair received Convair 340s from the United States in 1953. Satisfied with this type, the carrier took the next development into its fleet and operated the Convair 440 to Moscow in 1956.

In 1954 East Germany formed an airline and called it Deutsche Lufthansa! And it adopted the same insignia as West Germany. It began operations in 1956 with Il-14 airliners but, almost an ostracised country in the Western world, East Germany could not persuade anyone to recognise the name of its

airline. This particular aspect of the cold war ended in 1959 when the name Interflug was adopted but the airline remained small by any comparison and it has never become an accepted international airline.

In Spain, Iberia bought Lockheed Super Constellations and steadily expanded its network, concentrating on Spanish-speaking areas of the world, particularly Mexico and Cuba. In 1954 New York was added to Iberia's Atlantic network. Neighbouring Portugal's TAP enjoyed less success in the 1950s; indeed the decade opened with the airline in serious financial difficulties. TAP was bought by a syndicate of business interests in 1953 and began to recover; the following year it introduced the Super Constellation into service.

The collective strength which went to make up SAS allowed the airline to be more enterprising than separate Scandinavian airlines could ever have been. There are some disadvantages in being a Scandinavian-based airline, not least when it comes to negotiating traffic rights with a country which has no desire to serve Oslo, Copenhagen or Stockholm but there are geographical benefits, too. In 1953 SAS opened an Arctic route to Los Angeles via Greenland and Winnipeg. Exploiting the longer range of the DC-7C, SAS pioneered a polar service to Tokyo via Anchorage in 1957. This route has since become one of the accepted means of getting to Tokyo quickly and many other carriers followed the Scandinavian lead.

On short-haul routes SAS, like Swissair, was content to operate the Convair 440 and opted to miss the turboprop interval before the introduction of the jet airliner. In 1959

Despite the jets, the massive postwar buildup of air traffic on the main long-distance routes was carried by the big piston-engined airliners, typified by this KLM Flying Dutchman DC-4 'Groningen'

SAS introduced the French Caravelle onto its network. In 1957 SAS took a half-share in the Swedish domestic carrier, Linjeflyg which proceeded to expand its route network. Formed originally as Airtaco in 1950, the airline was mainly concerned with carrying newspapers to outlying districts. While that has remained an important part of its operation, Linjeflyg steadily built up its passenger services using Convair aircraft.

Norway also maintained independent domestic carriers although neither was allowed to compete with SAS on international routes. Braathens and Wideroe demonstrated the important part which air transport can play in serving isolated communities. Operating floatplanes, Wideroe maintained links with towns in the far north of Norway, towns to which SAS had no interest in operating. Thus independent Scandinavian airlines learned to live in harmony with the international SAS.

In the Netherlands KLM, as well as joining the growing number of Viscount operators, later also took the Lockheed Electra into its fleet, the only European carrier to do so. The Dutch airline has sometimes had a curious fleet policy, operating the products of several manufacturers. Most carriers prefer to standardise on one aircraft producer for the sake of economy. KLM had indeed been a consistent operator of Douglas aircraft but the Convair 340 and the Viscount, the DC-7C and the Lockheed Super Constellation indicate some overlapping in fleet types.

Belgian Sabena also was a DC-7C operator and put the type on a new service to Moscow in 1958. At that time more and more European airlines ventured to penetrate the Iron Curtain. Quite commonplace nowadays, in the 1950s services to Moscow were considered something of an adventure for Western passengers who found the stern airport procedures somewhat daunting. Before boarding aircraft for the return journey to the West, the passenger's passport photograph was carefully compared before permission to board the aircraft was granted.

Air France also opened a service to Moscow in the late 1950s, using Super Constellations, and in 1953 introduced the same type on a North Atlantic service. Sizeable independent airlines remained in France, unlike most other European countries where a national monopoly usually evolved. Some reorganisation was considered necessary, however, and in 1956 there was a reallocation of routes; Air France was granted a monopoly of Atlantic and polar routes but was obliged to share Far East services with the independent TAI, which was allowed to continue to Australasia and the French Pacific island colonies, using DC-6Bs on the long route from Paris to Noumea and Bora Bora, though Tahiti continued to be linked by Short Sandringham flying-boats for several

years thereafter. In 1959 TAI entered a multi-national Far East pool which included Air France, Lufthansa, Alitalia and, later, JAL. Finally in the reallocation of routes operated by the French long-distance carriers UAT was granted rights to South Africa as well as certain other African regions.

In 1955 Air France ordered the Caravelle, an aircraft destined to be as revolutionary as the Comet and Boeing 707. Airlines had barely adjusted to the idea of using jets on long-distance routes, when the Caravelle issued a challenge on short and medium routes too. Although not profitable on very short routes, the smooth fast and quiet flights quickly gained the approval of the travelling public. By the end of the decade Air France had become Europe's largest airline, with the greatest unduplicated route network in the world.

Although the Caravelle was France's principal contribution to the development of air transport in the 1950s, the country also produced one of the world's first business (executive) aircraft, the Morane Saulnier MS760 Paris. Executive travel will be dealt with in a later chapter but the Paris, which flew for the first time in 1954, was one of the first of a new breed.

Britain has long had an uncertain policy regarding air transport, veering from a rigid support of the national airline to the active encouragement of independent carriers. For some years after the establishment of BEA there was little opportunity for private airlines. Perhaps the challenge stimulated original thinking and unusual enterprise but whatever the reason, the 1950s saw some new endeavours in air transport. By 1954, for example, Silver City Airways had established the unique cross-Channel car ferry. From the terminal at Lympne, the Bristol Freighters of Silver City clattered and roared their way to Le Touquet and other French destinations, delivering their loads of private cars and passengers in a mere 20 minutes or so. Many passengers were glad to avoid the long and tedious sea crossing and, at the peak of the service, Silver City flew 220 cross-Channel flights in one day.

Silver City's success encouraged others to enter the cross-Channel market and in 1956 the Air Charter company started the Channel Air Bridge which operated from Southend. Led by Freddie Laker, Air Charter later extended the ferry service to inland Continental cities. Such routes required an aircraft with a longer range than the Bristol Freighter and Laker hit upon the idea of modifying a DC-4 for the task. Raising the flight deck to allow direct entry through a door in the nose, the Aviation Traders ATL-98 Carvair could accommodate a larger load than the Bristol Freighters and fly to Switzerland with ease. Such enterprise was typical of the British independents, excluded as they

Above: *In the medium airliner field the 1950s laurels undoubtedly went to the turboprop Vickers Viscount, represented here by one of the last to be built, a Viscount 837 of Austrian Airlines.*

Facing page: *By 1959 the Boeing 707 was swamping the market and was bought new by many charter companies as well as major airlines. This picture shows one delivered in September 1959 to the independent Laker Airways at London Gatwick.*

were from operating scheduled passenger flights in competition with BEA or BOAC.

The Air Transport Advisory Council was set up to allocate licences as it thought fit, and it allowed independent airlines to operate services which were not judged to be competitive with either of the nationalised airlines. The ATAC was charged by the government to ensure that new licences for independent airlines would not result in 'material diversion' of traffic from the two national corporations. One result of the advent of a new Conservative government in the early 1950s was a much more favourable view of the independents. With widespread colonial territories which required the presence of defence forces, Britain had need of a number of 'flying troopships'. To send troops to Singapore by ship, for example, resulted in an unacceptable number of men being 'unemployed' in transit. Air transport offered a solution to the problem and as RAF Transport Command had insufficient aircraft, the independents could fill the gap without 'materially diverting' traffic from BOAC. Indeed, at a return fare of £100, the trooping fares were more than £250 cheaper then the scheduled civilian passenger fare. Small wonder that trooping became a major part of the independents' activity.

The Conservative government took further steps to support the independents; in 1952 it was agreed that the national carriers would only seek charter business when it was clear that the independents lacked the necessary capacity. Thus the roles of the two sides of the British air transport industry were clearly defined and both were afforded some protection from outside competition.

Trooping accounted for a high percentage of the total business performed by the independents during the 1950s and was certainly profitable. However, as Britain's overseas interests slowly contracted, so too

the extent and value of trooping contracts declined. Other outlets for the independents' energy had to be found. In 1952 an Air Safari service was opened to East, West and Central Africa. Hunting-Clan and Airwork were allowed to run weekly Viking services which were known as Colonial Coach flights. Involving many stops en route, the 28-seat Viking was not considered to make 'material diversion' of passengers from the faster and more sophisticated aircraft flown by BOAC. Taking about three days to complete the journey, the Safari services were nonetheless very popular, for as well as offering a fare saving, the journeys recaptured some of the relaxed atmosphere of the old flying-boat schedules.

Using Avro Yorks, Skyways operated a similar low-cost service to Cyprus via Malta. Airwork and Hunting-Clan found another way to operate the York, carrying pigs and other livestock to a variety of destinations in Europe. It was the Berlin Air Lift which established many British independents in business; Harold Bamberg founded Eagle in 1948, for example, with a capital of just £100. His fleet of demobilised bombers helped the airline to grow so that in the 1950s new ventures could be undertaken. Unable to operate scheduled passenger services, Eagle pioneered a form of air travel which has since become commonplace: the inclusive tour. This consisted of selling the entire capacity of the aircraft to a tour operator which then organised such ground arrangements as hotel accommodation and sightseeing, selling the whole 'package' as an inclusive tour. Inevitably cheaper than a holiday arranged by a private individual, this type of travel grew at an astonishing pace so that by the end of the decade, independent airlines were carrying more passengers to Spain on inclusive tours than BEA and Iberia combined.

Other pioneering airline personalities of the day included Don Bennett who, faithful to his Tudors operated previously by BSAA, operated the aircraft in his charter company, Fairflight. Some disastrous crashes ended both the Tudors and Fairflight. Eric Rylands formed the Lancashire Aircraft Corporation which in turn operated Skyways. As a challenge to both air and sea operators to Paris, Skyways started a coach-air service in 1955. Passengers were taken by coach from London to Lympne where they were flown to Beauvais by DC-3. From the French airport a coach continued to Paris. Cheaper than normal air fares and much faster than the rail/sea services, the Skyways Coach Air service attracted considerable business. Silver City Airways provided competition by starting the Silver Arrow service which involved rail links in England and France with a short hop over the English Channel to Le Touquet.

In 1955 Starways opened a service between London and Liverpool; a route long neglected by BEA which was content to regard Manchester as the principal airport for the northwest region. Starways traffic grew rapidly although the DC-4 airliners could hardly be regarded as the latest equipment. In many countries air transport has eclipsed rail as the principal method of moving from city to city. In Britain, however, electrification of the West Coast main line resulted in faster and more reliable rail services. The Starways Liverpool service was one victim of the new improvement in rail travel and ultimately it was withdrawn.

Other airlines which came into existence in the 1950s include Dan-Air, BKS, Derby Airways and Don Everall Aviation. Some survived, others fell by the wayside or were absorbed into other airlines. All had a useful role to play, however, some operating scheduled services which did not interest BEA. For years BKS operated a Newcastle-London service but eventually the little airline was taken over by BEA which had meanwhile taken a minority holding to keep the operation going.

Air transport steadily eroded the seagoing passenger services of the shipping lines. The hustle and bustle of the second half of the twentieth century had no place for the plodding pace of ships even if they offered a standard of luxury unattainable by airliners. A 17-hour flight across the 3500 miles which separated the New World from the Old was considered by most to be preferable to a four-day sea voyage. Undaunted, the shipping lines took a logical step; they bought interests in airlines. The Clan Line took over Hunting Air Transport in 1953 and a year later Blue Star and Furness Withy took shares in Airwork. The General Steamship Navigation Company took over the Britavia group, started at the beginning of the decade by Air Commodore Powell. By 1959 only one of the five major independent airlines was not owned by a shipping company; Harold Bamburg's Eagle Airways.

Britain's two national carriers enjoyed mixed fortunes during the 1950s, pioneering new equipment and enduring setbacks but entering the next decade in good shape. BOAC had more than its share of bad luck, for as well as suffering the trauma of the Comet 1 episode, other aircraft types brought difficulties in their wake. The Handley Page Hermes 4 entered service with BOAC in 1950; it proved to be expensive in terms of engineering costs and after only a few years most of the fleet of 25 aircraft were cocooned, that is preserved under a protective plastic shell. When BOAC suffered an overnight 20-per cent loss of its fleet capacity with the grounding of the Comets, the Hermes were hurriedly pressed into service once more. The Britannia, which

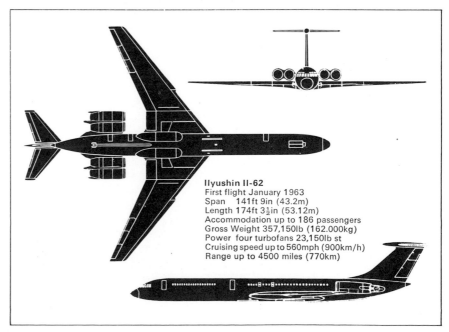

Ilyushin Il-62
First flight January 1963
Span 141ft 9in (43.2m)
Length 174ft 3½in (53.12m)
Accommodation up to 186 passengers
Gross Weight 357,150lb (162.000kg)
Power four turbofans 23,150lb st
Cruising speed up to 560mph (900km/h)
Range up to 4500 miles (770km)

eventually proved to be a fine airliner, failed to give BOAC the lead which the Viscount gave to BEA, but BOAC's 'Whispering Giant' became the first civil aircraft ever to achieve half a million flying hours without a fatal accident.

By and large, the Viscount helped BEA to success in the 1950s. Turboprop power brought new standards of comfort and safety, and then the Caravelle added yet another improvement to short-haul air travel. Indeed, the jet competition provided by the French aircraft obliged BEA to take the Comet 4B into its fleet.

In 1959 the first Vickers Vanguard took to the air. A greatly enlarged Viscount, the Vanguard had a 'double-bubble' fuselage which allowed good quantities of cargo to be carried 'below decks'. Although the machine subsequently gave good service both to BEA and TCA, it could be argued that the Britannia would have been just as suitable. Britain's aircraft industry has sometimes been charged with dissipating its energies and certainly it made little sense for two such similar aircraft to be developed in the same country.

The world's aircraft industry produced several new transport designs in the 1950s. In Britain in 1958 the Dart Herald flew for the first time. The 44-seat airliner was yet another in a long line of intended DC-3 replacements but it was overshadowed by the Dutch Fokker F27 which was well-established on the market by the time the Handley Page aircraft appeared. The Avro 748 which appeared later fared much better, finding favour with operators in many parts of the world. Like the Herald, the Avro 748 was powered by two Rolls-Royce Darts.

Four Darts were selected to power the Armstrong-Whitworth AW650 Argosy; a freight-carrying aircraft which flew for the first time in 1959. Heralded at the time as a breakthrough in cargo-aircraft design, the Argosy in fact found few civil customers, the bulk of the production run being taken by the RAF. Although many all-cargo aircraft have been designed, few have become a commercial success. Generally it has proved to be cheaper to operate 'retired' passenger aircraft which have plenty of life left in them but are no longer competitive with the latest passenger machines.

The Bristol Britannia design was taken by Canadair who modified the aircraft to become an unusual all-cargo machine. Rolls-Royce Tyne turboprops were substituted for the Bristol Proteus engines and the whole rear fuselage was hinged so that it could be swung to one side by the tail to permit the direct loading of bulky cargo. Although the CL-44 was not built in large numbers, it remained in service for many years and has become very popular with specialist operators.

Military cargo was the raison d'etre of the de Havilland (Canada) Caribou which first flew in 1958, although some aircraft did later come into the hands of airline operators. The Caribou was the first twin-engined design to emerge from the Canadian de Havilland company and it followed in the tradition of practical STOL aircraft established by the DHC Beaver and Otter machines. Although conceived to meet the special needs of Canadian civil operators, the DHC designs proved to be extremely adaptable. The little Beaver, which could carry up to seven people, was the company's first STOL design and it

Below: *Designed originally in the 1950s as a piston-engined pressurised airliner for medium stage lengths, the Handley Page Herald made little impression on buyers so it was rejigged as a turboprop with two Rolls-Royce Dart engines and first flew in March 1958. Here a British Air Ferries Dart Herald is seen at Blackbushe in 1977.*

was soon ordered by civil and military operators in many parts of the world, bringing air transport to hitherto unserved remote areas.

STOL machines first appeared in two other countries during the 1950s. In Switzerland the Pilatus Porter, which flew for the first time in 1959, was designed to fly slowly and safely into and out of Switzerland's deep valleys. At first powered by a single Lycoming piston engine, later variants offered a choice of turboprop engines—and quite remarkable performance. Requiring only a tiny take-off run, the Porter could climb steeply and so slowly as to appear to be on the point of stalling. Equally, the aircraft could point its nose to the ground at a sharp angle and be slowly and safely manoeuvred into a tiny airstrip. Deep valleys are not confined to Switzerland and many other countries found the exceptional flying qualities of the Pilatus Turbo-Porter invaluable.

The requirements of the colonial forces of France resulted in the design of another STOL transport, the Max Holste MH1521 Broussard six-seat utility transport. It became a useful addition to the transport aircraft operated by the French forces in Africa, and led to the twin-engined Super Broussard which in turn led to the Nord 260 and 262. Very much a refined aircraft, the Nord 262 could be described as yet another DC-3 replacement, having a capacity for 28 passengers. Fitted with two Turbomeca Bastan turboprops, the Nord 262 was operated in the United States by some feeder airlines.

Germany's return to aircraft production was closely supervised by the Allied powers. Indeed, Dornier, impatient to resume aircraft design, in 1955 produced the STOL Do27 in Spain. It was the forerunner of a series of STOL designs, and was later widely adopted by the German forces as a liaison transport. It was followed in 1959 by the twin-engined Do28, an unusual design which featured engines mounted on sponsons, or stub wings. A similar layout was adopted for the Sky-servant, which has joined the ranks of STOL aircraft in operation in many remote parts of the world.

The term STOL must be considered relative; the Lockheed C130 Hercules cannot get airborne in the take-off run required by the Porter. Nevertheless, for a heavy four-engined transport the Hercules has a remarkable performance. First flown in 1954, the Hercules has been adopted by the air forces of many lands. The four Allison turboprops power the Hercules into the air after a very short run for such an aircraft. Just as independent of runways as some smaller STOL designs, the Hercules can land on rough strips or even the icy 'runways' of the Antarctic. The ability of the Hercules to fly a load of supplies into the most elementary airfield had led to its being used to fly rescue teams and their equipment to many countries.

Fascinating though STOL designs are, it would not be right to close this chapter on this note, for by the end of the 1950s studies had already begun on supersonic transport aircraft. Many years were to elapse before the supersonic era of air transport was to open, but the seeds were already being sown in the research centres of Britain, France and the United States well before the end of the decade.

Above: *Earliest of the second-generation turbine-powered airliners were in production by the end of the decade. Here an ex-BEA Vanguard is shown in the livery of its second owner Merpati Nusantara Airlines of Indonesia.*

9. More Boom ~ and Crisis

THE AMERICAN BIG jets set a revolution in train which, perhaps inevitably, brought difficulties as well as positive advances. As airlines of all sizes clamoured to buy the latest equipment the first inevitable result was that too many airliners were chasing too few passengers. The greatly increased speed and capacity of the new jets was more than the market could bear, for the natural growth in passenger traffic could not possibly fill all the 707s and DC-8s offering seats on all the world's trunk routes. Statistics have shown that increases in speed generate traffic and this was certainly true of the new jet airliners, but lean years had to be endured until profitable loads were carried again.

Jet travel brought other problems to the airlines too; aircrew had to be 'converted' from piloting piston-engined aircraft to the new 150-ton jets. New techniques had to be learned and the weakness of jet aircraft discovered, sometimes the hard way. Jet engines (especially the early versions) do not respond so quickly as piston engines. A swept-wing aircraft lands at a much higher speed than one with a straight wing and therefore pilots had to react quickly if they found themselves approaching a stall at lower speeds. The necessary skills were quickly acquired, however, and the airlines of most countries eagerly entered the jet age.

With the transatlantic journey reduced to about seven hours, it was no longer necessary to provide sleeping accommodation but as there was room to spare on most jet airliners, the Boeing 707 and DC-8 were initially fitted with bars. Recalling the days of the down-stairs bar of the Stratocruiser, the new facility was popular with passengers as it gave them the opportunity to stretch their legs during the flight. In the succeeding years, as traffic grew and load factors increased, the airlines removed the bars and installed more seats.

The 1960s saw many developments both in the airline industry and the aircraft the air-lines used. The Viscount 800 grew in popularity as the largest and most economical of the popular Vickers design while, to face the challenge of the Caravelle, BEA took the Comet 4B into service. Perhaps to every-one's surprise, the Comet proved to be a profitable airliner and it sold to a number of airlines which wanted to 'go jet' without taking the leap in capacity represented by the American jets. BEA established a close relationship with Olympic Airways in 1960 under which the Greek airline leased Comets from the British carrier. A year later a similar arrangement was made with Cyprus

Airways in which BEA had a 23-per cent interest.

In 1961 BEA introduced the Vickers Vanguard into scheduled service and although it was a useful airliner for heavily booked routes, such as those to Spain, the 130-seat aircraft never achieved the popularity of the Viscount. A fleet of 20 for BEA was followed by an order from TCA for 23 but there sales stopped. When later retired from passenger service BEA's Vanguards continued to earn their living flying cargo. As the Merchantman, the voluminous cabin made it ideal for the air-freight role.

For BEA 1960 was an excellent year; profits reached £2-million for the first time and expansion was the watchword for the company. In anticipation of a need for more pilots in the future, the two British national carriers took a stake in the new College of Air Training at Hamble, where young students worked to obtain their commercial pilot's licences.

As part of its policy of attracting passengers BEA reduced fares on some routes; on the services to Glasgow and Edinburgh from London the fare of £3.15 was the lowest in the world for the distance. In the 1750s the journey from London to Edinburgh took 11 days by stage-coach; a century later it took about 11 hours by express train and two centuries later the BEA service took one hour—just one example of the extraordinary revolution brought about by air transport.

Another revolution of the early turbine era came about because of the poor weather often experienced in the British Isles, which encouraged BEA to experiment with an automatic landing system. Smiths Autoland, fitted to BEA Tridents, was proved by over 600 landings before the first passenger-carrying automatic landing took place in June 1965. The system uses triplicated components so that, should a failure occur, there are two back-up units arranged to take over automatically. The use of Autoland has been extended to other aircraft, enabling BEA (now British Airways) to operate fitted airliners to and from airports equipped for Autoland in weather conditions which keep other aircraft on the ground.

The Trident was the first 'second-generation' jet airliner, work on which began in 1957. De Havilland and Rolls-Royce were chosen to develop the new aircraft but the government of the day insisted that the DH121 Trident should be produced by a consortium consisting of de Havilland, Hunting Aircraft and Fairey Aviation. A new company named Airco (Aircraft Manu-

Previous page: *During the 1960s most major airports started what was to become an almost continual extension and expansion and virtual round-the-clock operation to cope with the traffic. This colourful shot of London Heathrow on a June night in the early 1970s features a BOAC super VC10, itself a product of the 1960s.*

facturing Company) recalled a similarly named aircraft builder of the 1914-18 war period, but a later government-induced restructuring of the aircraft industry ultimately resulted in different partners for de Havilland in the Hawker Siddeley Aviation group.

BEA ordered 24 of the Trident airliners, each powered by three Rolls-Royce Spey bypass turbojet engines. First flown in 1962, the Trident was ahead of its American rival, the Boeing 727, but although it was closely matched to the requirements of BEA, with a maximum capacity for 103 passengers on shorter stages, the British design had little appeal elsewhere. Both smaller and less powerful than the Boeing machine, the Trident won few orders from foreign airlines. Orders for developed versions, Marks 2 and 3, brought BEA Trident deliveries to 65 aircraft and a few others entered service with foreign airlines—PIA, Iraqi Airways and Kuwait Airways, and a fleet of Trident 2s and 3s was bought by CAAC, the Chinese airline.

As BEA enjoyed commercial success, BOAC by contrast entered the 1960s with an accumulated deficit of about £64 million. Although the pioneering spirit burnt no less brightly than for BEA, BOAC had paid a heavy penalty for opening the jet age and several of its British-built airliners had failed to realise their early promise. As the Boeing 707 demonstrated its reliability and money-making qualities, it is perhaps understandable that BOAC did not gladly assume the responsibility of supporting British industry by ordering new designs.

Nevertheless in 1957 the airline did order a substantial number of Vickers VC10 airliners, which were for Empire routes and hence able to use relatively short runways. The VC10 was powered by four Rolls-Royce Conway bypass turbojets mounted in pairs on the rear of the fuselage; it was first flown in 1962 and entered service in 1964 on the Lagos route. However, in the same year Sir Giles Guthrie assumed the chairmanship of BOAC and set about making the airline profitable. His first act was to reduce the order for the VC10, then an unknown quantity, which looked as if it would be more expensive to operate then the Boeing 707. Originally 12 Standard 135-seat VC10s and 30 175-seat Super VC10s had been ordered but the size of the Super fleet was reduced to 17 and a further 10 were to be held in suspense. By 1965 the 12 VC10s had been delivered, enabling BOAC to sell its Britannia aircraft. The government having agreed to write off BOAC's deficit, the airline turned in a profit of £8 million; Sir Giles had achieved his objective but at some cost to the aircraft industry. The suspended order for 10 Super VC10s was cancelled and although £7½ million was paid in compensation such a resounding vote of no confidence severely damaged the sales prospects of the type elsewhere.

The Super VC10 was introduced onto the North Atlantic in 1965 and soon became a very popular airliner. It was marginally more expensive to operate than the Boeing 707 but the British airliner consistently attracted considerably higher load factors than any

Above: *The Tu-134 short/medium-range twin-turbojet airliner introduced in the mid 1960s was stretched in the early 1970s to the 134A with more seats and baggage space. The one seen here is one of the earlier 64/72-seaters of the Polish airline LOT at Geneva Airport in 1970.*

Right upper: *Final development of the Hawker Siddeley Trident was the Super Trident 3B, two of which were, as the one pictured here, built for the Chinese airline CAAC in 1973 to join that operator's 33 Trident 2Es. The Super 3B is a development of the high-capacity 3B built for BEA, with extra tankage for longer range and normal seating increased to 152.*

Right lower: *A JAT-Jugoslav Airlines DC-9, one of about a dozen of the enlarged Series 30 105/115-seaters delivered to the airline in the early 1970s, at a loading bay of London Heathrow's European terminal.*

other type. Although rather noisy for those over whom it flew, inside the VC10 was the quietest of the big jets and its comfort continued to attract large numbers of passengers long after the novelty had worn off. The damage had been done, however, and few other airlines ordered the VC10; a 265-seat two-deck development of the Super VC10 did not get farther than the drawing board.

The advantages of fleet standardisation were at last open to BOAC as, with the delivery of the Super VC10, it could dispose of its Comet airliners. The Comets were bought by charter companies, notably Dan Air, and remained in profitable service for many years, fittingly rounding out the career of the world's pioneering jet airliner and, in the opinion of many, one whose graceful lines have never been surpassed.

The 1960s saw many changes in the position of the independent airlines in Great Britain. A series of mergers led to the formation of British United Airways in 1960; Airwork had bought Air Charter from Freddie Laker and along with Morton and Olley Air Services merged with Hunting Clan to form an airline of considerable size. A year later, BUA joined the Britavia group to form Air Holdings, one result of which was the merger of the two car-ferry airlines Channel Air Bridge and Silver City Airways.

Eagle too was bent upon a policy of expansion, forming Eagle Airways (Bermuda) in 1960 to operate a Viscount service into New York. To emphasise its new-found vigour, the company was renamed British Eagle International Airways but later the same year the company joined forces with the great Atlantic shipping line to form Cunard Eagle. The airline was awarded rights to Bermuda and the Bahamas, operating Britannias with some success. There followed one of those episodes which has dogged the development of the British airline industry since the earliest days. The Air Transport Licensing Board was encouraged to allow the expansion of the private sector of the airline industry and awarded Cunard

Eagle a licence to operate to New York from London. For years TWA and Pan American had shared the route and there was no logical reason why there should not be two British carriers on the route. Understandably BOAC did not agree and appealed to the Minister of Aviation to reverse the decision of the ATLB. To everyone's astonishment, in 1961 the appeal was allowed. With a Conservative government in power it had been expected that private enterprise would be encouraged to compete with the nationalised airlines. As a result of the Minister's decision, Cunard and BOAC formed a joint company to operate over the North Atlantic. The enterprise was short-lived, however, and BOAC soon resumed its monopoly.

British Eagle was allowed to operate domestic routes and introduced some interesting innovations. One was trickle-loading which permitted passengers to board the airliner as soon as they had checked in instead of having to wait in the terminal building before the customary undignified rush to the aircraft. The 1960s saw the failure of British Eagle, along with several other charter companies. Most tried to do too much with only the narrowest of profit margins; it often took only one setback to bring the airline to an end.

As some charter airlines went out of existence, others, like Caledonian Airways, quietly grew in strength. In an endeavour to bring some order to British air transport, in 1967 the government appointed a committee under Sir Ronald Edwards to consider the future organisation of civil aviation. Reporting two years later, the committee recommended that BEA and BOAC should remain the nation's principal carriers but that British United should be encouraged as a 'second force' airline. In 1970 the government issued a White Paper which indicated that BEA and BOAC should be merged, and

the proposal to build up BUA was accepted too. BUA had established an extensive network of services centred on Gatwick airport but although (or perhaps because) it was licensed to operate to New York it encountered financial difficulties and surprisingly offered to sell itself to BOAC. Freddie Laker had set himself up as a private operator and along with Caledonian Airways put in a counter-bid. Eventually the Scottish independent won the day and British Caledonian was formed, later to become a major carrier.

The boom in air transport brought about by jet airliners affected many areas of the world. In Pakistan, PIA became the first Asian jet operator by leasing a Boeing 707 from Pan American, opening a service to London in 1960 and extending it to New York a year later. Air Ceylon moved its management contract from KLM to BOAC in 1960 and the Comet 4 replaced the Electra as the island's main link to Europe.

Farther east, Taiwan's CAT took jets in 1961, putting the Convair 880 into service. A year later the same type of aircraft was selected for Hong Kong's Cathay Pacific Airways where it gave good service for several years. JAL steadily increased its DC-8 fleet and in 1961 opened a polar service to London. BOAC did not match the service until 1969 although the British company did open a polar service to Los Angeles in 1961. JAL's growing DC-8 fleet released DC-6Bs to domestic routes to link Tokyo with Fukuoka and Sapporo. The booming economy in Japan outgrew its slow narrow-gauge railway system and poor trunk roads and led to an astonishing growth in domestic air traffic. It recorded increases of between 30 and 60 per cent each year and by 1963 there were 30 services a day between Tokyo and Osaka. However, the following year the famous new Tokaido railway introduced a three-hour service on the 320-mile Tokyo-

Left: This Yak-40 was photographed at Norwich Airport during a demonstration tour of Britain in 1976. It was introduced in the late 1960s to replace the Li-2 (Russian DC-3) and is unusual for a small (up to 32 seats) airliner in having three jet engines. The Yak-40 can operate from rough airfields and production is probably approaching 1000 aircraft, mostly for Aeroflot, though some have been exported even to Western operators in France, Italy and W Germany.

Above: This Tunis Airport shot of a Boeing 727 is typical of scenes around the world since the middle 1960s. The 727 is one of the few commercial transports that has exceeded 1000 sales; in fact the total has now passed 1500. This one is a lengthened 163/189-passenger 727-200, one of 10 operated by Tunis Air.

Osaka route and there was a considerable decrease in air traffic. Even so, unlike the London-Liverpool route, the new rail service did not cause the collapse of the air service.

Densely populated Japan can support several domestic airlines and in 1960 All Nippon Airways introduced the Viscount followed later by the Friendship. Clearly satisfied with its foreign-built turboprop airliners, ANA ordered the Japanese-designed YS-11 into service. The YS-11 is a 60-passenger aircraft produced by the NAMC consortium of six aircraft companies and is powered by two Rolls-Royce Dart turbo-props. The YS-11 first flew in 1962 and sold in North and South America and Europe as well as Japan. In addition to ANA, another Japanese domestic carrier, TOA, ordered 20 YS-11s and the type became familiar at Japanese airports. Although the YS-11 can be counted a success as Japan's first postwar

commercial airliner, it did not sell in sufficient numbers to earn a profit for the NAMC group.

The 1960s saw considerable activity in Australia where Ansett-ANA and TAA took over New Guinea services from Qantas. The move momentarily placed TAA at an advantage as the airline took over also the Qantas domestic routes in the Territory. Reg Ansett was not to be outmanoeuvred, however, and he soon bought Mandated Airlines, which had previously taken over Gibbes Sepik and Madang Air Services in Papua. The enterprising Ansett bought South Pacific Airlines and, renaming it Airlines of New Zealand, opened a service between the North and South Islands using DC-3s, flying in competition with the government-owned New Zealand National Airways Corporation. Ansett later introduced Friendships onto the route; in fact,

117

the Dutch twin-turboprop airliner became widely used in Australia, operated by Ansett, TAA, MacRobertson Miller Aviation, East West Airlines and the New Zealand National Airways Corporation itself.

In Australia a curious, indeed unique, domestic airline system evolved; TAA and Ansett were each granted a strict 50/50 share of the market at least in terms of equipment and timings. Their aircraft departed within minutes of each other at the insistence of the Department of Transport, thus ensuring that competition on routes between the major cities was limited to the quality of service on the ground and in the air. Competition seems not to have been stifled by this unusual system; in fact there was still room for enterprise. A 'flexible cabin' system for example was introduced by TAA in which the bulkhead was moved and seats adapted according to the demand for first-class accommodation. Bulkheads and seats could be fixed in a matter of minutes and the configuration of an aircraft might be changed several times on a multi-stop service. Other Australian domestic carriers continued to play an important part in the country's transport system, even airlines considered small by most standards. For example Connellan Airways is an important airline which established a service to about 100 isolated stations in the 1960s, using four-engined de Havilland Herons as well as various smaller aircraft to serve a route network of about 10,000 miles.

As the wind of change blew through Africa, air transport underwent radical changes. The upheaval in the Belgian Congo resulted in the loss of a major part of Sabena's route network. At the height of the civil war in the Congo, Sabena flew out over 34,000 Belgians in 20 days. The new national carrier Air Congo was formed in 1961 when peace returned to the country and Sabena took a 30-per cent holding in the company and provided technical assistance.

As the Belgian airline reduced its African services, KLM extended its network, opening routes to Monrovia and Conakry. The Dutch airline's efforts to open services to Los Angeles and Hong Kong had been baulked by the Americans and British, obliging it to concentrate its efforts on broadening its Middle East and African network.

Newly independent Ghana embarked upon an expansion programme for its airline, ordering Herons, Viscounts, Il-18s, Boeing 707s and VC10s. Such expansion would have taxed a long-established airline and it proved to be too much for Ghana Airways. The Il-18s were not a success and eventually were returned to Russia; the VC10 on the other hand served the airline well and the Boeing order was eventually cancelled.

Above: The twin-Dart turboprop Hawker Siddeley (Avro) HS748 is a versatile short/medium-range airliner to accommodate up to 58 passengers and it has sold well around the world. Of a total production of more than 300, over 250 have sold overseas because of its ability to operate from unsophisticated airfields. This picture shows one of the many 748s in service with South American airlines climbing out of the Los Andes (2620ft asl) dirt runway.

Right: The Ilyushin Il-62 four-jet long-range airliner appeared about four years after the BAC (Vickers) VC10 and with its four turbojets, aft-mounted in pairs, it is quite difficult to distinguish between the two aeroplanes in the air. The Il-62 entered Aeroflot service in 1967 and in September that year provided the first Aeroflot transatlantic turbojet service.

Neighbouring Nigeria Airways grew at a more steady pace, using VC10s and Comets leased from BOAC, and ultimately buying its own Boeing 707 aircraft.

Air Guinée and Air Mali were founded in 1960 and both were donated Il-18s by the Soviet Union to mark their independence. Although much of French Africa was given its independence at this time, some countries in French West and Equatorial Africa combined to form Air Afrique in 1961 with the help of Air France and UAT. As the years progressed, a number of the member countries preferred to go their own way and withdrew from Air Afrique to form their own airlines.

In 1960 the government of the Central African Federation took over the operation of Central African Airways from BOAC, which had run the airline under an agreement signed in 1957. After the Federation broke up, the three countries formed their own airlines; Air Malawi has remained largely a regional carrier and Zambia Airways has grown with the assistance of a number of carriers including Alitalia, Aer Lingus and Lufthansa. Air Rhodesia might be called a clandestine airline, having obtained its Boeing 720s by devious means after the colony made its unilateral declaration of independence.

British United Airways helped Sierra Leone Airways by leasing a Britannia aircraft and providing technical assistance. Sudan Airways did not grow at a great pace in the 1960s but its equipment was updated by the provision of Comet 4Bs and F27s. These aircraft provided links with major cities in the region and Europe as well as serving scattered domestic airports. The three former French colonies in the Magreb formed Royal Air Maroc, Tunis Air and Air Algerie and all bought Caravelles.

The 1946 three-nation venture in Africa, East African Airways which was patterned on SAS, fell apart in failure in 1977. Kenya, Uganda and Tanzania, which retained close economic ties after they gained their independence, slowly drew apart in succeeding years and finally East African Airways collapsed under the strain of the economic difficulties which were a byproduct of political tension between the three nations.

As the Communist Bloc's principal long-distance international carrier, CSA the Czechoslovak airline, opened services to Conakry, Dakar and Rabat in the early 1960s using Il-18 aircraft. The Czech carrier also extended its network to Djakarta in Indonesia and, in 1963, to Havana in Cuba. The Havana service was interesting in that a Cubana Britannia was used by the Czech airline to link Havana with Prague via New York and Prestwick.

South America, too, rapidly entered the jet age and by 1961 the principal carriers had taken French, American or British jet air-

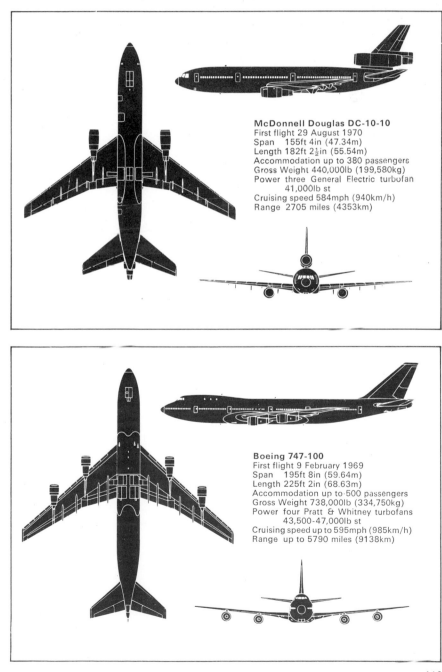

McDonnell Douglas DC-10-10
First flight 29 August 1970
Span 155ft 4in (47.34m)
Length 182ft 2¾in (55.54m)
Accommodation up to 380 passengers
Gross Weight 440,000lb (199,580kg)
Power three General Electric turbofan 41,000lb st
Cruising speed 584mph (940km/h)
Range 2705 miles (4353km)

Boeing 747-100
First flight 9 February 1969
Span 195ft 8in (59.64m)
Length 225ft 2in (68.63m)
Accommodation up to 500 passengers
Gross Weight 738,000lb (334,750kg)
Power four Pratt & Whitney turbofans 43,500-47,000lb st
Cruising speed up to 595mph (985km/h)
Range up to 5790 miles (9138km)

liners into their fleets. Varig gradually became the principal Brazilian carrier having taken the Caravelle into service in 1957 and the Boeing 707 in 1960. A year later the company took over Real Aerovias and in the process quadrupled its international mileage and doubled its domestic network. Convair 990A aircraft were taken into the Varig fleet as part of the Real assets. Four years later, Panair do Brasil also ceased operations and once more Varig increased in size almost overnight. Avianca and VIASA had acquired jets by 1961 and the principal American and European carriers soon introduced jets onto their services. As part of his economies Sir Giles Guthrie withdrew BOAC services to South America and British United eagerly took the opportunity to put VC10s onto the route.

It is hardly surprising that the greatest rate of growth took place in the United States. PanAm's order for Boeing 707 and DC-8 airliners opened a floodgate of orders from American domestic carriers. The absence of an American short-range jet airliner, however, obliged United Airlines to turn to France for a fleet of Caravelles. As

the world's largest airline, United could not afford to fall behind in terms of equipment and although American carriers traditionally support the home industry, the Caravelle order showed that competitiveness could be decisive in the matter of equipment. It was not, of course, the first purchase of a European airliner by an American airline; in 1954 Capital Air Lines ordered a large number of Viscounts. However, although the airline had grown to fifth place in the American domestic market, its mostly short routes proved to be unprofitable and in 1960 it collapsed, to be taken over by United. Although Vickers repossessed the Capital fleet of Viscounts, United repurchased a substantial number for its routes.

The third, and smallest, American jet airliner after the Boeing 707 and Douglas DC-8 was the Convair 880, which entered service with Delta in 1960 and with TWA and VIASA a year later. The slightly larger Convair 990 was developed for American Airlines but the builder had some difficulty in meeting the guaranteed performance and it was only after various modifications had been completed that the aircraft performed

Left upper: *Another short/medium-range British airliner that has won a high proportion of exports is the BAC twin-jet One-Eleven, which has logged sales totalling over 220, many in small numbers to charter and feeder airlines. Here is pictured a Series 400 One-Eleven, one of four delivered to Cambrian in 1967/68.*

Left lower: *This DC-8-63F of Saudia Saudi Arabian Airlines seen ingesting a load of freight packages is one of the Super Sixty series introduced in 1965 in all-passenger and cargo configurations.*

Above: *Picture shows one of about 70 Boeing 727s of various marks bought by Braniff over the period 1965-73, typical of the equipment programmes of many airlines around the world.*

well. The aerodynamic improvements gained by the modifications were embodied in the CV-990A, the production version of which proved to be the fastest jet airliner of its time. The lengthy development of the Convair gave its rivals the opportunity to scoop up more orders and few were sold. American Airlines took 20 and Swissair eight (leasing two to SAS). For Convair the project was a disaster; it resulted in a loss of about £150 million and took the company out of the airline business.

At last starting to learn the lesson that, despite the benefits of fleet standardisation, low seat-mile costs do not spell profitability unless most of the seats are filled, US domestic airlines raised a clamour for smaller aircraft. Boeing responded with a smaller version of the 707 in the Boeing 720, which was bought in substantial numbers by United and American. In 1960 the Boeing 720B flew for the first time and was to become the fastest of the 707 family, capable of cruising at 622mph. The 720B, like the later 707-320B, was fitted with the new Pratt & Whitney turbofans which were more efficient than earlier jets. The maiden flight of the 707-320B took place in 1962 and airlines soon took the variant into their fleets, PanAm ordering 21, TWA 20 and Lufthansa 11. With this aircraft and the cargo or 'mixed' version, the 707-320C, the airlines had an aircraft with which they could make money, and did until the Jumbos came and again interrupted profitable operation.

Having sensed the growing world demand for short/medium-range jet airliners, in 1960 Boeing announced plans for the 727 and two years later the prototype was rolled out at the Renton plant and made ready for its first flight. With a T-tail and three engines at the rear, the Boeing 727 bore a striking resemblance to the de Havilland Trident and inevitably there were suggestions that the British design had been copied. However, just as the 707, DC-8 and CV-880 were similar in appearance, so it was likely that the two trijets should look alike as they were designed to do a similar job. Boeing's 727 was somewhat larger than the Trident and it utilised some of the 707's components; the cabin width and nose were of the same dimensions, for example. In retrospect it would seem that the Trident was designed

too closely to the needs of BEA, for although it was produced before the American machine, it was the 727 which scooped the large orders. Certainly the aircraft was ordered in substantial numbers by Eastern and United and, after the American domestic carriers, Lufthansa became the first foreign airline to place a large order, for 21.

Initially some carriers had difficulty in converting pilots to the 727 and some unfortunate accidents resulted. The aircraft had a rapid rate of descent, a useful feature in joining a busy airport's approach zone from a high cruising altitude. However, with the slow response of jet engines to throttle movement, an inadequately trained pilot was liable to make a hole in the ground. The initial problems were soon overcome and the Boeing 727 went on to become a phenomenal success. The first version, the 100 series, was also produced in a Quick Change variant, enabling the airline to remove the seats at the end of the day and turn it over to cargo carrying at night.

The first series of 727s could be fitted to carry up to 130 passengers; as traffic increased Boeing responded to airlines' demands for still more capacity by producing the 200 series, which first flew in July 1967. It was about 10 feet longer than the 100 series, to take about 160 passengers in normal layout and up to 189 with high-density seating. In the 727-200 the airlines at last had a machine which was profitable to operate as well as being very popular with passengers, its rear-engined layout making for smooth and quiet flight. As it was steadily improved during the next decade, the Boeing 727 became more efficient and profitable, and more popular, reflecting the success of the DC-3; about 90 operators have ordered the type and total sales have exceeded 1500. The Boeing trijet has certainly won itself an honourable place in airline history. Built as a first-generation medium range airliner, it has sold in such numbers that it will undoubtedly be still going in the twenty-first century.

Expansion of United States domestic traffic in the 1960s was due partly to a new policy of the CAB, that of ' use it or lose it.' Some carriers held licences to operate routes but for some reason or other chose not to use them, preventing other carriers from expanding their network. The CAB policy succeeded in breathing new life into such carriers as National, Delta and Northeast.

As the new jets forced the older but still healthy piston-engined airliners into premature retirement, Eastern Air Lines found a new use for ' written-off ' aircraft. In 1960 the company started an Air Bus service between Boston and New York and this soon led to the Air Shuttle. Using Super-Constellations, Eastern offered a guaranteed seat for passengers who could not get on a scheduled departure. Bookings were not accepted; all the passengers had to do was to check in. Tickets were bought on the aircraft and if a flight was full, another aircraft would be put on to clear all passengers wanting to fly. Eastern extended the shuttle service to Washington and it drew interested glances from many other airlines. The service has continued to grow in popularity and a number of other airlines have since copied the system. In 1963 Allegheny Airlines offered a discount on certain routes for passengers who went to the airport to take a chance of getting on board. Seats could be booked at full fare but the 'standby' passenger could fly at a discount of 36 per cent. High-density routes on which some form of shuttle service operates now include the Rio de Janeiro Sao-Paulo Air Bridge operated by Varig of Brazil, the London-Glasgow/Edinburgh/Belfast shuttles by British Airways and a similar service between Riyadh and Jeddah flown by Saudia. Establishment of a co-operative London-Paris shuttle is being discussed by British Airways and Air France as this is written.

In 1965 Douglas flew the DC-9 80/90-passenger airliner for the first time, about 14 months after the BAC One-Eleven of similar capacity. To help finance the project, Douglas invited a number of manufacturers to share in the production and the risk. The twin-jet soon won orders from Delta, Eastern, Continental and others, but to broaden the appeal of the type in 1966 Douglas added 15 feet to the basic length, producing an aircraft with a capacity for up to 115 passengers. Early orders were placed by Ansett and TAA in Australia as well as Eastern in the US. Although by producing both the short-body Series 10 and the longer fuselage Series 30 Douglas won a large share of the market, it also overstrained its financial resources, with the result that the company was obliged to merge with McDonnell. It takes many years for most airliners to become profitable and the early period of a production run can impose a considerable burden upon a company.

The DC-9 clearly had a promising future and McDonnell's rescue of the Douglas project was to prove a sound investment. Other versions of the DC-9 followed, some with improved take-off performance, others with increased passenger capacity. The ability of the Douglas design team to adapt the DC-9 to the requirements of individual airlines is one reason why the aircraft has sold so well; the fuselage of the latest Super 80 model is over 43 feet longer than the original, with a capacity for 172 passengers, virtually double the capacity of the original design.

Similar flexibility was applied to the earlier DC-8, which was adapted for US long-range domestic passenger and cargo operations. In 1966 the basic DC-8 was

stretched by about 37 feet to provide accommodation for up to 275 passengers. The Super Sixty series consisted of three models; the -61 used the basic wing but had the new very long fuselage, the -62 had a wing of improved design and an increase in fuselage length of only seven feet and the -63 combined the new wing with the very long fuselage. The DC-8-61 was used mainly by US domestic carriers, entering service with United in 1967. The -62 was used mainly by SAS which needed the very long range offered by this variant to provide non-stop service from Copenhagen to Los Angeles and for a Copenhagen-Bangkok via Tashkent service. The Super-63 combined high capacity with long range and entered service in 1967 with KLM on its Amsterdam-New York route.

The Caravelle was the first short/medium-range twin-jet airliner, but it was a first-generation design and there was a requirement for a more economical and flexible aircraft. Hence the DC-9, but the American aircraft was preceded by the BAC One-Eleven which was first announced in 1961 when British United Airways made a launching order for 10 aircraft. The Series 200 was the first production One-Eleven; it could carry a maximum of 89 passengers and flew for the first time in 1963. During flight trials the first aircraft was lost in a deep stall accident. Essentially this means that, in normal test routine, the aircraft was deliberately put into a stall at altitude but as it fell almost vertically, the wings blanketed the high-tail unit which was thus prevented from responding to the pilot's attempts to lower the nose in the standard stall recovery procedure.

The accident delayed the introduction of the One-Eleven into service while its causes were investigated and a solution found. The stick-shaker stall warning device developed for the One-Eleven was adapted for other aircraft of similar configuration which might get into a deep stall, after the results of the investigations were made available to all other manufacturers.

The One-Eleven entered service in April 1965 with British United Airways and in America with Braniff International Airways, and its future looked bright. The Series 300 and 400 followed and more American orders came from Mohawk Airlines and American Airlines. But the DC-9 provided formidable competition, particularly as early introduction of the wider range of DC-9 variants ensured a better penetration of the market. It was not until 1968 that the first Series 500 version of the One-Eleven, for up to 119 passengers, entered service with BEA. The Series 500 is roughly the equivalent of the DC-9-30 which entered service a year earlier. The One-Eleven has sold in many parts of the world and production exceeds 200 but DC-9 sales

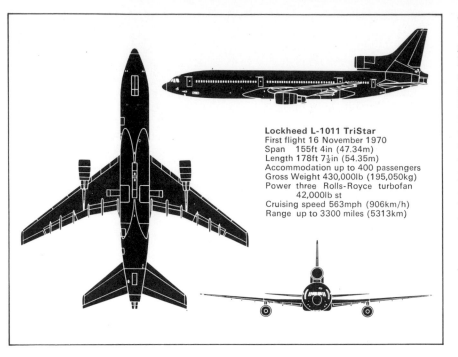

Lockheed L-1011 TriStar
First flight 16 November 1970
Span 155ft 4in (47.34m)
Length 178ft 7½in (54.35m)
Accommodation up to 400 passengers
Gross Weight 430,000lb (195,050kg)
Power three Rolls-Royce turbofan 42,000lb st
Cruising speed 563mph (906km/h)
Range up to 3300 miles (5313km)

are over four times that of the British design.

Boeing entered the short-haul market somewhat later than Douglas and BAC, flying the first Boeing 737 in 1967. Retaining as much as possible of the 707 and 727 designs, the twin-engined 737 took the same fuselage width as the earlier Boeings and did not adopt the rear-engined configuration. The Boeing baby was unusual in being launched by a foreign airline; Lufthansa ordered 21 Boeing 737s from the drawing-board and therefore was in a position to influence the design. In common with the earlier Boeing jets, the 737 was soon developed into a 'family.' A QC version was produced and a fuselage stretch resulted in the Series 200 variant. The aircraft has 'grown' from a 99 to 135-seater and sales exceed 500.

As well as bringing jet transport to short-distance services, the smaller jets brought about a revolution in the holiday charter business. The inclusive-tour package pioneered by Eagle Airways in the 1950s grew into an enormous air transport business and in the early days the aircraft used for charter work tended to be retired front-line equipment. Indeed, a number of scheduled airlines set up charter subsidiaries to use outdated piston-engined airliners rather than consign the aircraft to the scrap-heap. As a relative newcomer to the airline scene, Lufthansa could see the advantages of owning a charter subsidiary but decided to provide it with modern equipment from the outset. Condor's Viscounts were soon followed by Boeings of various types and the package-tour business in Germany grew apace.

Jet airliners proved to be capable of making money and holiday-makers demanded the latest in standards of comfort. Conse-quently airlines such as Britannia in the United Kingdom and Sterling in Denmark grew to be sizeable organisations, some having larger fleets than some European scheduled carriers. The influence of jet aircraft on the growth of the holiday charter business cannot be over-emphasised, for unlike scheduled airlines, which must operate their aircraft when passengers want to travel, to a large extent charter airlines can transport their passengers at 'unsocial' hours. A late night or early morning departure will be accepted by a holidaymaker who knows that the package price is a bargain and far cheaper than an independent arrangement using scheduled airlines.

Russia also followed the general trend in jet airliner development. In 1960 the short-range Tupolev Tu-124 appeared as a scaled-down version of the Tu-104. The Tu-124 was a 44-seater and it was followed by the rear-engined Tu-134 in the mid-1960s. With the exception of a sale to Iraqi Airways, Tu-134s have served only with Russian and Communist-bloc airlines.

To update Aeroflot's long-distance fleet, in 1962 Ilyushin produced the Il-62 four-jet airliner, rear-engined in the style of the VC-10. It provided an eventual capacity of 198 passengers and was bought by most Eastern-bloc nations, but has only seen brief service with one non-Communist airline—EgyptAir in the early 1970s. The Egyptian carrier, however, returned the aircraft to Russia and replaced them with Boeing 707s.

Another Western airliner development that was matched by the Russians is the twin-turboprop short-haul aircraft. The Antonov An-24 is similar to the Fokker Friendship and has been designed to do the same type of job, that is, fly passengers and cargo into airports of limited size. Since its appearance in 1960 the An-24 has been produced in many variants and is operated by many airlines and air forces, including some in Africa.

In this capacity the Rolls-Royce Dart turboprop has proved paramount. So powered, the Friendship has remained the market leader, with total sales exceeding 600 aircraft, and the twin-Dart-engined Avro (now Hawker Siddeley) 748, which first flew in 1960 and is still in production, has attracted sales exceeding 300 and is in service with many air forces and airlines. The HS748 has been built under licence in India, although Indian Airlines operates both the 748 and the Friendship. A development of the HS748, the Andover produced for the RAF as a tactical transport, has an upswept rear fuselage and tail to permit air-drops through a rear door.

Although the airliner industry continued to be dominated by America in the 1960s and 1970s, European manufacturers produced some interesting projects, though few found

Right: Typical scene at London's No 2 airport, Gatwick, in the early 1970s, with fleets of British Caledonian BAC One-Elevens, and Dan-Air and BEA Airtours Comet 4s busy day and night on holiday charters.

Below: Eastern Airlines was the first and biggest initial operator of the Lockheed L-1011 TriStar, having taken delivery of 26 during 1972-74, Eastern applied the tag 'whisper' to its Boeing 727s in the class name Whisperjet, which was hardly true, but it found justification in carrying on the tradition with Whisperliner for the TriStar, with its Rolls-Royce engines probably the least disturbing to airport neighbours of all the big airliners flying today.

commercial success. The search for a STOL airliner capable of flying into downtown airports led Breguet to design the Br941, a four-engined aircraft with large propellers designed to cover the entire wing with their thrust. A generous flap area provided a deflected airstream which enabled the aircraft to fly very slowly but safely and without fear of stalling. Each engine was linked to all propellers so that should one engine fail all four propellers would continue turning. In the late 1960s the Br941S was demonstrated in the United States to Eastern Air Lines and American Airlines and there were plans to produce the type under licence by McDonnell Douglas. The type never entered production, however, and the quest for an economical STOL airliner continues.

Beyond extending the fuselage of the Caravelle and fitting Pratt & Whitney JT-8 engines, French industry was not overly active in the 1960s in terms of new design work. Dassault began work on the Mercure short-haul transport aircraft in 1967 and the first prototype flew in 1971. The Mercure was designed to carry up to 162 passengers and was similar in appearance to the Boeing 737, though rather larger. The debut of the

Mercure came at an unfortunate time for by the time the first production machine flew in 1973, the world was suffering from an economic depression brought about by the fuel crisis. Production costs increased dramatically and suddenly well-established aircraft like the Boeing 727 had an advantage over new designs. With production in full swing and production costs amortised or written off, established aircraft have a lower unit cost than new machines; the early 1970s was clearly no time to introduce a new type. Only 10 Mercures were built and all were delivered to the French domestic airline Air Inter, which accepted them with some reluctance. In service the aircraft have performed well but the Mercure may be considered a victim of the oil crisis, for the production run ended with the tenth machine.

The Pratt & Whitney JT-8 is a widely-used jet engine, being fitted to the DC-9, Boeing 737 and many other types, and unquestionably it has played an important part in the development of jet transport. By fitting the JT-8 and extending the fuselage by three feet the life of the Caravelle was extended, but not by much and the 104-seat Super Caravelle was the last. Finnair was the first operator

of the Super Caravelle, trading in three earlier models as part payment. The Danish charter company Sterling was another operator but few other sales were achieved in the face of competition from more-recent designs.

The Rolls-Royce Spey turbofan engine, powering the Trident, One-Eleven and other aircraft, also made its contribution to air travel. With successive upratings, it enabled Hawker Siddeley to meet a BEA requirement for improved take-off performance and range with later versions of the Trident. The Trident 2E entered service with BEA in 1968 and a total of 33 were subsequently acquired by the Chinese airline CAAC which also took two Super Trident 3Bs. The 3B was a high-density development of the Trident with a 16-foot extension of the fuselage and a capacity for up to 160 passengers. It was announced in 1972 and BEA ordered 26 of the 3B variant.

The Spey also helped Fokker to stay in the airliner business with the aft-twin-engined F28 Fellowship short-haul jet airliner offering seats for up to about 80 passengers, the first of which entered service with the German charter company LTU in 1969. The Fellowship is, in fact, an international project produced in collaboration with Shorts in the UK and MBB in Germany. It has been steadily developed over the years to meet specific performance requirements and, although it has not sold in large numbers to any airline, total sales have topped 100 and it is still receiving orders. The Fellowship is a

remarkably quick and manoeuvrable airliner and two air-brakes on the rear-fuselage provide a useful ability to land on short airfields.

In 1970 Fokker made news by merging with the German aircraft group VFW, whereafter the two companies worked to develop and market the twin-turbofan short-haul VFW614 transport, which was unusual in having the engines mounted over the wings to reduce noise disturbance under its flight path. The VFW 614 was designed to carry about 40 passengers and was aimed at small third-level carriers; it first flew in 1971 and although it gained 16 orders it was finally abandoned in 1978.

As the 1960s gave way to the 1970s two new Russian designs entered service. Both have since been built in substantial numbers but, as with most previous Soviet designs, they have not made a significant impression on world markets. The little YAK-40 27/32-seater is unusual in being a small airliner with three turbofan engines and straight wings. Like many Russian aircraft, it has been designed to operate from rough airfields and with over 800 built the type is clearly in widespread use in the Soviet Union. Some were sold in the West, specifically to General Air in Germany and Aertirrena in Italy, but the expected flow of further orders has not materialised.

The Tu-154, first flown in 1968, is also a three-engined airliner but in the Boeing 727 category. It was designed as a replacement for the Tu-104, Il-18 and An-10 over medium to long ranges and has been in regular service with Aeroflot since 1972. The Tu-154 is available in five basic versions providing from 128 to 167 seats and it has been supplied to several other Eastern-bloc airlines.

Barely used to the pleasant sensation of actually making money, the airlines of the world received another shock when Pan American ordered 25 Boeing 747s in 1966. The giant aircraft was to be capable of carrying nearly 500 passengers in a very large fuselage, which appeared monstrous inside even when broken down into several cabins. The Jumbo, as it became known, flew for the first time in 1969 and entered service with PanAm less than a year later. Thus the new decade opened with yet another major upheaval in the airline industry. However, the Boeing 747 provided such a great increase in capacity that it was out of the question to replace all the first-generation jets with the new aircraft. Although the major airlines once more followed PanAm's lead in ordering the Jumbo, the numbers ordered tended to be quite small.

Perhaps surprisingly, people readily took to the new wide-bodied aeroplane. Although most of its passengers could not sit anywhere near a window and they were obliged to travel in the company of hundreds of others, the sheer spaciousness seemed to attract the travelling public.

For some airlines the 747's capacity was simply too much and in 1966 American Airlines invited manufacturers to submit proposals for an aircraft with a similar wide body but a maximum capacity for 380 passengers. The design submitted by McDonnell Douglas was accepted and in 1968 American Airlines ordered the DC-10. The

new aircraft had three aft-mounted turbofans and took to the air on its maiden flight in 1970, entering service a year later with American and United. In the tradition of modern airliner design, McDonnell Douglas quickly offered variants to fit the needs of particular carriers; the Series 10 was intended mainly for US domestic airlines while the Series 30 and 40 were capable of flying the longer ranges needed by international airlines. KLM and Swissair put the Series 30 into service in 1972. In terms of size the Boeing 747 is without a competitor as no other manufacturer has chosen to launch another Jumbo, but the DC-10 has established a firm place for itself and has won orders from airlines which had previously flown only Boeings.

Although McDonnell Douglas won the American Airlines competition, Lockheed believed that its design would establish itself too and in 1971 the L-1011 TriStar, powered by Rolls-Royce RB211 turbofans rather than American engines, made its maiden flight. The TriStar soon received orders from TWA and Eastern Air Lines but has since had a chequered career. Lockheed itself encountered severe financial difficulties and was only rescued by a government loan, said to be because of its importance as an arms manufacturer. Rolls-Royce overstretched itself and was put into the hands of a Receiver but the British government also recognised the importance of the engine manufacturer for the defence industry and in 1971 the company was nationalised. The TriStar survived both traumas but the lack of capital has prevented the type being developed in as many versions as the DC-10. However, despite difficulties over 200 TriStars have been sold and new variants are beginning to

Above: Pan American's Boeing 747SP 'Clipper Great Republic'. In May 1976 sister ship 'Clipper Liberty Bell' carried 96 passengers round the world in 46 hours, having made only two refuelling stops between taking off and landing at New York John F. Kennedy Airport. This flight beat the earlier record by 15½ hours. The 747SP (SP = special performance) is 47 feet shorter than the standard Jumbo and was developed for very long stages (partly to compete with Concorde's much shorter flight times). Pan Am uses its 747SPs on scheduled nonstop flights from Los Angeles to New Zealand and from New York to Tokyo.

Below right: Latest of the Russian big transports is the Ilyushin Il-86, a wide-bodied airliner which first flew in its production form in December 1976. The three-bogie main undercarriage is well illustrated in this picture. Available information indicates a maximum of about 350 passengers nine-abreast in three cabins and a gross weight of up to 454,000lb (203 tons).

McDonnell Douglas entered the wide-bodied field with the three-engined DC-10, which started in 1966 as a short/medium-range high-capacity design to meet an American Airlines requirement for its domestic services. The initial outcome was the DC-10 Series 10 with accommodation for up to 380 passengers over ranges of about 2700 miles, which first flew in August 1970. First deliveries were made on the same day in July 1971 to American Airlines and United Air Lines. The DC-10 role was extended with the introduction in June 1972 of the Series 30 of greater range and in July 1975 of the Series 40 with Pratt & Whitney in place of the basic General Electric engines. Convertible passenger/cargo variants are designated 10CF and 30CF. Pictured is one of Lufthansa's 10 DC-10-30s, the first of which was delivered in December 1973.

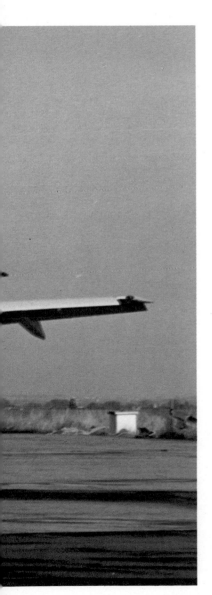

appear. The large PanAm order placed in 1978 gave a considerable boost to the TriStar programme. British Airways Tri-Stars, ordered by BEA before the merger with BOAC, are used extensively on both European and Middle East services.

With hundreds of Boeing 707 and DC-8 aircraft coming to the end of their useful lives, the DC-10 and TriStar may be expected to win many more orders but, of course, Boeing has a number of projects designed to fill the gap in its catalogue and follow on the success of the 707, 727 and 737. To broaden its share of the market for large aircraft, in 1975 Boeing produced a smaller version of the 747. The 747SP is 47 feet shorter than the standard aircraft and is designed to carry fewer passengers over very long ranges. PanAm, South African Airways and others ordered the SP and in 1976 one set up a long-distance record by flying 10,290 miles non-stop from Seattle to Cape Town in 17 hours 22 minutes.

For years various designs have been offered to the airlines, and other national industries (notably the British, Italian and Japanese) have been invited to take a major share in their development. The matter has been complicated, however, by an understandable desire to build up a strong European aircraft industry. So often in the past European companies have produced promising designs but have lacked the capital, and the large home market enjoyed by the Americans, to develop them to the full.

In the Airbus, which is built by an international consortium of French, German, Dutch, Spanish and British companies and flew for the first time in 1971, Europe at last has an aircraft with a promising future. The Airbus A300 is a wide-bodied airliner for short to medium ranges, powered by two General Electric CF-6 engines—the same type as fitted to the DC-10. The A300 entered service with Air France in 1974, but it was slow to win orders and it needed calm nerves for the management to sit out the lean years. Nevertheless, with only two engines and a capacity for up to 320 passengers, the Airbus is the smallest of the wide-bodied aircraft and, like the Boeing 747 at the other end of the scale, it is without a direct competitor. Before long, airlines all over the world realised its virtues and the order book started to look up. In 1978 an Eastern Air Lines order for a large number of A300s after a unique trial of four aircraft on free loan from the manufacturers, opened the important American market to the European airliner.

Not to be outdone by Western aircraft builders, Russia has also built a wide-bodied jet airliner, the Ilyushin Il-86. A 350-seat aircraft, the prototype was first revealed to the West at the 1977 Paris Air Show. Integral air-stairs are arranged for passengers to board through a lower deck, where coats and hand baggage will be stowed before reaching the cabins. The lack of an engine in the big turbofan class has hindered the development of an aircraft comparable to that of the Western wide-bodied airliners.

The oil crisis of 1973, which spelt the end for the Mercure, did not bring the same fate to the Airbus, although there was a period when airlines preferred to buy more Boeing 727s or DC-9s than opt for a new large aircraft. The world economic depression resulted in a decline in air traffic and airlines which had only recently bought the new big jets found that they had to stand idle for want of passengers. Secondhand Jumbos depressed the market for new aircraft, and earlier narrow-bodied airliners found a new lease of life. It was not until the late 1970s that demand for the large aircraft got under way again.

Ironically, the very oil crisis which caused a general down-turn in the world air traffic in fact stimulated routes serving the oil centres. Businessmen flocked to sell their goods to the new centres of wealth and charter companies mushroomed to carry cargo to cities often poorly served by harbour facilities. As the North Sea became a major oil-producing area, airlines such as Air Anglia grew to become strong regional carriers serving cities of importance to the oil companies. This pattern was reproduced in several parts of the world where small airlines suddenly found that they had a key role to play in the development of new oil-fields.

Slowly, as the airlines recovered from the years of depression, the growth in passenger and cargo traffic gathered pace. New methods of marketing helped to reduce the cost of air travel. Britain and the United States negotiated a new air traffic agreement designed to boost traffic between the two countries. President Carter and the chairman of the CAB, Alfred Kahn, introduced the new word deregulation into the airline industry. Determined to get lower fares and bring air travel to an even wider number of the population, the new administration considered that opening more routes to competition would provide the necessary climate for cheaper air travel. The same philosophy was applied to foreign routes and this brought some clashes with a number of governments, some of which are still to be argued out and settled. Nonetheless, the objective is being achieved; new low fares introduced on many routes in 1977/78 represent outstanding bargains in a world plagued by inflation and are indeed adding a new stimulus to air travel.

Granted freedom from further economic depression, air transport may be expected to grow steadily and continue to stimulate world trade and tourism.

10. Vertical Flight

The helicopter has yet to fulfil its potential as a profit-earning passenger vehicle for working into and out of city centres but helicopter lifting power has been increased remarkably in recent years. Russian designers, in particular M. L. Mil who has been prominent in VTOL development since about 1930, have produced helicopters of exceptional lifting power. Illustrated is the Mil Mi-10 which, as well as ability to accommodate passengers in the shallow cabin, can taxi over and pick up a large freight or passenger module weighing over 17,000lb.

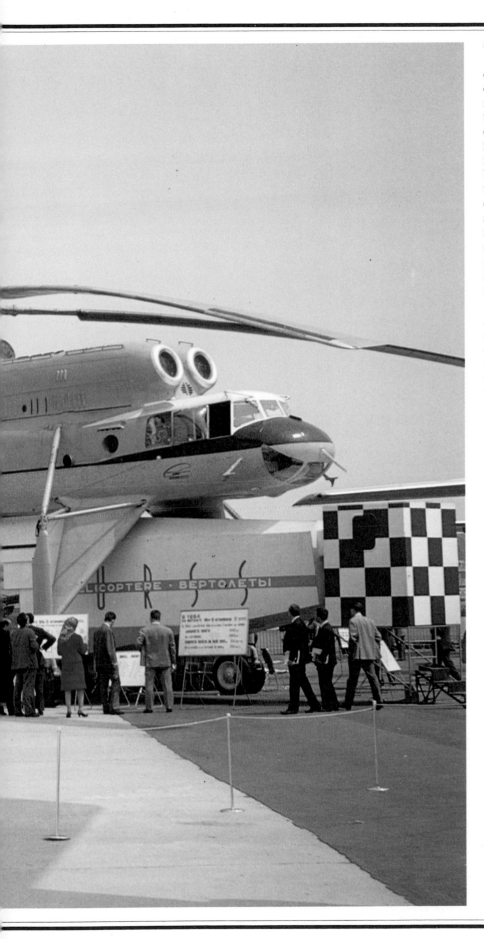

THE FIRST ROTARY-WING aircraft to achieve any commercial success was developed during the early 1920s by the Spaniard Juan de la Cierva, who originated the Autogiro as a machine that would provide very short take-off and landing runs and reduce the danger of crashing in the event of engine failure or a stall. The Autogiro was a normal aircraft with its main wing replaced by a rotor above the fuselage. Unlike the true helicopter, the Autogiro's rotor was not driven by the engine, but rotated itself as the aeroplane was pulled along by its propeller. So it provided lift for short take-off and the safety of autoration, as a kind of mechanical parachute, in landing but could not hover in still air or move in other directions than forward.

In the later production versions of the Autogiro the so-called jump start took it a short step nearer the helicopter; the rotor could be temporarily coupled to the engine to spin it up before starting the normal take-off, which was much shortened thereby, virtually to the point of vertical take-off when conditions were favourable. Cierva's first three models were failures, suffering instability; he learned that inflexible rotors produced unequal lift forces as they revolved, producing more lift when advancing that when retreating relative to the aircraft's direction. So the rotor blades of his fourth machine in 1922/23 were fitted with hinges that allowed the blades to flap, and stability was achieved. And so, in fact, was the principle of the flapping hinge which remains a feature of many of today's rotary-wing machines.

Quite clearly, the Autogiro had an advantage in using the main parts of any existing small aeroplane and it was certainly the first successful rotary-wing aircraft, deserving the commercial success it won during the interwar years. Cierva's sixth machine, the C6A based on an Avro trainer, was demonstrated to the British Air Ministry in 1925 and that led to an order with Avro to build a number of machines for the RAF. In September 1928 an Avro-based version, a two-seat C8L, became the first rotary-wing aircraft to cross the English Channel, piloted by Cierva himself. By 1928 the Autogiro was being built in America as well as Britain and, with others taking licences later, more than 500 had been produced before the true helicopter had been advanced sufficiently to replace it. Most Autogiros were produced for military use, but a fair number went into private use because they were easy to fly and for their STOL ability. In the United States Eastern Airlines inaugurated the world's first rotor-

borne mail service in July 1939 with a Kellett KD-1B on a service between the Philadelphia Post Office and nearby Camden Airport.

The practical helicopter took a long time to emerge. Louis Breguet returned to the field in 1929 and, with Rene Dorand, produced a new Gyroplane incorporating patented features in 1933. It had coaxial contrarotating rotors with flapping hinges and cyclic and collective pitch controls, making it one of the first true helicopters, but although it advanced all the existing world records, control problems persisted. Greater success was achieved in Germany by Dr Heinrich Focke, a director of the Focke-Wulf company when it took out a licence to build Cierva Autogiros. After removal from his company by the Nazis he formed Focke-Achgelis and continued work on a helicopter, using the fuselage of a FW Stieglitz training aircraft. It was fitted with two separate rotors on outriggers (the Cayley layout lived on) driven by the front-mounted engine and the pilot could vary the collective pitch of the rotors independently. The Focke-Achgelis FW61 was first flown in 1937 and its remarkable controllability was dramatically demonstrated in 1938 when the famous woman pilot Hanna Reitsch flew it inside the Deutschland Halle in Berlin. One by one, FW61s toppled the records established by the Breguet machine. A civil transport development might have ensued when Luft-

hansa placed an order for a six-seat development, the Fa266, but war obliged the venture to be shelved.

The war put an end to promising developments elsewhere, including those of C. G. Pullin in England and Ivan Bratukhin in Russia, and von Doblhoffs rotor-tip jets in Austria. However, in the United States, Igor Sikorsky, having designed several successful flying-boats, turned his hand once more to helicopter design and persuaded United Aircraft, his parent company, to fund the production of a prototype aircraft. The Vought-Sikorsky VS-300 appeared to be as crude as some of the other weird creations produced in Europe, but appearances were deceptive; after tethered tests in 1939 the VS-300 made its first free flight in May 1940 with Sikorsky at the controls. It was a single-rotor machine with the torque counteracted by a small vertical rotor on the tail, originating the classic 'penny-farthing' layout and the practical helicopter.

As the VS-300 took the records previously held by the FW61, the US Army asked Sikorsky to design a military helicopter. The result was the R-4, a bigger version of the VS-300 with an enclosed cabin. With customary American vigour, the R-4 was built in quantity and by 1944 it was in service in Europe and the Pacific. Sikorsky was asked to set up a separate company within the United Aircraft group and by the end of the

Above: *A Sikorsky S-61N helicopter, one of a fleet operated by British Airways mainly on North Sea oilfield services, maintains an intense summer passenger service between Cornwall and the Scilly Isles, one of the few profitable scheduled helicopter passenger services.*
The S-61N carries 28 passengers in normal airliner comfort on the 30-mile flight in 20 minutes and in high-summer season makes up to 14 round flights a day.

Right upper: *The Sikorsky S-58 12-passenger helicopter with which Sabena operated scheduled services between Brussels and Paris, here seen at Brussels Melsbroek in March 1957.*

Right lower: *KLM also uses the buoyant N version of the Sikorsky S61, as seen here taking off in a moderate chop.*

war about 400 R-4s and R-5 and R-6 derivatives had been produced.

As so often before in aviation, military needs had stimulated helicopter development but it was not long before airlines became interested in this fascinating form of transport. In theory, the prospect looked good; here was a machine which could take off vertically, even from the centre of a city, and deliver its passengers directly to their destination. In practice it was not quite so simple. Early helicopters were noisy and not designed with comfort as a principal requirement. Furthermore, the complexity of the design inevitably meant that they were, as they still are, expensive to buy and to operate.

The first commercial helicopter produced by Sikorsky was the S-51, a four-seat machine which was also manufactured under licence by Westland in Britain. Although licensed for civil operations by the CAB, once again it was military users who took most of the production. Some enterprising airlines were willing to experiment, although under no illusions as to the profitability of the helicopters then available. Los Angeles Airways started the first helicopter mail service in 1947 using an S-51 and in 1950 BEA opened an experimental service carrying passengers between Liverpool and Cardiff, again using the little S-51.

Demand by the US forces for a bigger helicopter led to the S-55 which flew for the first time in 1949 and was capable of carrying up to 12 passengers. Certificated in 1952 by the FAA as the world's first commercial transport helicopter, the S-55 could not be operated without a subsidy but it did represent a major step forward and was eagerly ordered into operation by a number of airlines. In 1952 New York Airways put the S-55 into service carrying mail and, later, passengers between the city's three airports.

Helicopter carriers were formed in other cities primarily to carry out the important function of linking major airports. Having started life as Helicopter Air Services in 1949 and using a Bell 47 to carry mail, Chicago Helicopter Airways was formed in 1956 and operated 16 flights a day between the city's Midway and O'Hare airports using S-55s. It progressed to the S-58 in 1957 and to the 25-passenger S-61 two years later. The relatively large S-61 is perhaps the first commercial helicopter with the potential to be operated profitably without a subsidy. On America's West Coast, San Francisco and Oakland Helicopter Airlines was established in 1961 using S-62s to ply between the airports and points in the San Francisco Bay area.

To Sabena in 1953 went the honour of opening the world's first scheduled international helicopter service between Brussels and Maastricht using S-55s. The airline began experimental services in 1950 using the

little Bell 47 to carry mail but with the delivery of the S-55 and later the larger S-58 Sabena had aircraft which could carry small numbers of passengers. Sabena set up a helicopter service between the centre of Brussels and the city's airport, a journey which took only six minutes by helicopter, and eventually built up a fleet of eight helicopters. Although it attracted much interest from other airlines, the venture was abandoned as there seemed little likelihood of a profitable helicopter appearing.

BEA used the Westland-built S-55 on experimental passenger services, including a short route from London's Heathrow airport to a site near Waterloo Station in the city. Passengers who flew on these early helicopter services often did so out of curiosity rather than from necessity. The strange 'whirlybirds' provided a new sensation in flying but those who expected to experience a rapid ascent were usually disappointed; generally passengers enjoyed a good view but the noise

Above and right: New York
Airways has been operating
passenger helicopter services
between New York area
airports since 1953 and now
links Newark, La Guardia and
Kennedy with Wall Street
Heliport using S-61Ls with
accommodation for 30 passengers.
Between 1966 and 1968 the
airline operated a service to the
roof of the PanAm building
using Boeing-Vertol 107s, as
these two pictures show, but the
service was suspended and
although reinstated for a few
months in 1977 with S-61s it is
again in suspense.

and vibration levels were somewhat higher than contemporary fixed-wing airliners.

Another American designer who made a profound mark on helicopter design was Frank Piasecki. He produced several designs principally for the American armed forces, the first of which flew in 1945. Piasecki left the company but, under the Vertol name, work continued on tandem-rotor helicopters. The Model 44 produced in 1956 offered up to 15 seats for airline operation and the type was used by Sabena and New York Airways.

The gas turbine produced as great an advance in helicopter design and performance as it did for fixed-wing aircraft. Vibration levels were considerably reduced and the noise produced by helicopters became rather more tolerable. In 1962 the twin-turbine Boeing-Vertol 107 (in 1960 Vertol became a division of Boeing) was introduced into service by New York Airways. Pan American had taken an interest in New York Airways in 1960, providing the capital necessary to buy new equipment and ensuring a regular service from Idlewild to La Guardia, Newark and downtown New York. The rooftop of the giant PanAm building became a terminal for the New York Airways services and in due course the Boeing-Vertol 107 was superseded by the bigger Sikorsky S-61.

Britain developed a thriving helicopter industry, but its products were largely for military users. During the war an Austrian refugee, Raoul Hafner, carried out several rotary-wing experiments for military projects but none went into production. Joining the Bristol Aeroplane Company after the war, Hafner designed the Sycamore helicopter. A single-rotor machine in the S-51 class, the Bristol 171 five-seat Sycamore flew for the first time in 1947 and was in production for several years, though only a few went to BEA. A tandem-rotor development, which appeared in 1957, fitted with Napier Gazelle gas turbines in place of the original Alvis Leonides piston engines, was ordered for the RAF and considered by BEA, but did not enter civilian service.

Much the most original and interesting rotary-wing research in Britain was carried out by the Fairey Aviation Company. A team led by J. Bennett produced the five-seat Gyrodyne in 1947; it was a stub-winged helicopter with a single Alvis Leonides piston engine driving both a tractor propeller on the starboard wing and a single main rotor. The off-centre propeller counteracted torque and the lift provided by the wings helped to relieve the load on the rotor. A member of the Austrian Doblhoff team joined Fairey to help in the development of the Jet Gyrodyne, the second prototype converted to investigate rotor-tip jet propulsion. In the Jet Gyrodyne, which first flew in 1954, the Leonides engine also drove a compressor which supplied air to the tips of the blades, where it was mixed with fuel and burnt. The tip jets were used only for take-off, landing and hovering; in the cruise forward power was provided by propellers at the tip of each wing.

Satisfied that the principle worked, Fairey began development of the Rotodyne transport aircraft in 1953. With a capacity for over 40 passengers, the Rotodyne really looked a serious contender for passenger services. At least New York Airways and BEA evidently thought so for they placed tentative orders for the type. The Rotodyne had two Napier Eland turboprop engines providing power both for the tip-jets and for tractor propellers; later variants were fitted with the higher-powered Rolls-Royce Tyne turboprop. Under the government's consolidation plans, Fairey was taken over by Westland in 1960 and although work on the Rotodyne continued for a while financial support was withdrawn two years later. This tragic change in government policy perhaps robbed Britain of the chance to become a major supplier of rotor craft to the world's airlines, for although very noisy the Rotodyne could probably have been developed into a practical airliner.

The vast majority of helicopters produced throughout the world have been for military or other specific tasks, particularly the servicing of the world's offshore oilfields. Very few have been able to supplant fixed-wing aircraft for regular scheduled passenger services but that is largely a matter of economics. As a means of transport, however, the helicopter is unique and in many ways can be regarded as the 'angel' of aviation. Only a helicopter can snatch shipwrecked sailors from a stormy sea, or injured climbers from a mountain ledge, or rescue flood victims from the roof of a house. Earthquakes, avalanches and disasters of many kinds bring helicopters quickly to the scene with medical help or to ferry injured people to hospital.

The introduction in the late 1950s of the larger helicopters powered by two gas turbines marked a step forward in practical helicopter transport design. The commercial versions of the Sikorsky S-61, for example, can carry up to 30 passengers in normal airline style. Los Angeles Airways was the first operator to employ the S-61 for scheduled passenger services and it has been followed by airlines in various parts of the world. In East Pakistan, PIA replaced fixed-wing aircraft with the S-61 for operation in remote areas but the services were withdrawn when the helicopter operations proved too costly. Ansett-ANA in Australia regularly uses an S-61 to ferry holidaymakers to one island resort off the coast of Queensland.

BEA (now British Airways Helicopters) has since 1974 successfully operated the S-61 (a 28-passenger amphibious version) to serve the Scilly Isles in place of DH89 Rapides. The helicopter provides a 20-minute flight on the 30 miles between Penzance in Cornwall and St Marys in the Scilly Isles and, with only a five-minute turnround in the busy summer season, makes up to 14 return trips a day, constituting what is possibly the only profitable scheduled helicopter service in the world. British Airways of course maintains many more than one helicopter. A fleet of about 20, largely S-61s, is used mainly in North Sea oil-rig support.

Another of the big helicopters with a commercial passenger version, the French Aerospatiale Super Frelon, has been operated by Olympic Airways on services between Athens and the neighbouring islands of Chios, Mykonos, Thera, Santorini and Skiathos. The Super Frelon is a single-rotor machine developed with Sikorsky technical assistance; it is powered by three gas turbines and can carry up to 37 passengers at 155mph over a range of about 500 miles.

Regardless of the method used, vertical take-off airliners will always be more expensive to operate than conventional aircraft but it is probable that eventually the helicopter will give way to a composite VTOL aircraft of some sort; despite their higher costs, there is likely to be a definite place for such aircraft in the future, as airways in the vicinity of airports become more congested and the ability to approach and leave vertically without the dangerous high horizontal speed component is made a necessity.

Various attempts have been made to produce a commercially viable composite aircraft in designs which combine the abilities of rotary-wing and fixed-wing formulas. That vertical flight without helicopter rotors

140

Above: *The Fairey Rotodyne looked promising as a 40-seat passenger helicopter using gas turbines to drive both rotor-tip jets and tractor propellers, but after about 10 years' work by Fairey and Westland and despite airline interest financial support dried up and the project was dropped.*

Left: *Unusual sight at San Francisco International Airport when the entire fleet of SFO Helicopter Airlines S61s took to the air together.*

is possible was first demonstrated in 1953 by Rolls-Royce with an extraordinary machine which was swiftly dubbed the Flying Bedstead. It consisted of two Nene turbojets mounted in a metal rig designed to investigate the control problems of vertical thrust. The four-legged apparatus was successfully flown and the principles originated in it were incorporated in the Short SC-1 which flew in 1960. It was much more a normal aeroplane, with a small delta wing and carrying four Rolls-Royce RB108 turbojet engines to provide vertical lift and a fifth for propulsion. It served the purpose of investigating the exceptionally demanding techniques of transition between vertical and horizontal flight. The American Ryan XV-5A of 1964 explored similar ground using two lift fans in the wings.

Also in the United States, a rather different principle has been pursued. Ling-Temco-Vought produced and tested a tilt-wing aircraft in 1964. Powered by four 2850shp General Electric turboprop engines, the XC-142A could tilt its wing vertically for a helicopter-like take-off and landing, and move it into a horizontal position to carry the aircraft in the normal way. In Montreal, the Canadair CL-84 Dynavert also investigated the tilt-wing principle and although these and other aircraft proved capable of vertical flight and transition, the complex mechanism is very expensive and none has entered production.

Hawker Siddeley adopted a different course for its P1127 Kestrel series of VTOL aircraft using a single Bristol Siddeley turbojet engine with swivelling jets to provide both lift and horizontal flight. That path eventually led to the HS Harrier fighter/ground-attack aircraft, several hundreds of which are now in service with British, United States and Spanish forces. The Harrier is the first, and still the only, successful application of jet power to provide VTOL performance, though the Russians have recently revealed an STOL carrier fighter using swivelling-jet lift.

Hawker Siddeley co-operated with Dornier in testing the latter's experimental DO31E VTOL transport aircraft. Using two Bristol Siddeley Pegasus swivel jets and two wing-tip pods each containing four Rolls-Royce RB162 lift jet engines, the DO31E performed well but was incredibly noisy. From that development came the DO31C 100-passenger civil transport project which would use two straightforward jets for normal propulsion and 12 lift engines grouped in wing-mounted pods and the fuselage.

Until the very serious noise problem of jet lift is overcome, it is unlikely that any other form of VTOL transport so far projected will seriously challenge the helicopter. However, aircraft designers have a long record of transforming hopeless-looking futuristic projects into practical hardware and doubtless, if the demand is there, economic VTOL airliners will appear in due course.

11. Small Airliners

Mainstay of many regional small carriers is the DHC6 Twin Otter, as this Californian tourist operator Golden West aircraft pictured at Santa Barbara in November 1973. The Twin Otter is a twin-turboprop machine able to take up to 20 passengers in its latest Series 300 development.

MANY OF THE aircraft which pioneered new routes in the 1920s and 1930s were small single-engined machines. They demonstrated that such aircraft could be flown safely and reliably over vast distances although when the airlines eventually exploited the routes they obviously had to use larger machines as traffic developed. Nevertheless some great aviation designers were convinced that small aircraft had a place in the air transport scene.

In the United States Jake Moellendick had become a rich man by finding oil but instead of retiring to a comfortable life, in 1920 he set up an aircraft manufacturing business in Wichita, Kansas. A gambler by nature, he was content to invest money in designs which one day might bring aviation to a wider public. In those heady days it was believed that light aeroplanes would become as widely used as motorcars, and although this forecast proved to be too optimistic, Wichita did indeed become the 'capital' of light aircraft construction. Moellendick attracted many talented young designers to his company but his business ability was lacking and although he faded from the scene and died penniless in 1940, some of the talent he had gathered at Wichita remained to become giants in what has become known as general aviation.

The company formed by Walter Beech, for example, went on to become a major force in the industry and after producing several single-engined designs he introduced the Model 18 in 1937. The twin-engined Beech 18 became a classic in the light transport category, remaining in production until after the 1939-45 war. In 1946 Beechcraft produced another classic in the V-tailed Bonanza, a single-engined aeroplane which has been built in large numbers and is still rolling off the production lines over 30 years later. Carrying up to six passengers, thousands of Bonanzas provide personal transport for those living in remote areas or who simply prefer to fly themselves instead of taking a seat on an airliner. Among many other Beechcraft types are the propjet King Air series of executive aircraft and the Model 99 Airliner—a 17-seat unpressurised aircraft which first flew in 1966 and has become an important third level or feeder airliner.

Feeder services mushroomed in the late 1960s when many mini-airlines were founded to serve smaller towns, particularly in the United States. There is no need to emphasise that America is an air-minded country and many towns there consider it essential that the municipality should run an airport. Such a facility helps to stimulate business so that in time it becomes necessary to provide scheduled feeder services to larger cities already served by trunk or regional carriers.

Another Wichita company which began its days in the 1920s is Cessna, now the largest manufacturer of light aircraft in the world. In the formative years the company concentrated on efficient single-engined aircraft but in recent years the range has included twin-engined and jet aircraft. Cessna products have become commonplace in many countries, customers choosing from a whole range of pressurised and unpressurised twin-engined aircraft developed for the burgeoning business and third-level market. With a total production to date of over 130,000 aircraft the Cessna company can truly be described as a giant in the general aviation industry.

One interesting and unusual operator is Scenic Airlines which was founded in 1967 with a single five-seat Cessna 205. The spectacular scenery of the Grand Canyon in the United States attracts thousands of visitors every year and Scenic's founder, John Seibold, correctly guessed that many would be willing to buy an airborne guided tour. In his first six months of operation Seibold carried fewer than 300 passengers, yet within three years the total had grown to more than 6000. After experimenting with various types of aircraft, Scenic built up a fleet of 12 Cessna 402 10-seat mini-airliners which have proved to be ideal for 'flightseeing'. With passenger totals now numbered in hundreds of thousands, Scenic has had to buy bigger aircraft and now operates some Swearingen Metro II 20-passenger aircraft to supplement the Cessna fleet.

Another successful oilman who left his mark on general aviation was William T. Piper. He was persuaded to invest in the Taylor Brothers Aircraft Corporation in 1931 when it became bankrupt and there followed the sort of conflict which has been

Below: *Designed as a simple capacious cargo transport for 2-ton loads using small airstrips, the Short SC7 Skyvan in its production turboprop form found numerous users aslo as a passenger aeroplane. Equipped to airline standards and named Skyliner, it could carry up to 20 passengers; it has been further developed into the Shorts 330 designed to carry 30 passengers.*

Right upper: *Big name on little ship, but as in so many other cases where there were backwoods communications to be maintained Qantas found the answer in de Havilland Canada products. The DHC2 Beaver was the first of the very successful range of DHC STOL light transport aircraft, introduced in 1947, and could carry up to 10 passengers.*

Right lower: *A jungle clearing in India forms the interface between old and new transport modes as a Hankyu Airlines Dornier Do28 twin-engined light utility transport pauses during its delivery flight.*

a feature of many an aircraft company; brilliant designer with no business sense versus hard-headed financier. Eventually Piper took control of the company and built up a sound business with a reputation for reliable easy-to-fly aeroplanes. Many single-engined designs have been produced by the company and after the 1939-45 war twin-engined aircraft began to broaden the Piper range. As well as private and business operators, Piper aircraft are also used by third-level operators in many countries. First produced in 1964, the twin-engined Navajo, for example, has become one of the most popular executive and commuter aircraft and is used by many small airlines. The Navajo has been produced in several versions including a turboprop variant called the Cheyenne.

The boom in light aviation during the 1930s was by no means confined to the United States; in England the de Havilland company established a reputation for build-ing fine 'sports' aircraft and the Moth series has become firmly established in the record books, for many were used to pioneer new routes. The Miles range of aircraft also helped to establish Britain as a leader in light aircraft design but the impetus was lost during the 1939-45 war and Britain's strength in this field has since all but disappeared.

Although after the war light aircraft were no longer a major part of de Havilland activity, the Dove, Heron and later DH125 kept alive the tradition established in the 1930s and these aircraft remain popular today, although the Dove and Heron are no longer produced. The four-engined Heron is one aircraft which brought third-level air transport to several countries long before

Overleaf: A successful entry into the feederliner and light utility market was made in the mid-1960s by Britten-Norman with the twin-engined nine-passenger BN2 Islander, of which the sales total, in well over 100 countries, is approaching 1000 aircraft. By adding a third engine, mounted in the tail unit, and an extended fuselage to seat up to 17 passengers the BN2 Mk 111 Trislander was created and introduced in 1970. The picture shows a Trislander in service with a small Jamaican airline.

the term third level was adopted. In 1957 BEA's Herons took over some of the Scottish Highlands and Islands services previously flown by the venerable de Havilland Rapide, and as passenger loads have grown and airports have been improved the Heron in turn has been replaced by bigger aircraft. One route served by the Heron for many years was that between Glasgow and the Hebridean islands of Tiree and Barra. Tiree has a runway but a beach is the landing strip on Barra and passengers were advised to check the tides when booking their flights. The air links do more than help to reduce the feeling of isolation on the remote islands; often the aircraft are used as ambulances and in other emergencies. Loganair took over some of the Scottish Highlands and Islands services from BEA in the early 1970s and introduced Britten-Norman new-generation Islander and Trislander third-level airliners. First flown in 1965, the Islander has become Britain's best-selling aircraft since the war, with total orders approaching

1000 machines. In the tradition of the Rapide, the Islander is a simple rugged design able to operate from short rough airstrips and it has found a ready welcome in many countries. The Israeli third-level carrier Kanaf-Arkia is an excellent example of an Islander operator; the 'mini-airline' maintains links with remote settlements in all parts of the country and the pilots fly their little aircraft with the verve and confidence of taxi-drivers. It is not uncommon to see one fix a small technical problem with a screwdriver before setting off on another flight. In 1970 the 10-seat Islander was enlarged by 7ft 6in to become the Trislander with a third Lycoming engine fitted to the tail. The extended fuselage increased the seat capacity to 17 and as a feeder-liner the aircraft has been exported to Africa, Australasia and the Americas.

What has become colloquially known as the 'bizjet' represents the top end of the general aviation scale. In 1962 de Havilland first flew its DH125 (later HS125) executive

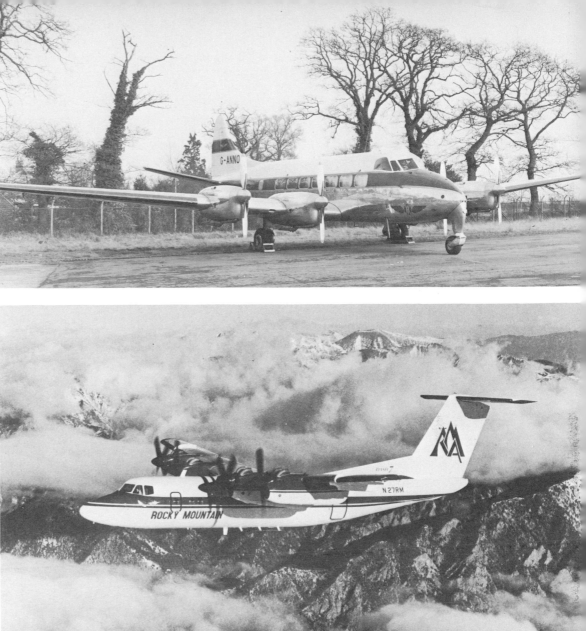

aircraft powered by two Rolls-Royce Viper turbojets. The HS125 can take up to as many as 14 passengers but is more usually equipped to carry about eight and operated mainly by large companies or corporations and government bodies. In 1976 the HS125 was offered with quieter and more economical turbofan engines, opening up a new lease of life for a design that had already sold more that 350 machines to customers around the world.

Executive jets have been developed on both sides of the Atlantic by companies which could draw upon military experience. North American, for example, produced the first swept-wing jet fighter for the USAF, the F-86 Sabre, and used experience gained to design the T-39 Sabreliner, which first flew in 1958. Bought mainly by military operators initially, in recent years the type has found an increasing number of civilian customers. It is still being developed over 20 years after its first appearance and the latest Sabreliner is fitted with a new design of wing said to permit higher speeds at lower operating costs.

The Dassault company has become one of Europe's most successful exporters, producing Mystère and Mirage fighters for the air forces of many countries. In 1963 the prototype Mystere 20 executive jet made its maiden flight. In the same year, Pan American World Airways (as it was called then) established a Business Jet Division and ordered over 50 Mystère 20s, marketing them in the United States as the Fan Jet Falcon. The 10-seat French bizjet sold well abroad and was followed in 1970 by the smaller Falcon 10 which could carry up to seven passengers at higher speeds than the older design.

Success did not attend the Aérospatiale SN601 Corvette produced in 1970. Intended to be used as a third-level airliner as well as a bizjet, the Corvette failed to attract many orders and total production was 40 aircraft. Similarly, Germany's attempt to enter the bizjet market in 1964 was not a success; the unusual HFB320 had swept-forward wings and was powered by two General Electric turbojets, but it was not produced in quantity. A joint American/Italian bizjet which flew in 1964 also was a failure. Douglas collaborated with Piaggio in the design of the PD808, a 10-seat jet transport which did not manage to gain a foothold in the highly competitive executive jet market.

In 1964 Bill Lear produced a business jet based on a Swiss fighter, the FFA P16. The fighter never entered production but the Learjet became the most elegant of bizjets, selling in large numbers to corporate and government users. It has been developed into a number of variants and well over 600 have been built. In 1967 Lear sold his interest in the company and set about designing another aircraft, the LearStar 600, now marketed as the Canadair Challenger. The Lear design could be described as a 'jumbo bizjet' for its wide cabin permits a major improvement in comfort. Even before its first flight in 1978, the Challenger had attracted over 100 orders. Lear's inventiveness was not yet at an end; he went on to design the Learfan, an unusual aircraft with a straight wing, an inverted V tail under the fuselage and a propeller at the rear.

The price of failure, even with small aircraft, could be heavy indeed. In 1967 Handley Page produced a twin-turboprop light transport called the Jetstream. It was a very attractive design that clearly appealed to the American market, for 100 were ordered 'off the drawing board', but when flight tests began it was found that the aircraft was overweight. Much money was spent in trying to improve the performance of the aircraft but the burden was too great and another great name in aviation faded from the scene. The Jetstream was later produced by Scottish Aviation for the RAF and Royal Navy for use as a trainer but its early promise has yet to be fulfilled.

De Havilland (Canada) had greater success with a development of its Otter 'bush' transport. The DHC6 Twin Otter first flew in 1965 and although intended for operation from small airstrips, it appeared at a time when third-level operations were growing rapidly in the United States. Consequently the type was adopted by many new operators which found its reliability and economy ideal for their requirements. Powered by the ubiquitous Canadian Pratt & Whitney PT6A turboprop engines, the Twin Otter has also found wide use with bush airlines. An unusual application has been made by the French third-level airline Air Alpes, a carrier which has specialised in bringing skiers to the heart of the winter sports resorts. The STOL performance of the Twin Otter enables Air Alpes to fly the aircraft onto short airstrips in the mountains. To date over 600 Twin Otters have been built.

Third level operations expanded in the Communist-bloc countries too, indeed it can be argued that the ungainly An-2 biplane could be considered one of the first aircraft to be used on this type of service in the Soviet Union. In Czechoslovakia the Let L410 Turbolet was produced in 1969. It is a 17-seat feeder-liner powered by two PT6A turboprops and was initially aimed at Western markets, but the type has so far sold only in the Soviet Union and other East European countries.

General aviation has been the means by which several nations have established aircraft industries. The Philippines assembles the Islander for example, for local distribution and Piper aircraft are licence-produced in several countries, including Brazil. Under the leadership of Max Holste, the Brazilian Embraer company produced a feeder-liner powered by PT6A turboprops, the Bandeirante, which first flew in 1968. It has since been produced in large numbers for airline and executive use and has even been exported to France and Great Britain, countries which previously manufactured this class of aircraft themselves.

Argentina also has a long-established but small aircraft industry including a military aircraft factory which designed and produced a twin-turboprop transport in 1962. Powered by two Turbomeca Bastan engines, the Guarani II can carry 15 passengers but the sole customer to date has been the Argentine Air Force.

Meanwhile in France the Nord 262 (developed from a Max Holste design), now called the Aérospatiale Frégate, is in service with the domestic airline Air Inter and in the United States. The type has been re-engined with the PT6A turboprop and thus powered is arousing the interest of several third-level carriers.

Japan's attempt to market an executive transport must be counted a success, for the Mitsubishi Mu-2 which first appeared in 1963 has been produced in large numbers. A subsidiary company was established in the US in Texas in 1967 for the assembly of the Mu-2 from parts supplied from Japan. It was originally powered by the Turbomeca Astazou turboprop but production machines are fitted with Garrett TPE331 engines.

Spain has had some experience in the design and production of transport aircraft having produced the 40-passenger Azor machine for the Spanish Air Force in the 1950s. More recently the CASA C212 Aviocar has enjoyed some success in world markets. It is a twin-turboprop machine and can carry passengers or freight in a boxlike fuselage. A number of C212s is being assembled in Indonesia.

The harsh terrain of the Australian outback has bred the country's first indigenous STOL design, the N22 Nomad, which is produced

Biggest of the wide range of Piper light aircraft is the PA31 Navajo, which can be equipped as a feederliner to seat up to eight passengers. The Navajo Chieftain here pictured at Eilat is operated on busy local routes by the El Al subsidiary Kanaf-Arkia.

by the Government Air Factories. The Nomad is powered by two Allison 250 turboprops and can carry up to 12 passengers, although a lengthened version will accommodate a total of 15 passengers. The little STOL transport attracted considerable custom in Australia and South East Asia and is yet another demonstration of the fact that the best STOL aircraft are designed in the countries which have the greatest need for this type of transport.

Israel has long had a strong aircraft industry producing many aircraft for its air force. In 1967 Israel Aircraft Industries took over the production and marketing rights of the American-designed Jet Commander, an executive jet which has since been further developed by the Israeli company. It is now named Westwind and continues in production. The Israeli-designed Arava is a STOL transport machine powered by two PT6A turboprops. It was first flown in 1969 and has sold well in Latin America.

As third-level carriers mature and their traffic increases they must find larger airliners, but most would still find the smallest of the domestic trunk machines uneconomic.

Carriers which were content with the Trislander or Twin Otter with 17 to 20 seats are growing into larger STOL airliners. One such is the de Havilland Canada four-engined Dash 7 offering up to 50 seats, one of a new generation of larger third-level or commuter airliners. Slightly smaller, with about 30 seats is the Shorts 330, a twin-turboprop aircraft which is particularly quiet enabling it to be operated into small airports without disturbing the built-up areas it is designed to serve.

General aviation has made a great contribution to the development of air transport. Indeed, there are primitive tribes in New Guinea and South America who are more familiar with the sight of small aircraft than they are with the motorcar. Missionaries in remote areas rely on light aircraft as a means of transport; many small communities see a doctor only when he comes in an aeroplane; and lumberjacks in the far north of Canada think nothing of taking a small aircraft to get to the next worksite. The applications for this type of air transport are endless and it can be said with certainty that it will continue to grow rapidly.

12. Merchantmen of the Air

ALTHOUGH THE FIRST recorded carriage of air cargo took place as long ago as 1911, this type of air transport has tended to be over–shadowed by the more glamorous passenger travel. In the United States air mail was flown in frail biplanes long before passengers were carried, but the driving ambition of designers was to produce an efficient airliner. In the DC-3 they succeeded and it was a flood of demobilised military C46, C47 and C54 aircraft which brought about the first real advance in air cargo. The war had demonstrated the value of air-craft used in the cargo transport role and it was logical that the same machines should be put into commercial use when the war ended.

Of the would-be air cargo carriers set up after 1945 only a few have survived as cargo-only airlines. The pattern of progress in air freighting is exemplified by one of the world's biggest all cargo carriers, the Flying

Above: *Many of the early big jet airliners were turned over to cargo as later developments appeared, either as conversions after a spell of passenger service or suitably modified during production. The DC-8F Jet Trader was a variant of the DC-8-50 with a big side-loading door introduced in 1961, of which Airlift International (one-time Riddle Airlines) as pictured is a notable operator.*

Left: *First specialised turboprop freighter was the Hawker Siddeley (Armstrong-Whitworth) AW650 Argosy, which first flew in January 1959 and had doors at both ends of its boxlike fuselage. Only 16 were built for civil use, seven going originally to Riddle Airlines in the US, but more were built as military transports.*

Tiger Line, which was founded in 1945 as the National Skyway Freight Corporation. An aircraft which played an important part in its success was the Douglas DC-8-63F. Now regarded as one of the most economical aircraft ever built, the Super Sixty version of the DC-8 featured a long and capacious fuselage which soon brought orders both from Flying Tiger and the other large American freight carrier, Seaboard & Western Airlines (now Seaboard World Airlines).

With 19 DC-8-63Fs in service, Flying Tiger's business grew so rapidly that by 1973 a further expansion of its fleet became necessary. The Super Sixty DC-8 was no longer in production (it is suggested that its operating costs were so competitive with the new DC-10 that the manufacturer thought it wise to delete the DC-8 from its range) so the airline turned to the Boeing 747. Second-hand 747s were becoming available from airlines suffering from the downturn in

business resulting from the world energy crisis. The ever-adaptable Boeing company designed and produced a conversion for early passenger versions of the Jumbo which enabled them to take the large international standard (ISO) containers, for the first time providing ISO containers with complete interchangeability between the four modes of transport—and a tremendous fillip to air freighting. The Boeing 747F has double the capacity of the DC-8; its enormous hold resembles a miniature railway marshalling yard with long rows of roller-bearing tracks and powered trolleys sunk into the floor to manoeuvre heavy containers and pallets.

Most of the many early attempts to produce a specialised cargo aircraft resulted in failure, with the exception of military transports, where economic considerations are not paramount. Of the civilian exceptions there is the Short Skyvan flown for the first time in 1963 powered by two Rolls-Royce Continental piston engines, but it was quickly converted to turbine power, first with Turbomeca and later with Garrett turboprops. The Skyvan has a high wing and easy-loading boxlike fuselage designed specifically for freight loads of up to about two tons, but to the company's initial surprise much of the success of the aircraft has been as a passenger transport, in which role it was later given the name Skyliner. From the same design team, and at the other end of the size scale, came the Short Belfast in 1964. It was powered by four Rolls-Royce Tyne turboprops and had a most capacious fuselage and loading facility, designed to carry particularly bulky cargo. Ten Belfasts purchased for the RAF were each capable of carrying over 150 fully equipped troops and a wide variety of military equipment; they gave excellent service as strategic freighters before being retired as a result of government defence cuts.

Also in Britain in the 1960s, Armstrong Whitworth produced the Argosy freighter, a twin-boom design with squarish fuselage and full-section doors at either or both ends, powered by four Rolls-Royce Dart turboprops. The design did not enjoy the sales success of the similarly powered Viscount, selling only to BEA for civil use and, in the United States to Riddle Airlines and Zantop for military charter work. Thus civilian sales were disappointing and the bulk of the production went to the RAF.

In 1963 an unusual task brought about a very unusual design in the Boeing Stratocruiser conversions named *Pregnant Guppy* and *Super Guppy*. They were extraordinary looking aircraft produced to carry US space

programme rockets from the manufacturers to Cape Kennedy. The rockets were too large to travel by rail or road and had to be delivered by slow sea transport before the Guppy was devised. Aero Space Lines had a Stratocruiser subjected to major surgery, making it over 16 feet longer with a cargo area 20 feet high. At some sacrifice of speed the *Pregnant Guppy* flew and considerably reduced the delivery time of the rockets. The *Super Guppy* differed in having turbo-prop engines and it has played an essential role in the production of the European Airbus, carrying large components to the assembly line in Toulouse from Britain and Germany.

Cargo aircraft built specifically for military customers fared better in the 1960s. The de Havilland (Canada) Buffalo, for example, was selected by the US Army in 1963 and flew for the first time a year later. Similar in appearance to the earlier piston-engined Caribou, the Buffalo is somewhat larger and powered by two General Electric T64 turbo-props. In the tradition of most designs produced by the company, the Buffalo is a STOL machine which is capable of flying into short rough strips. Consequently it has enjoyed steady sales to armed forces in several parts of the world, especially South America and Africa.

To meet a similar need in Europe, France and Germany collaborated in the design and construction of the Transall military freighter in 1963. Powered by two Rolls-Royce Tyne turboprops, the Transall owed its origins to Nord Aviation and the aircraft bears some resemblance to the N262. By 1959, however, when the Transporter Allianz group was formed, Nord had been swallowed up by Aérospatiale. The other partners in the group were Messerschmitt-Bolkow-Blohm and VFW-Fokker. Although primarily a military machine, some Transalls are operated by Air France for the French Post Office on domestic mail services.

Also designed for military transport and powered by GE T64 turboprops is the Aeritalia G222, which flew for the first time in 1970. The Italian and other air forces have taken delivery of the G222 as a STOL transport; the original intention to fit jet lift engines to provide VTOL capability having been dropped because of the expense and complexity.

Some notable Soviet cargo aircraft have been produced for both military and civil use, with the Antonov design team making the biggest (literally) impact in this category. In the 1960s the company produced the An-12 four-turboprop design which has found application in several air forces but, although in the same category as the Lock-heed C-130 Hercules, the An-12 has not enjoyed the American aircraft's commercial success. Of similar configuration to the An-12 but very much bigger is the long-range An-22 powered by four 15,000shp Kuznetsov turboprop engines. It was introduced at the 1965 Paris Air Show with a maximum pay-load of 176,350lb; with a wing-span of 210 feet and a length of 167 feet it is a giant by any standards.

In response to a USAF requirement for a strategic freighter, Lockheed followed up the turboprop Hercules with the turbojet C-141. StarLifter in 1963. Eventually over 250

Left: Like a miniature railway marshalling yard, the main deck of a Lufthansa Boeing 747F taking aboard a load of 13 radio vans for transport from Frankfurt to Indonesia. The 747-200F can take pallet or container loads weighing up to 90 imperial tons over a range of more than 4500 miles.

Above: The method of efficient loading adopted for the Canadair CL44, the long-range turboprop freighter derived from the Bristol Britannia, was to hinge the fuselage so that the whole tail unit could be swung aside, as demonstrated here by one of several CL44Ds operated by Transmeridian Air Cargo Ltd.

were produced and widely used to supply American forces in Europe and the Far East. A 1977 modification of the C-141 increased its volumetric capacity. The fuselage was extended by 23 feet, enabling it to carry 13 pallets instead of 10 in the standard aircraft.

Also for the USAF in 1964, Boeing, Douglas and Lockheed all submitted design proposals for the C-5A giant cargo aircraft. The result of the competition was to have far-reaching effects both for the aircraft industry and for airlines. Lockheed's submission was successful and in June 1968 the Galaxy made its first flight. It was similar in appearance to the C-141 but dwarfed it and all other aircraft, with maximum take-off weight well over 700,000 lb or around 340 long tons. The engine developed for the Galaxy was the General Electric TF-39 turbofan of 41,000lb static thrust; it led to the highly successful CF-6 series of turbofans used by many of today's wide-bodied airliners.

Although they lost the military contract, Boeing and Pratt & Whitney refused to waste the effort they had put into their C-5A proposals and in 1966 they persuaded Pan American to order the Boeing 747. With the cockpit perched high above the cabin, the cargo origins of the Boeing 747 are clear and indeed the freighter version produced for Lufthansa in 1971 opened a new era in commercial air transport. The Boeing 747F featured the upward-hinging nose of the military design to allow up to 200,000lb of palletised/containerised cargo to be swallowed up in the cavernous hold.

The rapid expansion of air cargo traffic was not confined to long-distance routes. Although it may be argued that the Boeing

155

707-320C opened the way to an enormous increase in the air movement of freight, smaller jet aircraft played an important part too. In the mid-1960s, encouraged by the reliability and efficiency of the Boeing 727, several airlines took QC (Quick Change) versions into their fleets. The 727QC was fitted with a large side-loading door and a strengthened floor and could be quickly converted from a passenger airliner into an all-cargo machine. At the end of the day, the seats and galleys were quickly removed leaving the cabin clear to receive palletised freight. Thus transformed the aircraft could fly through the night operating scheduled cargo services. Douglas shortly responded with the DC-9RC (Rapid Change) but an increasing sensitivity to airport noise has led to the abandonment of this type of operation.

A big advance in air cargo transport was the introduction of the jumbo-sized passenger aircraft. The Boeing 747, Lockheed Tri-Star, McDonnell Douglas DC-10 and Airbus A300 all have enough underfloor space to accommodate freight previously flown in cargo versions of first-generation jet airliners. Introduction of the wide-bodied fleets in the 1970s had another effect on the air cargo business. Numbers of redundant Boeing 707 and DC-8 aircraft were converted to carry cargo, for the aircraft had plenty of life left in them but passengers preferred the Jumbos. The late 1970s therefore saw a growing number of air cargo carriers formed to carry charter loads around the world, especially to countries with booming economies and limited port facilities. The swing-tail CL-44 and retired RAF Britannias were joined by converted DC-8s and 707s to boost the air cargo business.

In the United States an interesting development took place in 1972 when the Federal Express Corporation began a fast parcels service using converted Fan Jet Falcons (Mystere 20s). Little Rock Airmotive began converting Falcons to provide a large side door in the manner of the larger Boeing and Douglas airliners and the Memphis-based airline soon built up a large network to utilise its 33-strong fleet. Federal Express obviously fulfilled a need, for demand for its services grew apace, and the company planned to introduce larger aircraft. It concluded that the Canadair Challenger was ideally suited for its needs and contracted to purchase five standard models and 25 stretched variants.

Deregulation is a word which will become associated with the 1970s for it was a cornerstone of the Carter Administration's air transport policy. In a nutshell, deregulation entails the removal of restrictions in running scheduled services, in fact opening the door to maximum competition. First to feel the benefit of this policy was the cargo business in the United States and it enabled carriers such as Federal Express to expand its

Above: *A PanAm Cargo Boeing 747-100F, one of five of the type operated by the company since the first conversion of some of its original 747 passenger fleet was completed in May 1975. The 100F has a big cargo door in the port side to allow pallet and container loading and has a maximum taxi weight of 753,000lb (336 tons).*

Right: *The raised nose of the Boeing 747-200F permits the loading of containers of international standard dimensions; with the Jumbo's massive load capacity, this provides full interchange of ISO containers between the four main transport modes for the first time.*

services and acquire bigger airliners like the Boeing 727.

Many exotic cargo transport designs are being considered for the future but two recent American designs may point the way to the next step. As a replacement for the Lockheed C-130, the USAF invited tenders for an advanced medium short take-off and landing transport (AMST). Boeing and McDonnell Douglas submitted designs and built prototypes to take part in a ' fly off ' competition. The YC-15 produced by McDonnell Douglas is powered by four Pratt & Whitney JT8D-17 engines and flew for the first time in 1975. Boeing's YC-14 flew some time after the McDonnell Douglas aircraft but was more advanced in concept, featuring two over-wing engines and very generous flap area arranged so that the engine's thrust is induced to hug the wing and produce almost vertical lift. There is little to choose between the extraordinary performance of these aircraft; both are capable of landing slowly on short airstrips carrying heavy loads, but neither has yet been ordered into production. Meanwhile the Lockheed C-130 remains in production, the total number built having exceeded 1500 machines.

Other technological advances have recently been put into the service of air cargo. Computers, for instance, help to sort the cargo at large terminals, eliminating human error as far as possible. No longer the poor relation of passenger services, air cargo is now a highly sophisticated element of air transport which is sure to grow in importance.

13. Flying's Many Facets

Modern aircraft need sophisticated
ground equipment to support
them.   This British made
Reliance Mercury 40-ton tug
operated by the Dutch airline
Martinair is capable of hauling
the DC-10-30 at its maximum
take-off weight of 555,000lb and
also incorporates a 60kVA
generator to augment the aircraft's
own supply for engine starting.

IN THE SIXTY years or so of air transport, technology has brought about many changes. If the needle-sharp Concorde is compared with the clumsy frail aircraft of the 1920s, the changes are, of course, obvious but there are many other aspects of air transport which have changed just as much over the years.

The first passengers often bargained with the owner/pilot over the fare and on safety grounds alone it soon became clear that some order had to be brought to air transport. In 1919 six European airlines formed IATA, an organisation which has grown to include over 100 airlines today. To prevent cut-throat fare levels IATA set about arranging annual tariff conferences at which the conflicting requirements of member airlines were resolved. Setting fare levels has not been the only function of IATA however; common reservations and ticketing procedures have been devised to enable passengers to travel in any part of the world without difficulty. The movement of cargo and mail has also been simplified so that the necessary paperwork is common to all parts of the world. Some countries still impose a jungle of bureaucratic formalities for both passengers and cargo but IATA provides a medium for discussion which helps to facilitate the flow of traffic.

Fares play a major part in the development of air transport and IATA has often been considered to be responsible for maintaining high rates. Certainly IATA has tended to move at the pace of the most conservative member airline and dramatic reductions in fares have often come about as a result of government action or the efforts of an enterprising airline. The North Atlantic has usually been the crucible in which new fare policies have been fused. Until 1953 a standard rate was charged but in that year tourist class fares were introduced and first class was set aside for the limited number of passengers who could afford some luxury. A further reduction took place in 1958 when economy class was introduced, providing a return fare from London to New York of £162 compared with the £254 of the standard tourist fare in 1949.

When economy-class services were introduced in 1958, IATA airlines made a number of rules which included the distance in inches between each seat-row and the type of food which could be served. The rules prescribed 'sandwiches', which put the Scandinavians at some advantage because open sandwiches from that part of the world are meals in themselves.

With the introduction in 1959 of jet airliners on the North Atlantic, a surcharge was levied on jet passengers in fairness to the piston-engined aircraft which continued to operate the route. The surcharge remained in force until there were hardly any propeller-driven airliners left. Similarly, a heavy surcharge over normal first-class fares has been enforced on British Airways and Air France for their supersonic services.

Excursion fares were introduced on trans-atlantic routes in 1962, providing a further opportunity for saving and encouraging more people to travel. The new fares were designed in particular to persuade passengers to travel in off-peak times and in the low season, when many airlines flew the main trunk routes half or more empty. Nothing is so perishable as a seat on a public transport vehicle; an unsold seat is revenue lost for ever. A successful airline has to calculate correctly the percentage of seats it will sell to be certain that the fares charged will earn profits, so the airlines' efforts to attract off-peak business is understandable. More recently agreement on advanced purchase excursion (APEX) fares has helped airlines to match capacity to demand, as well as providing a welcome increase in revenue.

Non-IATA airlines offering low fares have caused minor upsets in the past; Loftleidir on the North Atlantic in 1952, for example. But when Laker was finally allowed to introduce the Skytrain London-New York service a new chapter opened in air transport. Skytrain fares are not very much lower than APEX fares, but they are for walk-on, not advance-booking advance-payment, services and their introduction forced IATA scheduled

airlines to respond by cutting their own fares, putting the balance of profit or loss on a knife-edge. The drive for lower fares presents a danger which could result in a radical change in the pattern of air travel. Business travellers need scheduled services in order to be able to arrange their affairs but the pressures to get economic utilisation out of the big new airliners encourages a trend towards non-scheduled services aimed at carrying ever greater numbers of tourists and private travellers. Doubtless the airlines will resolve the problem.

Safety is an emotive subject and aircraft crashes are generally spectacular. Although the early days of air transport were exceedingly hazardous, crashes often occurred at such low speeds that passengers and crew escaped without serious injury. As aircraft increased in size and travelled faster an accident became more likely to have disastrous results. The many lessons which have been learned in all aspects of air travel have led to constantly improved standards of safety.

When the earliest airliners plied their way from city to city, there were no radio communication or beacons to guide them. Paraffin flares were used to light runways by night and a flag might be used to give permission for an airliner to take off. The coming of radio provided a great step forward in air safety; step by step communications and air traffic control have improved to the point where automatic computer controlled flights cannot be far away. Computers, of course, aid air traffic controllers today and radar provides a ' picture ' of the air traffic pattern as the

aircraft make their way along the 'corridors' called airways which lead to the zones surrounding cities and their airports. The airways system was first evolved in the United States in the 1920s and has since become accepted worldwide.

The improvements in automatic navigational aids which came about after the 1939-45 war ultimately made airborne navigators redundant. Airliners today carry 'black boxes' galore to guide the aircraft with an uncanny accuracy and the instrument landing system (ILS) is used to bring the journey to a safe end. ILS was preceded after 1945 by ground controlled approach (GCA) a system by which a ground controller 'talked down' an approaching aircraft calling for considerable skill on the part of both pilot and controller; an automatic landing system was even then considered inevitable as a means of eliminating human errors. 'Stacking' is an accepted method of safely separating airliners which are approaching an airport to land. At peak periods at busy airports, or if the regular flow of landing aircraft is interrupted for any

length of time, queues are likely to form. On such occasions airliner pilots are instructed to circle a beacon, each one being given a particular height to ensure a safe vertical separation from others in the queue. The air traffic controllers have to keep constant watch on their radar screens as they take aircraft from the 'stack' to feed them into the approach to the airport's runways.

In building aeroplanes, manufacturers have progressed from the trial and error days of the 1920s to the computer-aided design techniques of the present day. Much has been learned over the years but mistakes still sometimes happen. However, when an accident does occur it sometimes results in an extensive modification programme. As a result of the Paris DC-10 accident caused by an insecure cargo door, all wide-bodied jets underwent a series of modifications to prevent repetition of such a disaster. Today all aircraft undergo years of tests and trials before service and an advanced airliner like Concorde has to be proved even more stringently before it is allowed to carry passengers. Many government research

centres are devoted to the task of exploring the frontiers of aeronautical knowledge so that future generations of airliners can carry their passengers in even greater safety than is the case today. It is ironical that the worst airliner disaster ever should have taken place on the ground, when an air traffic control misunderstanding caused two Jumbos to collide on the runway at Teneriffe, tragically pointing to the need for further improvements in airport control techniques.

Airports were once little more than flat fields with some sheds but as traffic grew architects started to consider the special needs of airline passengers. Many of the early purpose-built airports have been swallowed up by the relentless spread of urban development. Croydon was London's first civil airport (although air services to Paris had begun earlier from Hounslow) and it was at Croydon that what came to be regarded as standard airport facilities, including a hotel, were first established as the airport grew to become one of Europe's major terminals. It was closely matched by Le Bourget at Paris, scene of Lindbergh's triumphant end to his solo Atlantic crossing, which remained in use long after Croydon was closed, and whose distinctive architecture has served airlines and passengers well.

An interesting airport built before the 1939-45 war is Berlin's Templehof, noted for its large curved terminal building which permits an aircraft to bring its passengers to a point beneath a canopy. Templehof too finally had to close as it became hemmed in by buildings. Stockholm's Bromma airport opened in 1936 and its use today is restricted to light aircraft and the airliners of Linjeflyg whose F28 Fellowship jets are quiet enough not to disturb the airport's neighbours. In the 1970s Arlanda became the principal airport of the Swedish capital and, like successive airports as they appear, its buildings are claimed to be the last word in advanced design—although Paris Charles de Gaulle airport at Paris might be regarded as the most futuristic. There passengers are trundled for long distances on moving belts and escalators housed in metal and glass tubes between the series of circular terminals built as satellites to the main multi-storey complex.

In America, cities like New York and Chicago quickly outgrew their first airports, which, unlike most countries, handle large volumes of general as well as airline traffic, and additional ones had to be provided. A measure of the immensity of the task today is Chicago O'Hare airport, the busiest in the world, which handles about 2000 take-offs and landings a day and 44 million passengers a year.

Many attempts have been made to produce the ideal airport shape. Some modern designs, such as Cologne, have attempted to reduce the distance between the aircraft and

the entrance to the terminal to a minimum. Others have grown to enormous size by building new extensions and wings, obliging passengers to walk long distances to their aircraft. Clearly the volume of passengers to be handled influences the design of airports and their terminals, some, such as Washington Dulles and Montreal Mirabelle, use mobile lounges to carry passengers to airliners parked away from the terminal building; others have to maintain fleets of buses for the purpose. Manoeuvrable finger-like covered ways became popular after the war as they permitted passengers to walk directly between terminal buildings and aircraft.

Rail connections to city centres are one method of overcoming the sometimes long road traffic delays to and from airports. Brussels has long had a rail link with its airport and it has been joined by Frankfurt, Dusseldorf, Paris Charles de Gaulle and London Heathrow. Since its inception as London's second airport Gatwick has enjoyed a direct rail link to the city and British United Airways established its passenger terminal at Victoria railway station early in its career.

Weighing machines were used initially at airports or terminals for passengers as well as baggage, but as aircraft grew in size a method of averaging out passengers' weight was devised. Already on some routes baggage is no longer weighed in a necessary step to speed up passenger handling. An adverse factor in the speedy movement of passengers is the very necessary security check, airliners having become a natural target for terrorists and the mentally unstable. Some do not hesitate to place passengers' lives in jeopardy. The destruction of three airliners in 1970 at Dawson's Field, a desert strip in Jordan, was but the first of many spectacular and costly acts of destruction. Some ground has been recovered by the adoption of mechanical systems to speed up the security checks, using X-rays, metal detectors and explosive-'sniffing' devices. Some airlines have become especially vulnerable to the attentions of political terrorists and as a result their security standards have to be even more stringent to retain the confidence of their passengers.

Catering is another area in which giant strides have been taken since the birth of air transport. For many years, of course, cabin attendants were not carried in the tiny aircraft which could accommodate few passengers anyway. As 'real' airliners entered service, stewards and air hostesses became regular members of the crew. Sandwiches and biscuits were the most that could be served initially for there were no facilities for heating food on board, but coffee and tea were often provided from thermos flasks which were replenished at each

port of call. On longer trips in those early relaxed days of air travel, food and overnight accommodation were provided at suitable stops along the route. As aircraft have become bigger and efficient galleys have been designed full meals can be served. Food is usually prepared in large kitchens, by the airlines themselves or by specialist caterers, and delivered to the aircraft in containers; meals need little attention from the cabin crew, apart from reheating where necessary in special ovens in the aircraft's galley. In some of the wide-bodied airliners the food is prepared in an underfloor kitchen and sent up to the passenger cabins in lifts, which allows more room for passenger seats but restricts the amount of cargo space.

Some cabin service traditions have disappeared long since—handing out rugs or blankets against the chill, for example; others have persisted to outlive their usefulness— a few airlines continue to serve sweets, for example. Originally introduced as a means of avoiding discomfort in unpressurised aircraft during the climb and descent (the action of chewing and swallowing helps to relieve pressure in the ears), the introduction of pressurised aircraft practically removed the need for such aids to comfort.

Cabin interiors have changed enormously since the days of the converted bomber. Chintz curtains, flowerpots and wicker seats helped to provide a 'homely' atmosphere reminiscent of a Pullman railway carriage and in the earliest of passenger aircraft additional ventilation was made possible by opening windows. The big British biplanes started the move towards much greater cabin comforts and the DC-3 provided a new standard of cabin environment, although even the airliners of the 1930s lacked really comfortable appointments. Gradually sound-proofing and seat design have improved to the point where it is now possible to talk

with one's neighbour in comparative comfort or sit and enjoy a Mozart symphony through earphones as the airliner wings its way to its destination at 500 or 600mph. In-flight entertainment can now extend to a choice of several music programmes and a film show. Cinema was introduced to aircraft before the advent of the Jumbos, for although jet travel greatly speeded up the journey time between major cities, a seven-hour flight across the Atlantic, for example, could still be very tedious, but the wide-bodied aircraft give much greater scope for providing a variety of entertainment.

Apart from obvious safety factors such as seat belts, introduced in the late 1930s, life-belts over water routes and emergency oxygen in aircraft that fly outside a breathable atmosphere, in recent years an increasing amount of attention has had to be given to cabin safety. For example, the choice of furnishing materials can be important as it has been found that, in a fire, flameproof materials may give off noxious gases, or perhaps when two individually harmless materials are put together they become lethal at certain temperatures. Every new airliner is required to be tested in respect of its cabin safety. The strengths of seat fastenings and belts and the position and operation of emergency exits are prescribed, and emergency evacuation of a full aircraft has to be carried out and timed. Inflatable escape shutes facilitate the speedy exit from a crashed aircraft and there have been remarkable cases of survival from totally destroyed machines in which the passengers have been able to get out before fire consumed the wreckage.

Air transport has spawned a whole industry of special support vehicles. At most, a van to deliver mail to the aircraft would have been used in the early days but as airliners have become increasingly complex

Luxury and spaciousness are airborne in today's airliners; compare the wide aisles and easy chairs of the first-class cabin of a Douglas DC-10 (above left) *and the carpeted spaciousness of a section of a Boeing 747 with the picture on page 161.*

more and more specialist vehicles have been produced. Catering trucks with a scissors-lift action deliver new food containers and take away empty meal trays. Rubbish is taken away by another vehicle while yet another empties the toilets. Fresh water has to be put into the tanks on board the aircraft and sometimes a mobile generator is needed to provide power for the many electrical devices which are in use even when the airliner is on the ground. Passengers and baggage have their own mobile means of entry and exit and mobile conveyor belts carry packages into the freight hold. Most likely today, cargo and baggage are carried in containers and they too will be handled by special vehicles. To manoeuvre an aircraft the size of a Boeing 747, weighing around 200 tons even unladen, around the parking area needs a special and very powerful tractor indeed.

Although airliners have grown enormously in size, the controls used by the pilots have diminished. The control wheel on the HP42, for example, would not seem out of place on a present-day bus or heavy truck but a DC-10, say, needs only small controls because its many movable flight control surfaces are powered by a hydraulic, pneumatic or electric system. The instruments on the control panel on the other hand have multiplied many times since even the first airliners of the 1930s. All the essential instruments are duplicated, either so that they can be seen by both pilots or as a safety measure should one fail. Although a present day flight deck looks daunting it must be remembered that each of the many engine instruments are duplicated, triplicated or quadruplicated, depending on the number of engines fitted. Indeed, there is a noticeable absence of drama on a flight deck; most

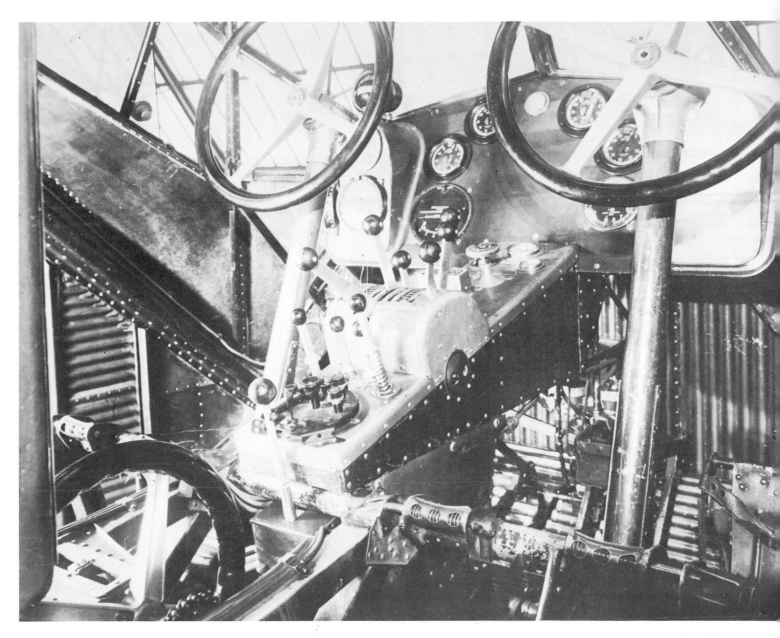

These two pictures illustrate dramatically the great changes that have taken place in aircraft flight decks in the space of about 30 years. The picture above shows that of the Junkers G38 of the early 1930s, with extremely heavy manual control columns and trim-tab wheel and sparse instruments. On the left the camera overlooks a landing approach of a BAC One-Eleven.

parts of the journey are flown by the automatic pilot which responds to the command of the captain. If a new heading is required, the necessary buttons are pushed to bring the airliner steadily onto course and it is only during take-off and landing phases that the aircraft is controlled manually. With the Autoland system installed on British Airways aircraft even the approach and landing to touchdown at suitably equipped airports can safely be left to automatics.

As well as controls, the flight decks of airliners have also diminished in size. Modern navigational aids have removed the need for navigators, leaving no more than three in most airliner crews; pilot, co-pilot and engineer. In comparison, the Empire flying-boats, for example, had very large flight decks.

It may be said that flying an aeroplane is much like driving a vehicle; once you have mastered the technique you should be able to

fly anything. In reality it is not quite like that. The earliest pilots taught themselves or received their instruction on the ground before venturing forth in a single-seat aircraft. Military requirements led to the formation of flying schools and the basic techniques of instruction have changed little over the years. For the present-day airline pilot, however, there are many advanced training aids, the most impressive of which are the flight simulators which reproduce the characteristics of particular airliners. Consisting of a flight deck which faithfully reproduces the original, a flight simulator provides movement, noise and even smell (in the event of a cabin fire, for example), giving a pilot the atmosphere of the real aircraft it represents. As a visual aid to the deception, a large model of the area around an airport is scanned by a television camera which transmits the scene as seen from the aircraft as it flies over the land. This system is now being superseded

by a computer generated image (CGI) arranged to reproduce the characteristics of any one of several airports by day or night, in a wide range of weather conditions. Thus pilots can become familiar with particular airports and practise landings in all sorts of weather. (Some simulators allow pilots to perform aerobatics, something which is clearly not allowed on the real airliner!)

Training schools such as the Oxford Flying School provide instruction for students from all parts of the world, the often poor weather and crowded skies of Southern England providing an ideal testing environment in which to acquire the skills necessary for today's airline pilots. English has long been the standard language of communication in aviation and it is a further benefit for foreign students to attend English or American

flying schools and receive instruction in the English language.

Just as computers are used extensively in the design of modern aircraft and in their navigation in service, so they have speeded up communications and simplified seat booking in the airline industry. Before the advent of computerised reservations systems, flight bookings were recorded, often manually, on cards or sheets maintained in each airline's central office. The system was cumbersome and prone to delay and error. The use of computers in the reservation system provides virtually immediate access to continuously updated records of all bookings from any of the airline's, and even other airlines' and agents' offices. For example, a client in New York can be told the booking position on, say, an airliner scheduled to fly from London to

Right upper: *At Delta Airlines terminal at Atlanta Airport fingers probe out onto the tarmac from the main terminal building, to provide passengers with direct access to their aircraft by means of pedestrian conveyors and telescopic couplings with aircraft doorways.*

Right lower: *Airports have always been noisy neighbours and more so since the coming of jets. Some relief during protracted ground engine running is afforded by jet muffles, four of which are here seen being adjusted into position on traverse rails as a Balair Convair 990 Coronado prepares to start up in the maintenance area of Zurich Airport.*

Tehran, in a matter of seconds. Airline computers perform many other tasks previously undertaken by expert clerks; the most economical flight routes used to be calculated by flight despatchers, a complex task requiring hours. A computer provides the correct information in minutes. Servicing and maintenance have also been simplified by the use of computers helping to keep down the cost of operating the complex modern airliner.

The growth of scheduled air traffic over the past 30 years or so is indicated by the *ABC World Airways Guide* which contains details of all scheduled airline services and is used throughout the world by travel agents and airlines. In 1949 it detailed the services of 247 airlines and the current issue lists 475, nearly doubled. In the same period the number of departure airports has increased from 2412 to 3774 and the number of aircraft types from 47 to 115. To contain all the necessary entries, the number of pages has increased from 390 in 1949 to 1944 today.

In 1892 Lawrence Hargrave in a paper given before the Royal Society in Australia, forecast: " . . . that the flying machine will tend to bring peace and goodwill to all, that it will throw light on the few unexplored corners of the earth, and that it will herald the downfall of all restrictions to the free intercourse of nations." Much of his prophecy has yet to come true, but his patient experiments played a part in the ultimate achievement of manned flight, and the subsequent giant strides in air transport history. The aeroplane, however, is only one of the essential elements in the mosaic which goes to make up today's airline industry.

14. Faster, Bigger ~ or Both?

IN TERMS OF size and speed, the frontiers of aviation technology have been relentlessly pushed to their limits.

Many will wonder when air transport will reach a plateau, a levelling-off in development in much the same way as the motorcar, railway train and ship. Doubtless all these methods of transport are capable of greater development but there are restraints which discourage major improvements in performance. Road conditions and traffic density have led to speed restrictions on motor vehicles, and there is a limit to the size of truck or bus which can be manoeuvred through towns and villages. There are many who feel that air transport has also reached reasonable limits; London to New York in 3½ hours is surely fast enough for the busiest executive and nearly 500 passengers on one aircraft seems as much as airports can handle. Tempting though it might be to cry enough the indications are that even greater advances in air travel will be achieved in the future.

Although Concorde entered service only in 1976, basic research on supersonic airliner design was being carried out 20 years before. Independent work was initiated in both Britain and France some years before the two countries agreed to pool their resources. With America firmly in control of about 80 per cent of the world's airliner market, some aviation leaders in Britain and France considered that only by pioneering a major step forward would they be able to win back customers who had got into the habit of shopping in the United States whenever they wanted a long-haul airliner.

Initially, the aims of Britain and France in embarking on the design of a supersonic air transport (SST) were at variance. The French wanted to build a medium-range airliner to follow the undoubted success of the Caravelle. While acknowledging the achievement of the Caravelle, the British correctly pointed out that it was not a notably profitable airliner; an airliner capable of flying over the North Atlantic was the aim of Sir George Edwards of BAC and others who wanted to build an SST in Britain. Headed by Sir Morien Morgan of the Royal Aircraft Establishment, a Supersonic Transport Aircraft Committee (STAC) was set up to consider all aspects of the subject. All sides of the industry including BEA and BOAC, the Air Registration Board and manufacturers were represented on the committee. Two alternative SST designs were considered; a delta and an M-shaped aircraft, but before long the delta showed

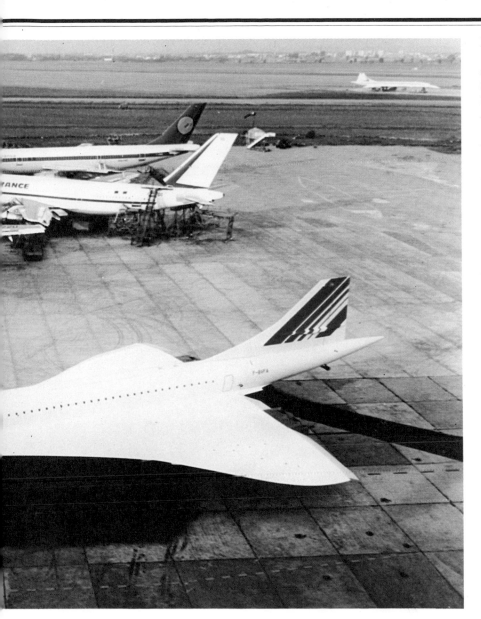

Above: *Concorde 101 F-BVFA, first of four production aircraft delivered to Air France with which scheduled service between France and South America was started on 21 January 1976.*

Left: *French assembled Concorde 02 pictured in Alaska for cold-weather tests.*

British, at least in terms of shape, and at the 1960 Paris Air Show Sud Aviation caused a stir by displaying a model of its proposed Super Caravelle. Led by Georges Hereil, Sud Aviation was by no means enthusiastic at the prospect of collaborating with the British, for although the Caravelle made extensive use of British equipment BEA did not follow the example of most other European airlines in ordering the aircraft, preferring to take the Comet 4B instead.

Nevertheless exploratory discussions did take place in 1961 after behind-the-scenes pressure from the Aviation Ministers of Britain and France. Co-operation on the project clearly made sense, for considerable technical and financial resources would be needed to achieve success. Both countries had displayed inventiveness in aviation and researched delta-winged design several years earlier. Indeed, Britain's Fairey Delta 2 first flown in 1954 went on to establish a world speed record of 1132 mph two years later. The French Durandel and Griffon delta-winged research aircraft had exceeded Mach 1 in the mid-1950s, and the later Mirage series of delta-winged fighter aircraft was to become one of Europe's most successful aircraft.

Although prodded by their governments, the talks between BAC and Sud Aviation made little progress, failing at first to agree on even an outline project. The failure was reflected later in the squabble over the English or French spelling of Concord(e). Finally a meeting between BAC's chief designer Dr Strang and Sud's Lucien Servanty resulted in a draft design. It was enough for the Aviation Ministers and in November 1962 they signed the Anglo-French Supersonic Aircraft Agreement. It was a short document containing only seven Articles but it did not include a break clause—a fact which was later to save the project on more than one occasion. The cost estimates in 1962 for the SST were £150 million, to be divided equally between the two nations.

French industry was apportioned 60 per cent of the airframe design to balance the fact that Bristol Siddeley Olympus engines, already well developed for the Avro Vulcan bomber, were to power the projected SST. It was an entirely logical choice of power plant—in fact, the only one—and found agreement on both sides of the Channel. Agreement on the size and range of the Concorde, as it was eventually named, proved harder to find. The French were still keen on building a medium-range aircraft and valuable time was lost until they

superior characteristics as models were tested in the Farnborough wind tunnel.

In 1959 the STAC reported its findings to the government, which proceeded to award design study contracts to Hawker Siddeley Aviation and Bristol Aircraft (Bristol soon afterwards became part of the British Aircraft Corporation). Hawker Siddeley was to consider a medium-range aircraft and Bristol studied a long-distance airliner. It is perhaps ironic that it was Duncan Sandys who, as Minister of Aviation, so vigourously supported the SST project, having dealt a severe blow to the aircraft industry two years previously by declaring that manned fighters and bombers were things of the past and that missiles would take over the tasks of both attack and defence.

Meanwhile the French design studies had reached similar conclusions to those of the

were finally persuaded to agree on a long-range airliner. Nevertheless, by mid-1963 the design was sufficiently advanced to encourage BOAC, Air France and Pan American to sign options on the Concorde.

Although the concept of the SST excited the imagination of many in the airline industry, the enthusiasm stopped short at the prospect of actually buying the Concorde. Airlines had enjoyed only a few profitable years before the Jumbo era was forced upon them. The pattern of excess capacity provided by the introduction of the Boeing 747 had been a repetition of the situation which existed in the early 1960s when the Boeing 707 and Douglas DC-8 replaced piston-engined airliners. Consequently there was little enthusiasm for yet another major step forward which might well lead to the premature retirement of the Jumbos.

Small wonder therefore that the airlines had an ambivalent attitude to Concorde and did not exactly welcome its coming. Although there was no SST operating experience to draw upon, the high development costs of the Convair B-58 Hustler and North American B-70 supersonic bombers gave clear indication of the expense involved in producing a large supersonic aircraft. The Hustler did at least see service with the USAF, but the B-70, which first flew in 1958 and was built of steel and titanium to fly at Mach 3, failed to make the grade. It was well known that at the very high temperatures generated at high Mach numbers, aluminium would not be suitable, and indeed, the heat barrier was regarded by British experts with far greater concern than the so-called sound barrier.

The B-70 was considered by many to be the basis for a future American-built SST but severe problems were encountered and it is generally conceded that the extensive use of steel and titanium proved to be its undoing.

Right: Concorde 102 G-BOAC, one of five production aircraft for British Airways with which scheduled service was started between the UK and Bahrain on 21 January 1976. Completion of delivery of the nine Concordes for the French and British national airlines leaves seven of the 16 production aircraft unsold, though one or two sales prospects remain active and the possibility of leases or charters is under discussion as this is written.

Below: The Russian SST Tu-144 pictured at the end of its first scheduled passenger service from Moscow to Alma Ata on 1 November 1977. It covered the 2050 miles in just under two hours. Tu-144s had spent nearly two years prior to the opening of passenger service regularly flying the Moscow-Alma Ata route with mail.

The programme was cancelled by the American government and with it the chance of producing an SST 'on the back of a military project'. It has been seen that many successful American air transport designs owed their existence to military forebears which helped to reduce the overall costs of design and production. Consequently, although much remained to be done, the Anglo-French SST project remained the only one likely to reach fruition.

A political aspect to the Concorde programme has run like a thread throughout its turbulent life; for France the SST soon became a symbol of the country's leadership. American dominance of the world's airline market was to be challenged by France which, with de Gaulle at its head, had assumed the political leadership of the European Economic Community. Although Winston Churchill had advocated European unity in a speech soon after the war, Britain had been

torn between her Imperial role and her desire to join Europe. By the time she had made up her mind, the Common Market had been formed and France certainly had no desire to surrender her dominant position by allowing Britain to become a member. Quite apart from the obvious advantages in pooling technical and financial resources, Britain firmly believed that her commitment to the Anglo-French SST project would be an entry ticket into the EEC.

From the outset, therefore, the Concorde was the subject of controversy; some regarded it with pride as a symbol of national prestige, others considered it to be a very expensive toy which would create unwelcome noise and smoke. It was even cast in the villainous role of placing human life at risk by upsetting the earth's protective ozone layer; the fact that military supersonic aircraft had long been regularly flying at extreme altitudes was largely ignored.

The year 1962 was a fateful one for the SST; in the year in which the Anglo-French Agreement was signed the Council of Ministers of the Supreme Soviet decided that Russia, too, would build an SST. The Tupolev design team was chosen to carry out the task and it soon reached the same conclusion as the British and French; a slender delta offered the best prospect of success.

Anxious that the United States would be outshone by the European projects, some aviation leaders urged the American government to support the construction of an SST. The head of the FAA, Najeeb Halaby led the chorus of SST supporters in the United States, but the opposition was equally vociferous. There was no precedent for government aid on such a scale; hitherto the airlines had funded new projects along with the manufacturers but it was clear that the SST would call for an investment far beyond the resources of the industry.

As the Concorde began to take shape, at least on paper, airlines were persuaded to commit themselves. BOAC had tended to

176

The great stride forward in commercial aviation represented by Concorde is not reflected either in the quiet calm of the passenger cabin, where the machmeter gives the only evidence of passage of the once-dreaded sound barrier, or the flight deck. Here the camera overlooks the flight crew's shoulders to show a quite normal instrument display as a British Airways Concorde approaches the runway.

drag its heels on the subject of the SST but in 1963 the airline took out an option along with Air France. When Pan American followed suit, Congress was galvanised into action. Encouraged by President Kennedy who had introduced a new vigour into the United States, the FAA was authorised to get an SST programme under way and the major manufacturers were invited to submit proposals.

Predictably North American offered an airliner version of the B-70, while the Lockheed team concluded that a delta design was the correct one for a Mach 3 airliner. Mach 3 was indeed the target set for American designers; if the Concorde was to be upstaged the US SST would have to be superior both in speed and size. In retrospect it was an unreasonable target to set even America's aircraft industry, for an aircraft capable of around 1800 mph would have to cope with temperatures of 260 degrees Centigrade.

Boeing's submission featured a swing-wing, which had been proposed for very high-speed aircraft by Sir Barnes Wallis of Vickers (BAC) years earlier; the ability of a swing-wing to adjust to optimal positions for varying flying speeds appeared to offer an ideal answer to the SST design problem, so the Boeing 2707 was selected by the FAA as worthy of government support. Airlines were invited to take out options on the Boeing 2707 and among the many which joined the queue was BOAC. Although understandable, BOAC's action was considered by some to show a lack of faith in Concorde. Experience, however, had taught the airline not to rely on one type of aeroplane. As it turned out this time the insurance proved to be unnecessary, for ultimately Concorde entered service and the Boeing 2707 failed to become more than a ' paper ' airliner.

Slowly the Super-Caravelle and the Bristol Type 223 projections merged to become the Concorde and in 1964 the design was ' frozen ' to allow construction of the prototype to proceed. In the same year a Labour government was returned to power and the aircraft industry awaited its actions with foreboding, for the Labour Party had been severely critical of British aviation. Soon the axe fell on major military aircraft projects and inevitably the Concorde came under close scrutiny too. Indeed, a decision was taken to pull out of the project—until it was realised that the Anglo-French Agreement did not permit such action. Slowly the crisis passed and construction of the prototypes began.

Test flights of several experimental aircraft continued in order to increase knowledge of high-speed flight. The Handley Page HP115 investigated the slow-speed characteristics of slender delta aircraft, the Bristol Type 188 built of stainless steel explored the effects of speeds over 1500mph and confirmed that

heat at such speeds was indeed a problem. The record-breaking Fairey FD2 was given a new wing and, as the BAC221, first flew in May 1964. The ' wineglass ' shape adopted for Concorde was shown to be the most efficient for Mach 2 SST operation.

The construction of the prototypes proceeded at a seemingly painfully slow pace, for the Anglo-French team was breaking new ground in aircraft design. The fuel for example was put to a number of uses; as well as simply feeding the engines, fuel was used to maintain the balance of the aircraft. For as the Concorde builds up speed, the centre of aerodynamic pressure moves towards the rear. By pumping fuel from tanks ahead of the centre of gravity to the rear of the fuselage, the aircraft can be trimmed so that balance is maintained. The fuel also acts as a heat sink, absorbing some of the high temperatures generated at supersonic speeds. A full-scale fuel rig was built at the BAC Concorde assembly plant at Filton to ensure that the balance system would work.

To investigate the fatigue qualities of the special aluminium/copper alloy selected for Concorde, a special thermal test rig was built at Farnborough. With an expected skin temperature of 120 degrees Centigrade quite clearly the performance of the metal had to be thoroughly investigated. Alternate heating and cooling cycles were applied to a complete Concorde airframe, while in France another airframe was subjected to static and further thermal tests. The engine would have to provide power over a wide speed range and a system of intake flaps and ramps was devised to ensure optimum performance.

In 1967 Concorde 001 was rolled out at Toulouse but the first flight did not take place until March 1969, by which time the Tupolev Tu-144 had already made its maiden flight. The Russian SST flew on 31 December 1968 but it was to encounter many difficulties before it entered service.

In 1968 Boeing abandoned the swing-wing design in favour of a slender delta, to the understandable annoyance of Lockheed which had submitted such a design to the FAA in the first place. The added weight and complexity of the swing-wing system finally defeated Boeing, for the company's designers simply could not reduce the weight of the aircraft so that it could carry a reasonable payload. As the cost of the American programme grew, so the anti-SST campaign got under way. Led by Senator William Proxmire, the programme was attacked relentlessly until in 1971 the Senate finally decided to discontinue funding the SST. With over one billion dollars spent, only wooden mock-ups had been built and America had bowed out of the race.

The Concorde was by no means without its critics, especially as the cost of the programme continued to mount. Unhappily the aircraft industry had traditionally shown an unwillingness to disclose details of rising costs. Perhaps fearing that the unvarnished truth would lead politicians to kill the project, the cost-estimates were rarely accurate. As it happened, the Concorde programme reached a stage where its cancellation could not be contemplated. For so much had already been invested, the aircraft was performing well, that to abandon the project seemed a defeatist move.

By 1972 four Concordes were flying, two prototypes and two preproduction aircraft. In the same year BOAC converted its option into a firm order for five machines. Predictably, Air France also ordered Concordes but efforts to persuade TWA and Pan American to place orders failed. In 1973 both American airlines announced their decision to reject Concorde and once more the future of the project was placed in jeopardy. The American decision could have

been anticipated, for Pan American was in poor shape financially having invested millions in a large fleet of Jumbos. The airline simply could not afford to buy another new and complex airliner regardless of the prospect of surrendering its position as a world leader if it did not operate an SST.

In 1973 Russia suffered a setback when a Tu-144 broke up before crowds of visitors at the Paris Air Show. The cause of the crash has never been revealed but it is generally considered that the pilot was performing manoeuvres for which the aircraft was not designed. Unfortunately the competitive atmosphere at international air shows is apt to encourage pilots to exceed the capability both of their aircraft and themselves, occasionally with disastrous results.

In 1974 a Labour government was once again returned to power and once more Concorde was a candidate for cancellation. In the midst of a severe economic crisis, the

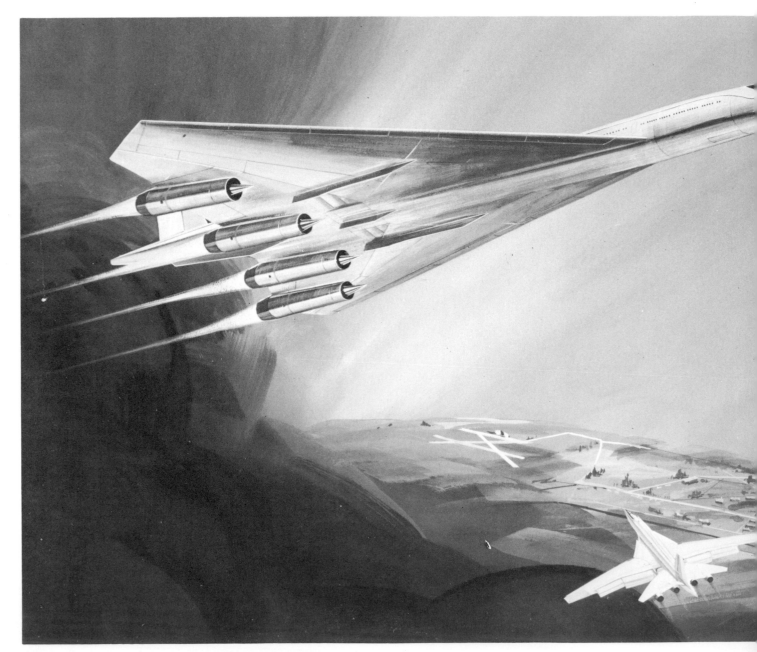

Below: *Artist's impression of the first proposed Boeing Mach 3 SST in low-speed flight with wings fully extended and in supersonic configuration with wings folded back to integrate with the tail unit to form a single surface. After spending many millions of dollars on preparatory research and development and an invitation to airlines to place purchase options, the project was considered commercially impractical and dropped.*

Right: *The Russian SST in typical early dramatic air show climb-out demonstration of the sort which might have accounted for the break-up of a demonstration aircraft over the Paris show in 1973. Although first into the air, on the last day of 1968, the Tu-144 was later into service than Concorde.*

government was determined to trim costs. The previous year the Arab oil embargo and subsequent price rise had thrown the world into turmoil. Overnight the cost of industrial production had rocketed and the world found itself in a severe economic crisis. The cost of operating airlines had shot up, too. Whereas fuel had not been the largest single item in direct operating costs (DOC), suddenly fuel economy had become a major item. This was unfortunate for Concorde to say the least, for airlines were clearly interested in buying the most economical aircraft and Concorde was selling speed, not economy.

Once more by careful diplomacy and skilful political manoeuvring, Concorde was saved, although no more than 16 aircraft were to be built unless further orders were forthcoming. Such a number makes a sad comparison with the original estimate of 250 sales. The final cost differed somewhat from the initial estimate; at £1070 million it represented a considerable cost to the taxpayer but at least the Anglo-French team could point to the technical success of the programme; in January 1976 an Air France Concorde left for Rio de Janeiro at the same time as a BOAC machine lifted off the runway at Heathrow bound for Bahrain. In the following May both airliners started to serve Washington. Immediately it started to fulfil its promise of halving travel times and considerably reducing the tedium of long flights. Moreover, it has operated with exemplary reliability and, on the transatlantic routes at consistently higher load factors than any other scheduled airliner.

However, Concorde's progress to the primary goal for which it had been developed, London/Paris-New York routes, was not smooth. The anti-SST lobby, having killed off the American project, turned its attention to Concorde. Noise and smoke pollution were but two of the evils which the lobby intended to keep from American shores. Secretary of Transport William Coleman held hearings in Washington at which the case for allowing Concorde flights into the United States was considered. Coleman later judged that the aircraft should be permitted to operate into Washington and New York for a 16-month trial period. The New York Port Authority chose to ignore the Federal ruling and many months of litigation passed before British Airways and Air France were finally allowed to fly into New York. On 22 November 1977 Concorde at last touched down at J. F. Kennedy airport to bring to fruition the work of over 20 years.

To some critics, Concorde has appeared as a step backward in some aspects of air travel. To the casual traveller the narrow cabin seems rather cramped in comparison with the spaciousness of modern wide-bodied aircraft and the windows also appear rather small. Another noticeable difference in looking out of a window is seeing the wing tip only a few feet away. But, apart from the VIP treatment at airports at present accorded to Concorde passengers, there is little in supersonic flight itself which can be considered unusual; beyond an indication on the machmeter on the cabin bulkhead, there is no sensation of flying at the speed of a bullet. It is a considerable achievement that passengers can travel faster than many military aircraft without experiencing any unusual sensation.

Although the Concorde has had to overcome many difficulties, it is not regarded as the ultimate in air travel. Within 20 years SST aircraft considerably larger than Concorde might well be commonplace. The cost of producing such a machine would certainly exceed the capability of any one company, or possibly any single country. Most likely the pattern of international co-operation established by the Concorde and later by the Airbus will be followed for all major airliner projects in the future.

Hypersonic aircraft are being studied by Lockheed under a contract from the National Aeronautics and Space Administration (NASA). A 200-seat airliner powered by five turbojets and five ramjets using liquid hydrogen and capable of flying at 4000mph for over 5000 miles is envisaged. The aircraft could fly from London to New York in rather less than two hours, again approximately halving today's time by Concorde. The aircraft would perhaps resemble the space shuttle built for NASA and undergoing tests as this is written. It has been designed to leave and re-enter the earth's atmosphere; as a hypersonic airliner flying at over 5000 mph it would 'bounce' around the rarified fringes of the earth's atmosphere until it reached the point of re-entry for its destination.

Whether or not Concorde and its like do represent the ultimate in speed, it seems certain that today's Jumbo will have a bigger brother in due course. Already a 'stretched' Boeing 747 featuring a double-deck fuselage is being planned and aircraft with a capacity for over 1000 passengers are confidently expected by the end of the century. Such giants will call for a radical re-thinking in airport design and management but few doubt that answers to the problem of ' processing' 1000-passenger airliners will be found.

Various possibilities for improving aircraft performance are already well researched. New materials such as carbon-fibres will replace metal presently used in many components, to result in lighter, stronger airframes capable of carrying greater payloads. Greater use of laminar flow, which involves sucking air from the wing surface to improve the airflow and reduce skin friction, would further reduce the cost of operating airliners. It has been shown that great economies can be made simply by cleaning up the surface of an airliner; making sure that doors are perfectly flush with the fuselage, for example. So-called active control technology (ACT) offers yet another opportunity for reducing operating costs. ACT involves transferring some of the control functions to a computer and using sensors to ensure that the controls are moved automatically to precisely the right position. One thing that experience with ACT has shown is that a reduction in the size of tail and wings is possible because of the very fast response of the automatic sensors and controls.

Among present researches that could affect air travel is the search for a substitute for oil-based fuels. Liquid methane is only one of the fuels under consideration but as it boils at minus 160 degrees Centigrade its use is certainly a challenge to aircraft designers.

Interesting work is being carried out in Germany involving the delta-wing theories of Dr Alexander Lippisch. An experimental aircraft is being used to investigate the benefits of an ' inverted V ' delta, with which an aircraft obtains support from an air bubble trapped in the inverted V of the wing. Such a design is said to offer great benefits in terms of operating costs.

Air transport history has taught us not to be surprised at the inventiveness of airliner designers, it has also shown that new methods of using air transport can bring great advances. Drastic reductions in fares have been made possible by a fresh approach to marketing and there can be little doubt that further advances in this field will match the ingenuity of engine and aircraft designers. Whatever happens, the amazing advances which have taken place in the short history of air transport will doubtless be mirrored in the years to come.

181

Index

Abbreviations

ABA	Aktiebolaget Aerotransport
ALI	Avio-Linee Italiane
ANA	Australian National Airways
ANA	All Nippon Airways
AOA	American Overseas Airways
APEX	Advance Purchase Excursion (fare)
ATAC	Air Transport Advisory Council
AT&T	Air Transport and Travel
ATLB	Air Transport Licensing Board
BAC	British Aircraft Corporation
B Cal	British Caledonian Airways Ltd.
BEAC	(BEA) British European Airways Corporation
BOAC	British Overseas Airways Corporation
BSAAC	(BSAA) British South African Airways Corporation
BUA	British United Airways
BWIA	British West Indian Airways
CAA	Central African Airways
CAA	Civil Aviation Authority
CAAC	Civil Aviation Administration of China
CAB	Civil Aeronautics Board
CLS	Ceskoslovenske Letecka Spolecnost
CMA	Compania Mexicana de Aviacion SA
CPA	Canadian Pacific Airlines (now CP Air)
CPAL	(CPA) Cathay Pacific Airways Ltd.
CSA	Ceskoslovenske Statni Aerolinie
DDL	Det Danske Luftfartselskab
DELAG	Deutsche Luftschiffahrt AG
DH	de Havilland
DHC	de Havilland of Canada
DLH	Deutsche Luft Hansa
DLR	Deutsche Luft Reederei
DNL	Det Norske Luftfartselskap
EAAC	East African Airways Corporation
EAL	Eastern Air Lines
IAC	Indian Airlines Corporation
IATA	International Air Transport Association (formerly Int Air Traffic Assn.)
JAL	Japan Air Lines (formerly Japanese A L)
JAT	Jugoslovenski Aerotransport
KLM	Koninklijke Luchtvaart Maatschappij voor Nederland an Kolonien
LAI	Linee Aeree Italiane
LAV	Linea Aeropostal Venezolana
MEA	Middle East Airlines AirLiban
NZNAC	New Zealand National Airways Corporation
PAA	Pan American Airways
PAL	Philippine Air Lines
PIA	Pakistan International Airlines
Qantas	Queensland and Northern Territories Aerial Services
SAA	South African Airways
Sabena	Société Anonyme Belge d'Exploitation de la Navigation Aérienne
SAM	Societa Aerea Mediterranea
SAS	Scandinavian Airlines System
TAA	Trans-Australia Airlines
TAI	Cie de Transports Aériens Intercontinentaux
TAP	Transportes Aereos Portugueses
Tarom	Transporturile Aeriene Romane
TCA	Trans-Canada Air Lines (now Air Canada)
TEAL	Tasman Empire Airways Ltd.
TWA	Trans World Airlines (formerly Transcontinental & Western Airlines)
UAT	Union Aeromaritime de Transport (later combined with TAI to become UTA)
UTA	Union de Transports Aériens
Varig	Empresa de Viacao Aerea Rio-Grandense
VASP	Viacao Areea Sao Paulo
Viasa	Venezolana de Aviacion SA

Pictures supplied by

185